WHO WAS "ROSIE THE RIVETER"?

To free men for military service during World War II, American munitions, shipbuilding, and airplane plants recruited "Rosie the Riveter" and her sisters to jobs that had been closed to them only a few short years before. After the war many remained in the workforce, and by 1978, half of the American women were employed outside the home.

WHERE IS "MANKILLER" A TER~~~~~~~~~~~~T?

Among Native American~~~~~~~~~~~~~~~~~~~ho elected Wilma Mankille~~~~~~~~~~~~~~~~~~er Cherokee Nation.

WHICH AMERICA~~~~~~~~~WON THE NOBEL PRI~~~~~~ERATURE?

Pearl Buck and Toni Morrison. Pearl Buck's most famous novel, *The Good Earth,* was published in 1931 and won the Pulitzer Prize for its portrayal of a Chinese peasant family. A prolific writer, Buck published over 100 books and won the Nobel Prize in 1938, the first American woman ever so honored. Toni Morrison's work reaches into her own African-American heritage. Her Pulitzer Prize-winning novel, *Beloved,* was based on an 1851 incident in which a fugitive slave woman killed her daughter to prevent her return to slavery. Morrison's Nobel award was announced in 1993 and was celebrated by many women for her refusal to gloss over the rough truths of women's lives.

WHEN DID BLONDES HAVE MORE FUN?

When they beat the Brunettes, 42–38, in the first baseball game women played for pay, in 1875.

KAY MILLS worked as a newspaper journalist for more than 25 years, many of them as an editorial writer at the *Los Angeles Times.* She has held a Knight Journalism Fellowship and a Rockefeller Foundation Humanities Research Fellowship, and has won awards from Planned Parenthood and the National Women's Political Caucus. She is the author of *This Little Light of Mine: The Life of Fannie Lou Hamer* and *A Place in the News: From the Women's Pages to the Front Page.*

Also by Kay Mills

This Little Light of Mine: The Life of Fannie Lou Hamer

A Place in the News: From the Women's Pages to the Front Page

FROM POCAHONTAS —TO— POWER SUITS

Everything You Need to Know About Women's History in America

KAY MILLS

For Anna Maria —
With best wishes
for your sojourn with
Margaret Fuller and
all her pals! All the best!
Kay Mills

A PLUME BOOK

PLUME
Published by the Penguin Group
Penguin Books USA Inc., 375 Hudson Street,
New York, New York 10014, U.S.A.
Penguin Books Ltd, 27 Wrights Lane,
London W8 5TZ, England
Penguin Books Australia Ltd, Ringwood,
Victoria, Australia
Penguin Books Canada Ltd, 10 Alcorn Avenue,
Toronto, Ontario, Canada M4V 3B2
Penguin Books (N.Z.) Ltd, 182–190 Wairau Road,
Auckland 10, New Zealand

Penguin Books Ltd, Registered Offices:
Harmondsworth, Middlesex, England

First published by Plume, an imprint of Dutton Signet,
a division of Penguin Books USA Inc.

First Printing, March, 1995
10 9 8 7 6 5 4 3 2 1

Poems 404 and 1078 from *The Complete Poems of Emily Dickinson*, edited by Thomas H.
Johnson. Copyright © 1929 by Martha Dickinson Bianchi; copyright © renewed 1957 by
Mary L. Hampson. By permission of Little, Brown and Company.

Library of Congress Cataloging-in-Publication Data

Mills, Kay.
    From Pocahontas to power suits : everything you need to know about women's
history in America / Kay Mills.
        p.   cm.
    Includes bibliographical references and index.
    ISBN 0-452-27152-5
    1. Women—United States—History.   I. Title.
HQ1410.M56   1995
305.4′0973—dc20   94-34521
                                                                        CIP

Printed in the United States of America
Set in New Baskerville
Designed by Leonard A. Telesca

Contents

Introduction

> Well-behaved women rarely make
> history.
>
> —LAUREL THATCHER ULRICH

From Pocahontas to Hillary Rodham Clinton, from Anne
Hutchinson to Anita Hill, women have asserted themselves and
paid a price. At the same time, women who risked much have
become honored heroines. If there is one clear message from
almost four centuries of women's history in America, it is that
the country still has not resolved its age-old ambivalence about
a woman's place. We are a nation that may consider a woman's
challenge radical or revolutionary today, take her for granted
tomorrow, and forget her the day after that. This book seeks to
keep alive the stories of women who challenged the world as
they knew it.

Nobody ever said it was going to be easy, this notion of
achieving a place in a society that preaches equality but often
fails to practice it. The Constitution laid out an elegant democratic system of government but left out the rights of the governed to free speech, press, and religion. Even with the Bill of
Rights, however, the Constitution remained flawed because only
white men could fully exercise those rights and call themselves
equal. Women and people of color have challenged that inequality throughout American history, and this book taps into
some of those struggles. It is a story both frustrating and glori-
ous, one too often unknown to too many people. The history of

women in America is a rich pageant, peopled with women of intellect, courage, and the necessary sense of themselves to survive.

When I was a child, I loved to read biographies. There was a set of books with orange covers—if you are of a certain age you will remember them, too. The series included George Washington and Abraham Lincoln and Lou Gehrig and, as I recall, Clara Barton and Juliette Low. Where were Deborah Sampson and Catharine Beecher and Elizabeth Cady Stanton and Sojourner Truth and Mary Lyon and Maria Mitchell? The history we studied was of wars and presidents, treaties and tariffs. Smoot and Hawley were men. But the real stuff of history—the people who made homes on the prairies, whose families were torn apart by slavery, who worked in the canneries and the garment factories, who were quietly writing poetry and novels, in short, who built our daily lives—escaped the schoolgirl.

The lone exception to this neglect of women's history in my early education was a report I did in eighth grade on women's rights. That report evolved more from a church women's society play that my mother directed about the Seneca Falls meeting than from any classroom encouragement. I still have the report, on lined paper carefully filled with a fourteen-year-old's penmanship. In the introduction, I pointed to the increasing number of women elected and assigned to government posts—Margaret Chase Smith, Oveta Culp Hobby, Ivy Baker Priest, and Clare Booth Luce. "But this has not always been so," I concluded that section, written in 1955. How frustrated I would have been had I known how long it would take for truly measurable increases in the number of women in government to occur, how many years it would be before we would see today's senators, congresswomen and cabinet secretaries in their stylish power suits debating, legislating, governing.

The saddest element of the history of women in America is the fact that the wheel has had to be reinvented so often. Who knew about the activity of women supporting the American Revolution when the Civil War started? Who knew about the early women's historians when women's colleges were founded? Who fully appreciated the nineteenth-century divisions in the women's movement when it splintered again in the 1920s? Why do the vast majority of young women today assume that life and opportunity has always been as it is today? Why, within the past decade, were young college students surprised when I mentioned that distributing birth control information had once been illegal? If we do not know, will we forget and must we reinvent yet again? Of all the questions this book raises and seeks to answer about women's history, that may be the most vital.

What is heartening about the history of women in America, however, is the thread of ingenuity that weaves throughout it. Whether black or white, native born or immigrant, when women lacked household goods that they needed, they made them; when they lacked moral support, they went in search of it. What they could not do by themselves, they formed associations to try to do together. And when they had no models for their lives, they charted their own independent course. As steep as obstacles may sometimes seem in the twentieth century, they were far higher in the nineteenth. That Mary Lyon persevered and founded Mount Holyoke College, that Harriet Tubman ferried slaves north from the South, that Susan B. Anthony crusaded for votes and other rights for women, and that Jane Addams overcame ennui and plunged into settlement work and political life in the broadest sense—all demonstrate stubborn courage in addition to intellect that would not be stifled. The twentieth century has also demanded such resilience, and doubtless the twenty-first will as well.

CHAPTER 1

~

The Early Years: From Pocahontas to the American Revolution

Whatever happened to Pocahontas?

What do Pocahontas and Anne Hutchinson have in common?

Who were the witches of colonial America?

Who was the first woman to cast a vote in America?

Why did a woman print the first official copy of the Declaration of Independence?

What did women have against British tea, and what did their spinning bees have to do with patriotism?

What was General Washington's Sewing Circle?

Who was the first woman to wear an American military uniform?

What did Abigail Adams mean when she urged husband John to "Remember the Ladies"?

Did the wives and daughters of American revolutionaries really enjoy the liberty that the men so loudly proclaimed?

How did the American Revolution change society's attitude toward educating women?

Who was the playwright of the American Revolution—without ever having seen a play herself?

~

Whatever happened to Pocahontas?

Despite what every schoolchild learns about **Pocahontas** throwing herself between the English settler **John Smith** and her tribesmen who were preparing to execute him, the story may not be completely true. As scholars have pointed out, the story of an explorer encountering native people and being captured, only to be saved by the daughter of the local ruler, was a common theme well before Smith reached colonial Virginia in the early seventeenth century. His account was remarkably similar to the legend. There is also the possibility that Smith's captors had decided not to execute him and that his "rescue" by Pocahontas was part of their ritual to adopt him into the tribe.

Pocahontas (1595?–1617) herself was no myth. The daughter of Tidewater Virginia's legendary chief **Powhatan,** she was lured aboard a British ship in the Jamestown area and held captive for more than a year. She was dressed in the English fashion and took religious instructions, becoming baptized as a Christian. In 1614, Pocahontas married British colonist **John Rolfe.** In 1616, as part of a plan to revive support for the Virginia colony, the couple traveled to England with their infant son. There Pocahontas met **King James I** and **Queen Anne.** Just as she and Rolfe were setting sail back to America the following

March, Pocahontas died, perhaps because of smallpox, perhaps because of the foul English weather. She was buried in a British churchyard.

What do Pocahontas and Anne Hutchinson have in common?

Pocahontas and **Anne Hutchinson** are the first women named in virtually every American history book. Both took unusually visible roles in their own communities.

In 1634, Anne Hutchinson and her husband, **William,** followed **John Cotton,** their spiritual leader, to Boston from England after the Anglican authorities forced him to leave the country. Cotton subtly questioned the basic teachings of Puritanism regarding conditions that might predict a follower's prospects for the eternal life after physical death. Anne Hutchinson (1591–1643), of nimbler wit than most around her, carried Cotton's thinking further than he did—in the direction of divine revelation to individuals. She met with devoted followers each week, and they talked about the previous Sunday's sermons. That alone made the authorities distrust her because women had little religious role except as worshipful followers. Hutchinson argued that God saved souls by placing the Holy Ghost within each person and, if that were the case, then outward behavior wasn't necessarily a sign of prospects for the afterlife. This state of grace, rather than demonstration of worldly success, must have been especially attractive to women, for it gave them authorization, usually denied them, for talking about their beliefs. These arguments raised a host of red flags to Puritan authorities, especially Governor **John Winthrop.** If God dwelt within individuals, as Hutchinson argued, then who needed clergymen and churches to direct the study of the Bible to discover God's will?

The Puritans may have come to the colonies to practice religious freedom, but it was religious freedom as their leaders would interpret it, not as pronounced by upstarts, especially not upstart women. Free speech was not compatible with religious and government control. In an attempt to stamp out what was viewed as potentially separatist doctrine, authorities charged Hutchinson with sedition and accused her of insulting ministers.

As Edmund S. Morgan wrote in *The Puritan Dilemma: The Story of John Winthrop,* the record of Anne Hutchinson's trial "reveals a proud woman put down by men who had judged her in advance." Hutchinson was Winthrop's intellectual superior except in her lack of political judgment, superior "in everything except the sense of what was possible in this world." Hutchinson bested her judges in every exchange. At one point she cited two biblical passages to support her belief that she, a woman, was qualified to hold the weekly meetings that she had conducted in her home. When the judges said neither one really suited her practice, she asked sarcastically whether her name had to appear in the Bible to prove her point.

She had almost outwitted the judges and beaten the charges with the help of supporting testimony from John Cotton, still a respected minister, when something in her reservoir of patience must have snapped. She started to gloat and then talk about all the revelations she had had directly from God, including a pledge to destroy those who persecuted her. On and on she raced. "Her owne mouth" delivered her into the power of the court, said John Winthrop, confirming she was "guilty of that which all suspected her for." She was excommunicated and left Massachusetts for Rhode Island. Later she moved with her youngest children to a village near Long Island Sound and was killed in an Indian raid in 1643.

Who were the witches of colonial America?

Witches in early New England weren't people with pointed hats, bewhiskered chins, and scratchy voices who rode on broomsticks carrying black cats behind them. Witches were the truly bedeviled, those who had lost their souls to Satan. Belief in witchcraft in New England was the product of a religious cul-

ture that taught about a struggle for the soul between God and
Satan. God won the virtuous; Satan captured the weak. Those
who questioned either the power of religion over their lives or
their own lot in life—usually women—might conduct themselves in ways that convinced their communities that they were
witches.

The seventeenth century was a disquieting time in colonial
America as religious and political leaders sought to exercise
their control in the newly settled country. The land and nature
were themselves often unforgiving, so life was economically per-
ilous. Amid such uncertainties, those who were different, especially women who were not submissive, might fall victim to a
convenient social control: an accusation of witchcraft. It was an
acceptable, religiously based explanation for events that in
those less-scientific times otherwise seemed inexplicable.

Although witchcraft had been prosecuted in England in the
seventeenth century, no one was tried for witchcraft in the colonies until 1647; **Anne Hutchinson** was informally accused of
witchcraft but never tried on those grounds. Two women were
executed on witchcraft charges in 1648. Between 1647 and
1663, fifteen people were hanged as witches, thirteen of them
women. The two men hanged were married to women said to
be witches. Major outbreaks of witchcraft accusations occurred
in 1662 in Hartford, Connecticut, and in 1692 in Salem, Massachusetts, where, again, more women than men were executed.

Carol F. Karlsen, author of *The Devil in the Shape of a Woman:
Witchcraft in Colonial New England,* found economic and demo-
graphic patterns in accusations and executions for witchcraft.
While poor women were not a majority of those accused of
witchcraft, they were overrepresented in comparison with their
numbers among the general population. Once accused, if they
lacked the protection of their own wealth or of wealthy relatives, they were most likely to be prosecuted and convicted.

Women more comfortably situated because they had inherited property were not necessarily immune from witchcraft
accusations. New England had a carefully ordered society in
which the eldest sons traditionally inherited a double portion
of family property. When there were no male heirs or when

men left to their wives the bulk of their estates, the female heirs upset the natural order of life. If some women had property, others might ask why they, too, might not manage their lands, especially if they had brought the property into their marriages. It was not unusual for women in families with no male heirs to be accused of witchcraft not long after their fathers or husbands died. Perhaps their accusers felt they had been in league with the devil to cause the death.

Some of the women accused of witchcraft were assertive, taking on their neighbors in disputes over boundaries, fences, or stray animals. One, **Mary Staplies,** was accused of being a witch because she questioned the judgment of local magistrates that a neighbor was a witch. Another woman was angry over being investigated as the cause of her husband's death. Many were speaking up for their rights. Some were angry over their situation and downright rude; others were simply too successful in their domestic work, which caused jealousy. One had a thriving butter business. Still others had become a threat by asserting independence because they ran taverns or boardinghouses. These women threatened the sexual order, although that threat was described by the clergy in terms of "subversion of the order of Creation," Karlsen wrote. For a time, Quaker women were especially vulnerable to accusations of witchcraft because of their church's belief that women as well as men could know the truth and speak it.

Puritan clergymen linked women with what they considered the sins of anger, envy, malice, and pride, understandable reactions to the stresses of social and economic change occurring in that era. In other words, it was easy to call women "witches" and blame them for problems that seemed to defy explanation.

Who was the first woman to cast a vote in America?

Lady Deborah Moody (d. 1659?), daughter of a member of the British parliament, became the first white woman to vote in

America during town council meetings in Gravesend, New York.

After her husband, a baronet who had also served in the British Parliament, died, Lady Moody migrated to America to seek greater personal liberty. She tangled with religious authorities in Massachusetts because she did not believe that infant baptism was necessarily ordained by God. She felt that those baptized should be old enough to understand the faith into which they were being received. In those days, however, baptism was viewed as essential to salvation—even though sometimes ice had to be broken in the church baptismal fonts before the ceremony could continue. Although Governor **John Winthrop** described her as "wise and anciently religious," she was excommunicated.

Moving to New Amsterdam in 1643, she led the founding of the Gravesend settlement on Long Island in what is now Kings County, New York, and helped draw the town plan and obtain its charter from the Dutch colonial governor. One of the first Quaker meetings in the New World occurred at her home. In 1655, she became the only woman to vote in early America during council proceedings in the community she had helped organize. She died in late 1658 or early 1659.

Why did a woman print the first official copy of the Declaration of Independence?

Mary Katherine Goddard was in the right place at the right time—and she had a printing press. In January 1777, she and the Continental Congress, which had drafted the Declaration of Independence the previous summer, were both in Baltimore. The Continental Congress had moved its operations there, and Goddard was in Baltimore running the *Maryland Journal*. As the first woman appointed to a federal job, she was also operating the fledgling postal service. She not only printed the document but also paid the post riders to carry it throughout the rebellious colonies.

Goddard had been a printer for many years by the time her services were needed to further the revolutionary acts of John Hancock and Co. Goddard's mother, **Sarah,** widowed when her physician husband died in 1757, had had enough money to finance a Providence, Rhode Island, newspaper and print shop for her twenty-two-year-old son **William.** She and daughter Mary Katherine took over the print shop when William took off; he was better at ideas than execution and had a hot temper to boot.

The Goddards, mother and daughter, moved to Philadelphia in 1768 to manage the *Pennsylvania Chronicle, and Universal Advertiser,* which William had established. It was considered the best-edited newspaper of the era just before the American Revolution. Sarah died in 1769 and by 1773, William was in Baltimore, where he started the *Maryland Journal.* During the war, Mary Katherine, taking over her brother's business again, found it difficult to hire good assistants, so she often ran the presses by herself. Her paper was pro-patriot, reporting with outrage news about British attacks and also urging women to be frugal and raise their own wool, the better to be independent from Britain and the rest of Europe. Goddard also defended freedom of the press by taking an abusive reader to court.

Mary Katherine Goddard was bounced from her job as postmistress (brother William had also helped set up the Constitutional Post Office) when **George Washington** became president in 1789. The new postmaster, **Samuel Osgood,** said that the job, involving travel as it would, was too strenuous and inappropriate for a woman. Goddard had, of course, been running the presses and packing and moving boxes in her shop as well as supervising the postal-delivery service that she had set up, but no matter. Her brother forced her to sell the profitable *Maryland Journal* to him, only to sell it himself years later for bad debts. She died in 1816.

What did women have against British tea, and what did their spinning bees have to do with patriotism?

In colonial times, the beverage of choice for many women was tea. So it was a sacrifice for them when the American patriots decided that the colonies should boycott tea and other goods after the British government's Townshend Act of 1767 imposed new import taxes. The colonials also started wearing simple fabrics made at home as part of the protests against imported linens and broadcloth. Who had to make the herbal tea to replace the British product? Not the men who were down at the port of Boston in 1773, dumping 342 chests of tea into the harbor, but their wives or their daughters. Who had to do the spinning to make the new cloth? Not the 115 Princeton University freshmen who were wearing homespun, but their mothers or their sisters.

During the Revolutionary War, there were many patriotic appeals to women, especially in terms of the economic boycott of British goods. As Mary Beth Norton wrote in *Liberty's Daughters: The Revolutionary Experience of American Women, 1750–1800,* women could not help but think differently about themselves after playing such a direct role in the success of a revolutionary enterprise. Sometimes resistance was individual, sometimes collective. In 1770, for example, Norton wrote, the *Boston Evening Post* reported that some three hundred women had decided to abstain from using tea. In North Carolina, fifty-one women signed an agreement in 1774 to do all they could to support both the public good and the resolutions passed by the provincial congress. Men applauded women who supported these economic causes, but belittled those who dared join in such a collective activity as petitioning. That evidently was a line that women were not to cross.

By the late 1760s, newspapers that would never have written about spinning bees started playing the stories on their front pages because of the patriotic angle. The spinning parties would usually involve from twenty to forty women, who would spend the day at their spinning wheels, drinking local herbal teas when they took a break. Sometimes people came to watch the spinning; sometimes the women competed to see how much an individual could produce in one day. While men and women alike knew how vital women's spinning was to their daily lives, women had rarely won public plaudits for their efforts nor had they been the subject of newspaper exhortations. It was truly an early case of the personal becoming political. Even though the idea of women's political participation receded after the crisis was past, the seed had been planted.

What was General Washington's Sewing Circle?

The so-called sewing circle started out as something quite different: a fund-raising effort to support the American revolutionary troops. The campaign started in June 1780 with the publication of *The Sentiments of an American Woman,* by **Esther DeBerdt Reed.** She and her female allies wanted not just to talk about patriotism but also to do something concrete for the soldiers. Reed's carefully argued broadside spoke of the patriotic contributions of women from the days of the Bible, then suggested that women renounce fancy clothing and hairstyles and give the money saved to the American troops.

Reed and her followers, working in Philadelphia, set about canvassing the city. They clearly were moving beyond boycotting tea and other domestic economies. They appointed treasurers, kept careful records, and planned to send the money collected to **Martha Washington,** the general's wife. There were, of course, those who felt this new role inappropriate, but in a few weeks the women raised about $7,500, an extraordinary amount in those days. The campaign not only showed their organizational skills but also was a morale boost for a country at war. Women in New Jersey, Maryland, and Virginia followed suit.

Unfortunately for the women, General **George Washington**

wanted the money to go into the country's general fund; the women had intended that it go directly to the troops and not for any goods that the army should be providing them. Washington was afraid that if the men were given cash, they might spend it on liquor. The matter ended with a compromise, and the women provided shirts for the soldiers. Esther DeBerdt Reed died in a dysentery epidemic before the shirts could be made. **Benjamin Franklin**'s daughter, **Sarah Franklin Bache,** and several other women took charge of making some 2,200 shirts.

The women had undertaken a political act, only to see their efforts converted into a virtual sewing circle, part of their normal domestic role. But although some of the male patriots like **John Adams** might make sarcastic comments about the drive, the women had taken it seriously and had organized their canvassing in a practical manner but with the philosophical base contained in Esther Reed's writing. And time has a way of bringing matters full circle: Years later, John Adams's son, **John Quincy Adams,** found himself quoting from Reed's broadside in congressional debate supporting women's patriotism and their right to petition Congress.

Who was the first woman to wear an American military uniform?

Deborah Sampson (1760–1827), a twenty-two-year-old teacher and seamstress, enlisted in the Continental army in 1782. Toughened by the farm and household work that she had done as an indentured servant and skilled in firing a musket, she was tall enough (five feet nine inches) and slender enough to pass as a youth who wanted to serve his country. She used the name of a brother who had died when he was eight years old, Robert Shurtliff, and she served with distinction for a year and a half.

Sampson was stationed in the West Point, New York, area where key strategic forts blocked British ambitions to seize the Hudson River valley. She feared exposure as a woman and possible execution for lying to the army in order to enlist. Having bound her chest so her breasts would not give away her sex, Sampson was aided in her deception by the soldiers' habit of sleeping in their uniforms and going off into the woods to relieve themselves. Her closest call occurred when two musket balls lodged in her leg after she had volunteered for a special mission against Tories loyal to Britain. Bleeding profusely, she was taken to a nearby field hospital where a surgeon, preparing to treat her, suggested she go into another room to remove her bloody trousers. She did and, finding a probe, removed one of the musket balls herself and bandaged the wound, thus avoiding having her trousers removed by the doctor and her true identity discovered.

Her principal service involved raids against Tories and Indians who had been plundering homesteads in upstate New York. She was selected for an elite ranger unit that was given special scouting assignments. Finally, during an epidemic of malignant fever in 1783, a doctor treating her discovered she was a woman but did not betray her secret. He helped her back to health, financed a trip for her through the Blue Ridge Mountains with a surveyor so that she could see more of the country, then wrote her commander about her bravery—and her identity. The war was over; there were no repercussions. Sampson had mixed feelings about returning to the submissive role that most women played after the excitement and equality that she had known.

She married **Benjamin Gannett, Jr.,** a Massachusetts farmer, in 1785, and had three children and raised a fourth whose mother had died when the child was an infant. In 1802, Sampson became one of the first women to embark on a lecture tour, speaking in three states about her army service. Never paid for that service, she had petitioned Massachusetts for back pay in 1792, supported by her regimental commander. She received the equivalent of one hundred dollars. Later, with the help of revolutionary leader **Paul Revere,** she asked Congress for a disability pension because of her war wound and was granted four dollars a month. In 1818, she became eligible for an additional eight-dollar monthly federal pension. She died in 1827.

I desire you would Remember the Ladies, and be more generous and favourable to them than your ancestors. Do not put such unlimited power into the hands of the Husbands. Remember all Men would be tyrants if they could. If perticuliar care and attention is not paid to the Laidies we are determined to foment a Rebellion, and will not hold ourselves bound by any Laws in which we have no voice, or Representation.

—Abigail Adams to John Adams, 1776

What did Abigail Adams mean when she urged husband John to "Remember the Ladies"?

John Adams was serving in the Continental Congress in 1776, separated by hundreds of miles from his wife and family in Massachusetts, when he received the letter that contains **Abigail Adams**'s most famous admonition. Asking her husband not to put all power in men's hands—and even offering him advice in the first place—was typical of Abigail Adams (1744–1818) in many ways. While she believed women could lose their femininity if they participated in politics, she was a keen observer of the turbulent scene surrounding the American Revolution and not afraid to express her opinions to her husband—whom she hailed as "Dearest Friend"—in regular correspondence during his absences. She managed the family finances, its farm, and the children's educations, and she wanted Congress not to adopt the British laws that gave men total authority over their wives.

She grew increasingly conservative politically once independence from Britain was achieved, so one probably should not read more feminism into her statement about women's rebellion than was actually intended. This famous passage, like other parts of her correspondence, also reveals that Abigail Adams spelled poorly. Knowing that her own education had been inferior, she always supported better schooling for girls.

The daughter of a Congregational minister, young Abigail Smith was a stubborn and clever child. She learned the household tasks that girls of her era were supposed to master and also spent hours in her father's library. She enjoyed reading Shakespeare, although she never saw one of his plays performed until she went to London with her husband, who was representing the new United States as minister to Great Britain.

She met John Adams, a young lawyer, when she was fifteen, and began to see him regularly by the time she was eighteen. Adams was initially put off by her, but he admired people of intelligence and was soon drawn to her. Their revealing and enduring correspondence began during their courtship, with John at one point comparing their attraction to "the steel and the magnet or the Glass and the feather." Married when Abigail was almost twenty and John twenty-nine in October 1764, the Adamses had four children, plus a daughter who died in infancy and one who was stillborn.

John Adams became increasingly involved in politics, serving in the Massachusetts legislature and later in the Continental Congress. He agonized over his long absences from home, but public service seemed essential if he was to back up his commitment to independence from an increasingly tyrannical British royal government. Abigail hated their separations but supported the revolutionary cause and would not directly demand that John leave politics.

While he served in Philadelphia or Baltimore, she became his political eyes and ears in Massachusetts. Adams quoted one of her letters in a speech before Congress and once said of her: "There is a Lady at the Foot of Pens Hill, who obliges me . . . with clearer and fuller intelligence, than I can get from a whole Committee of Gentlemen." Abigail also maintained a brisk correspondence with her sisters and other women, including the playwright and poet **Mercy Otis Warren.** In these letters, she not only talked about people and politics but also consulted about health problems, household concerns, and the children's education.

When John left for Europe, first to help negotiate France's entry into the war and then the peace treaty at war's end, Abigail continued to write, never knowing whether letters reached their destination. Left alone with the children to raise, Abigail felt that she and John were losing their best years together. Their longest separation by distance was four years; at one point, she received no letter from him for ten months. When he was named ambassador to France at war's end, she decided to make the hazardous ocean crossing to join him. The ship was filthy and the food worse than her most pessimistic expectations, wrote biographer Lynne Withey in *Dearest Friend: A Life of Abigail Adams.* After she recovered from her initial seasickness, Abigail asserted herself, and one of her servants traveling with her organized the crewmen to clean the ship. Then she turned to the food, helping the cook make edible pudding and prepare other dishes. Abigail's residence in Paris and later in London reinforced her belief that America was best—its government more democratic and its people more moral and harder working.

The Adamses returned to the United States in 1788, and that fall John was elected vice president. It was not a job he liked, but failure to win reelection in 1792 would have been a repudiation of his role in public service and a victory by those who wanted less centralized government. In 1796, he was elected president. Abigail followed **Martha Washington** as First Lady and, after so many years, still had great ambivalence about the demands of entertaining, but she enjoyed the reflected limelight. The nation's capital moved from Philadelphia to Washington during the Adams administration. While Abigail thought the president's mansion would become grand "for ages to come," in 1800 she found that the building was not finished and was difficult to heat and keep clean. She hung the laundry in the east room.

Forced into retirement by defeat in 1800, John and Abigail returned to Massachusetts, where she was happy to gather her family around her again, including many grandchildren. Abigail Adams remained active until she died of typhoid fever in 1818, only a few days shy of her seventy-fourth birthday. She was the only woman in American history married to one president and mother of another. She did not, however, live to see her son, **John Quincy Adams,** elected to the top office in 1824.

Did the wives and daughters of American revolutionaries really enjoy the liberty that the men so loudly proclaimed?

Americans still adhered to the practice of coverture, which meant that married women were considered one with their husbands in terms of accounting for property (or political opinions, for that matter). "The very being or legal existence of the woman is suspended" after marriage, said English common law. In colonial times some women had managed their own property with no overt problems and had signed prenuptial contracts outlining what they brought to the marriage and what could—and couldn't—be done with it by their husbands. Another common law provision protected a widow's rights to one-third of her husband's real estate. After the Revolution, however, the inequities of coverture were not corrected. Whatever protections women had enjoyed often disappeared. Supposedly promoting an equality of property in the true republican spirit, the North Carolina legislature, for example, said in 1784 that widows had to share their inheritance equally with all their children.

Women who had exercised some independence of judgment during the Revolution became somewhat more willing to seek divorces after the war, although divorce laws varied widely from state to state. Pennsylvania changed its divorce laws after the war so that courts rather than the legislature would hear the cases. In most other areas of the country, however, women seeking divorces had to win passage of private bills in legislatures, which, of course, were all male. Men had preached divorce from the British crown, but usually weren't willing to grant it to the women with whom they lived.

Anytime women were involved in legal disputes, they faced,

both before and after the Revolution, courtrooms in which they were neither lawyers, judges, clerks, nor members of the jury. Men may have gotten freedom from the crown, but women still lived with many of the same inequities.

How did the American Revolution change society's attitude toward educating women?

The notion of Republican Motherhood sprang from the Revolutionary War—not Republican as in members of a political party, but republican as in preparing for life in a republic. After years of rule by a monarchy, the citizens of the new republic would need education. They would need to read in order to stay informed and to be aware of the history and philosophies that had formed their government; they would need also to write in order to communicate their thoughts on public concerns, and to add and subtract to manage community and personal budgets. Mothers had traditionally taught their children basic skills and, even though formal education became more generally available after the Revolution, women were still charged with teaching their children morality and patriotism.

An educated mother could escape the criticism usually leveled at learned females, as historian Linda K. Kerber wrote, "because she placed her learning at her family's service." The concept proved a double-edged sword, however. It enhanced the value of women's work at home, but it also evolved into the tighter constraints of the "cult of domesticity," the idea that woman's place was *only* in the home, as the revolutionary fervor faded.

Before the Revolution, girls occasionally might have been taught with their brothers but, unless they were children of the upper class, their chores in helping to run the household usually took precedence over schooling. Unlike their brothers, they received no education beyond the primary level and never went away to college. Even for well-off young women, schooling usually focused on the skills needed to be a lady—needlepoint, a smattering of French, perhaps. Giving women more education ran the risk, so the conservative argument went, of "unsexing" them, of making them too masculine.

But the idea of Republican Motherhood—bringing up the citizens of a new republic—meant women needed to read, to study history, to be able to keep accounts. The informal "dame" schools where children had been educated, often poorly, gave way to academies for young women, including **Sarah Pierce**'s school in Litchfield, Connecticut, which started at Pierce's dining room table in 1792, and the highly successful Moravian Young Ladies Seminary in Bethlehem, Pennsylvania, opened to non-Moravian girls in 1785. These schools offered reading, grammar, geography, history, music, arithmetic, and sometimes astronomy and foreign languages. The young women educated soon after the Revolution in turn became the founders of higher education for women and leaders in the fights to abolish slavery and establish women's rights.

Who was the playwright of the American Revolution—without ever having seen a play herself?

Mercy Otis Warren (1728–1814) was a political satirist whose plays appeared in Massachusetts newspapers, so they were meant to be read as opposed to being performed. That was just as well because the city of Boston didn't allow performance of plays (it didn't even have a theater) because of its puritanical laws. Warren had, however, read Shakespeare and Molière as part of her youthful studies.

Educated with her brother but not allowed to go to college, Mercy Otis married one of his classmates, **James Warren,** and circulated in the society of the early American patriots such as **John** and **Abigail Adams** and **Samuel Adams.** Between 1772 and 1775, she published three plays. The first, *The Adulateur,* which appeared anonymously, satirized the royal colonial government—headed by a character whom she named "Rapatio" but who was clearly the governor. In her play, the government tried, unsuccessfully, to crush the patriots, who believed in self-government and in the common man and his dignity. They were headed by a character who was obviously Warren's brother. Rapatio appeared in her next play, *The Defeat*, in which the royals lost to the patriots again. Finally, in 1775, she wrote a play, also sold in pamphlet form, called *The Group*. Its characters were all Tories, men loyal to the king who had refused to give up their posts as appointed councillors when the patriots wanted to elect their own government.

For several decades, Warren worked off and on writing a vividly personal, three-volume *History of the Rise, Progress, and Termination of the American Revolution*, which was published in 1805. She and John Adams, who had encouraged her writing, had a falling out over her portrayal of him as a man of ambition who had forgotten the democratic principles of the Revolution. Later they had a rapprochement, although Adams harrumphed to a friend that "history is not the province of the ladies." Adams did, however, vouch for Warren's authorship of *The Group* when it came under question in 1814, shortly before she died.

CHAPTER 2

~

Life in the Young Nation

Who birthed most of the babies in early America?

Who first started writing women into American history?

Who was America's first female dramatic star?

How did slavery affect black women in the South?

Who put women on a pedestal, and why?

What was "Fanny Wrightism," and why was the woman after whom it was named so vilified?

Who was Harriet Tubman and why was she called the "Black Moses"?

How did Sojourner Truth get her name?

Who were the first Southern white women to speak out against slavery?

Why was medical school especially tough for Elizabeth Blackwell?

Could the Blackwells be called the "First Family of Women's Rights"?

~

Who birthed most of the babies in early America?

Midwives delivered most babies in the late eighteenth century because there were few doctors—and those doctors attended only a few births each year, especially in less urban areas. Some families might call in doctors for the late stages of a delivery or in a particularly difficult birth. But for the preparations, for the waiting, and usually for the birth—not to mention, sadly, sometimes to prepare the corpse of a stillborn infant for burial—it was the midwives who left home at all hours, crossed the river on the ice, and sat up with the expectant mother. Usually they were assisted during the birth by several other female family members or local women.

Midwives like **Martha Ballard** of Hallowell, Maine, also treated children who had scarlet fever or those who had been badly burned, cared for women with sore or abscessed breasts, and created herbal brews or poultices for anyone in need of relief from a sore throat or perhaps rheumatism. But mostly Martha Ballard delivered babies—814 of them in the twenty-seven years in which she kept a careful diary of the dailiness of life in her small town along the Kennebec River near Augusta, which would become the state capital.

It is Martha Ballard's diary, housed now in a vault at the Maine State Library and interpreted by historian Laurel Thatcher Ulrich, that has allowed a unique close-up of the workings of one community—especially the women's work usually ignored in men's accounts of that day. The fatigue of a woman often called in the middle of the night to attend to another's labor, even into the midwife's seventies. The family quarrels. The regularity of Martha Ballard's work in her vegetable and herb garden. All are captured in *A Midwife's Tale: The Life of Martha Ballard, Based on Her Diary, 1785–1812.*

In her diary, Martha Ballard (1785–1812) recorded her earnings from midwifery—sometimes cash, sometimes credit at a local store, sometimes cloth or foodstuffs. She usually earned about two dollars for a delivery; a local doctor charged six dollars. Not only was midwifery her calling, her way of helping the women in her community, but it also gave her an independent identity and means of contributing to her family's income. Much of the women's economy in a town like Hallowell has rarely been recorded, yet the trading of quince or herbs, eggs or pork, stretched families' incomes and added variety to their diets.

The unusual element in Martha Ballard's life was that she recorded it. Ulrich made the point that while "she was an important healer, and without question the busiest midwife in Hallowell during the most active years of her practice, . . . she was one among many women with acknowledged medical skills." Had she not felt compelled for whatever reason to record the births, the adventures in reaching the mother's side, and her own family's comings and goings, little would ever have been known of her; there is no gravestone, and there is only her husband's name on all the local documents. "Outside her own diary, Martha has no history."

Thanks to Ulrich, she does now.

Who first started writing women into American history?

Not even **Mercy Otis Warren**'s history of the American Revolution (see page 19) had any women as leading figures. It took until 1850 before women's activities in the Revolution went into book form, courtesy of author **Elizabeth Ellett** (1812?–1877).

After concentrating in her early writing on poetry, Ellett discovered that none of the histories of the American Revolution told of women's struggles. So she examined women's letters, talked with their descendants, and wrote *The Women of the American Revolution*. The first two volumes were published in 1848 and another in 1850. She also wrote *The Domestic History of the American Revolution*, published in 1850, and *Pioneer Women of the West*, published in 1852.

Other early writings on women's history include Samuel Knapp's *Female Biography* (1834) and Lydia Maria Child's *Brief History of the Condition of Women* (1845).

Who was America's first female dramatic star?

British-born **Ann Brunton Merry** (1769–1808), daughter of a grocer turned actor, was a seasoned veteran of seven years on the Covent Garden Stage in London when, at twenty-seven, she was offered a chance to perform in America. She needed the money because of family financial difficulties, so she and her husband set sail for the United States. She debuted on December 5, 1796, in *Romeo and Juliet.* One critic described her death scene as "inimitably fine." It was the first time any leading actor from the principal British stages had appeared in America, and she remained in the United States as a star.

Merry's husband died in 1798 and in January 1803 she married **Thomas Wignell,** manager of Philadelphia's Chestnut Street Theatre. They were considered a sound match, but Wignell died seven weeks after the wedding due to an infection he contracted during bloodletting, the means used to treat many ailments. His widow became co-manager of the theater, setting high standards for performance and also seeking to import well-known actors. She eventually returned to the stage, leaving management to **William Warren,** whom she later married. She became one of the first actors whose guest appearances could become gala (and lucrative) events. She died at thirty-nine in Alexandria, Virginia, after having delivered a still-born son.

How did slavery affect black women in the South?

The first Africans arrived in Virginia as slaves in 1619. Initially, at least some of these servants were able to work their way into freedom, but that system quickly changed and became particularly exploitive of women. For example, under some of the earliest laws that affected black women, their status dictated that if they were slaves, so were their babies, even if the father was white and free.

Slaves received no education; that was against the law. They worked for whichever whites owned them and they could be separated from their spouse and children and sold. It was therefore perfectly normal for a Virginia woman to write in 1863: "I am anxious to buy a small healthy negro girl—ten or twelve years old, and would like to know if you could let me have one." Slaves lived where they were told to live, performing whatever job they were assigned by the white owner or his overseer. Working from before sunup to after sundown, slave women did both their tasks in the white household or in the fields, and then fed their own families and did their own washing, cleaning, and sewing. Their white owners, or the owners' sons, or the owners' overseers could and did demand sexual relations with them; slave women had no recourse but to submit or occasionally to flee.

When they were as little as four years old, females born into slavery might be assigned to care for their master's children. They might be selected as a maid for their owner's daughter and therefore sleep in her room, wake before dawn to build a fire, and wait on the girl during the day. Sometimes the children would play together, but it was always clear who was mistress and who was not. This status might bring with it better clothing and diet, but it came at the cost of ties with the slave child's own mother. It did not protect the slave child from banishment to the harder field labor if plantation needs changed or if her mistress grew angry with her. And it did not guarantee immunity from sexual advances from the white men of the family as the slave girl grew into a young woman.

Other young slave women helped clean the plantation house and prepare the meals under the sharp eye of the owner's wife. Some household servants rose to positions of considerable influence as cooks and nurses, especially if the mistress of the household was inexperienced or incapable of managing her home—but these women were still slaves. Their value and experience did them little good if a comparatively good master died and his heirs were not benign or fell on hard times. Slaves were property and in these circumstances might easily be sold away from the only homes and jobs they had known.

Women who worked in the fields chopped weeds away from cotton plants early in the growing season, then later picked the crop. Plowing was generally a man's task but some strong women managed to obtain that job, sometimes because they preferred working standing up rather than stooped over tending to crops. Others liked the independence they felt while doing the plowing. But they were still slaves.

As slaves became the main workforce in the South and as laws supposedly suppressed the legal import of slaves, emphasis was placed on producing more workers. On the auction block, slave women might be stripped and sold as "good breeders." Slave owners, who sometimes recognized marriages between black couples and sometimes did not, often picked out men and women to mate to produce the strongest children. Once pregnant, women might have their workloads lightened somewhat during the last month before the child was born; when they had their babies, they would be given a month away from the fields and then had to return to work, taking breaks several times a day to nurse their infants. Later the babies would be taken into the fields because, as one owner said, it cost the women too much time to go home to nurse.

Resisting the will of slave owners or overseers often led to whippings or worse. Abolitionist **Sarah Grimké** wrote of a young seamstress who frequently ran away, only to be caught and turned over to the overseer of the Charleston, South Carolina, workhouse to be whipped. "This had been done with such inhuman severity, as to lacerate her back in a shocking manner; a finger could not be laid between the cuts." Yet women did resist, sometimes privately by poisoning their owners or setting fires, and sometimes publicly as they figured in slave revolts of the seventeenth and eighteenth centuries. For example, in 1732, a black woman was hanged for conspiring with four men in Louisiana; in 1766, a Maryland slave woman was executed for burning her owner's home and tobacco house; and in 1800, **Nancy** and **Gabriel Prosser** led a thousand slaves on a march on Richmond before their revolt was put down by the militia.

Black male slaves were often powerless to block exploitation of black women by white landowners although they sometimes resisted at the cost of their own lives. The presence of mixed race, or mulatto, children on many plantations proved the dalliances of the white owners and overseers. Plantation wives either looked the other way or vented their frustrations on the black women themselves. As **Mary Chesnut,** daughter of an antebellum South Carolina governor and wife of a U.S. Senator, commented: "Like the patriarchs of old, our men live all in one house with their wives and their concubines; and the mulattoes one sees in every family partly resemble the white children. Any lady is ready to tell you who is the father of all the mulatto children in everybody's household but her own. Those, she seems to think, drop from the clouds."

Who put women on a pedestal, and why?

Catharine Beecher (1800–1878), an independent woman of the nineteenth century, sought through her writings and lecturing to elevate the role of women in the home and balance it with men's control of the public sphere, that is, business and politics. She extolled the civilizing role of women, which was considered especially important as the United States entered an uncertain period of transition from an agrarian world to one centering on the factory and the office. When she spoke of the purity of women, it was not so much to elevate them on a pedestal above the fray—although that certainly was one interpretation of her thought; rather, she wanted to ensure that women played more than a menial role.

Beecher was one of those women who did one thing and said another. The daughter of a leading Calvinist, **Lyman Beecher,** she was engaged to a young Yale professor who died in a shipwreck; she never married in an age in which being single was both pitied and scorned. She had to wrestle free of her father's relentless attempts to win her full conversion to his faith and thus her submission to it. Once she did, she opened what became the celebrated Hartford Female Seminary in 1823, lectured, wrote, and traveled widely. Although she was the expert of her day on domesticity, she never made a permanent home for herself. Beecher, who had no children, wrote about childrearing, detailed plans for efficient homes, and outlined her philosophy that would have women be the moral guardians of the age. Women would make the home a sanctuary for men who went to business every day, and they would instill in their children the universal values that would seek to knit together an increasingly diverse country.

A good student, Beecher had won prizes and excelled in drama. But it was not until after her fiancé died and she was sorting through his papers that she discovered that she enjoyed reading mathematics, logic, and philosophy. A job as a tutor showed her that she could make her way as a teacher—which she had to do because her family lacked financial resources. In the 1830s and 1840s, she toured the country to recruit women to teach in the developing western United States—Iowa, Illinois, and Kentucky still being considered western at the time— and to raise money to help support them. As the population in these regions increased, communities needed more teachers but often lacked the money to pay men, who commanded higher salaries because they could get other jobs. They turned to women, partly for economic reasons and partly because Beecher had been extolling their ability to transmit the culture to the next generation. Beecher saw women as ideal to teach children "neatness, order and thrift" as well as morality, mathematics, and grammar.

Beecher supported lower pay as a way to encourage schools to hire women. During her campaign to prod Congress to create free teachers' colleges for women, she said that women could afford to work for less than men because female teachers did not have to worry about supporting families if they married and had only themselves to look out for if they did not. But by the 1870s, according to her biographer, Kathryn Kish Sklar, Beecher had come to believe that female teachers were "unjustly denied equal compensation" with men. She felt all girls should be educated so that they could support themselves if they had to do so.

Beecher believed that women would have their greatest influence as moral arbiters. The other school of feminist thought in the mid-nineteenth century, that led by the Grimké sisters and then by **Elizabeth Cady Stanton** and **Susan B. Anthony,** held that women needed to vote and be politically involved, especially in efforts to abolish slavery. Beecher, however, felt that a woman's place was in the home, a vantage point from which she would have the most civilizing impact. In the short run, Beecher's views won out because most women had few career options and therefore remained in the home. In the long run, however, the political feminists held sway as the economic situation changed and more women went to work outside the home. They would demand political rights to protect their interests. Nonetheless, Beecher had helped shape the debate. She did not sit docilely at home, waiting to influence husband and children, having none. Rather, through lectures and the printed word, she defined the terms of the argument. For women in America, that was a new role.

What was "Fanny Wrightism," and why was the woman after whom it was named so vilified?

Scottish-born **Frances Wright** (1795–1852) came to America in 1818 and, in 1825, became the first woman in the United States to act publicly against slavery when she established a commune of black and white farmworkers, called Nashoba, in Tennessee. Because she spoke frankly about sexuality, religion, and virtually everything else, her name was used to discredit liberal causes. "The fear of female deviance was reaching deep into the culture," wrote her biographer, Celia Morris, in *Fanny Wright: Rebel in America,* "and Fanny had become the symbol of most things women should not be." As a measure of the vehement reactions that Wright and her ideas engendered, Morris recorded that in 1836 a British abolitionist, George Thompson, was ridiculed as a Fanny Wrightist and almost killed.

Fanny Wright caught the public eye in 1821 when she published *Views of Society and Manners in America* about her first trip to the young United States. In that book she recognized all the issues with which she would later deal, such as the condition of women in America and the evils of slavery.

In 1824, three years after meeting the **Marquis de Lafayette,** the famous French general, and becoming so devoted to him that his family became openly annoyed, Wright accompanied him on his triumphal farewell trip through the United States. While she was in Philadelphia, she met with the mulatto representative of the Haitian government, thus breaking a taboo against social mixing between blacks and whites. Her disregard for convention eased the process by which jealous friends and relatives were able to separate her from Lafayette.

Later, while traveling along the Mississippi River, Wright and her sister **Camilla** saw along the shores the porticoed plantation homes of cotton barons. Writing of Mississippi's beauty, Wright said that she could have wept as she thought "that such a garden was wrought by the hands of slaves." She believed that many Americans wanted to rid the country of slavery if a way to do so could only be found. Her idea was to establish plantations on which blacks who worked hard could earn their freedom. She expected that that goal would stimulate them to prodigies of effort that would show up slave labor as unprofitable. To assure slave owners that they would not lose money, her plan called for slaves to work off their purchase price, which she calculated would take about five years. In 1825, Wright bought ten slaves and 640 acres of land not far from what is now Memphis, Tennessee. Land was cleared and worked, but prosperity was not to be. Wright overworked herself and became ill.

While traveling in Europe to regain her health, she learned that an abolitionist newspaper had published an account of Nashoba by her associate **James Richardson** in which he described lashing several slaves and admitted to living with a free black woman. Wright never disavowed what Richardson wrote and Nashoba's image became tarnished with the scandal over "free love," race-mixing, and inhumanity to the people who were supposedly being helped.

Rather than back away from controversy, Wright published her views. As Celia Morris wrote: "Against her culture's insistence that sexuality was shameful, she wrote that sexual passion was 'the strongest and . . . the noblest of the human passions,' the basis of 'the best joys of our existence,' and 'the best source of human happiness.' Self-denial could not lead to goodness."

On returning from Europe, Wright found that the Nashoba slaves had not worked as well as she had hoped and that the system she designed had been abandoned. As she put it: "Cooperation . . . has well nigh killed us all." She gave up on Nashoba and, at thirty-three, moved to Robert Owen's colony at New Harmony, Indiana, where she became co-editor with his son, **Robert Dale Owen,** of the *New Harmony Gazette*. In that paper over the next two years, Wright wrote about politics and religion, subjects on which American women had been almost completely barred from expressing themselves since the Revolutionary War.

On July 4, 1828, Wright became the first woman to speak in public before a large mixed audience of men and women. She was an imposing and eloquent speaker. That, plus the novelty of hearing a woman speak in public, drew large crowds as she moved on to lecture in Cincinnati and subsequently in Baltimore, Philadelphia, and New York City. Wright contended that women were men's equals and that, according to biographer Morris, "if women were unenlightened, they would injure and debase the men with whom they lived." In order for affection to prevail, power had to be "annihilated on one side, fear and obedience on the other."

Wright herself had vowed never to marry. But in 1830, following a trip to Haiti, she had to face the fact that she was pregnant and that any illegitimate child of hers would face an especially vicious world. In considering her decision to marry her lover, **William Phiquepal D'Arusmont,** a French doctor she had met at New Harmony, "Fanny now confronted her ultimate vulnerability as a woman, and she confronted it at a time when she had triumphed over every other restraint on women's lives," according to Morris. Wright soon returned to Europe, where she had a daughter, Sylva, and several months later married Phiquepal. Although she returned to the lecture circuit, she was rarely the public figure she had once been. Divorced in 1850, she died in Cincinnati in 1852.

Who was Harriet Tubman, and why was she called the "Black Moses"?

Just like Moses with the Israelites, **Harriet Tubman** (1820?–1913) not only said to let her people go but also helped them escape. She may not have had to part the waters of the Red Sea, but she faced many dangers in returning repeatedly to Maryland and helping slaves reach freedom in Canada.

Born a slave herself in Dorchester County, Maryland, Tubman spent a great deal of time as a young girl praying and thinking about slavery while recovering from a head injury. She had been hit by a two-pound weight thrown by an angry overseer. She came to realize that she should trust herself and God in trying to overcome the obstacles of her daily life as a slave. She took matters into her own hands at last when she heard that her young master's slaves might be sold into the Deep South. She fled to Philadelphia in 1849 and found work at a hotel.

The next year she went to Baltimore to free her sister and her sister's two children. The following year she rescued two brothers and their families, and finally, in 1857, she was able to bring her elderly parents north from the Eastern Shore of Maryland. The route north for this illegal and hazardous smuggling of slaves was called the Underground Railroad, and Harriet Tubman was one conductor who boasted that she never lost a passenger. In all, she made some nineteen trips into slave territory before the Civil War and may have brought out as many as three hundred people. To outsmart potential pursuers, she once bought tickets on a southbound train for herself and her passengers, figuring that no one would suspect them if they were seemingly heading farther south. Rewards for her capture reached forty thousand dollars. Her work was supported by many of the leading northern abolitionists who helped her with money, supplies, and shelter.

During the Civil War, she volunteered as a spy and a scout in South Carolina, often obtaining information from slaves who still lived behind Confederate lines. Once she came under fire during a battle with rebel troops.

After the war, she returned to Auburn, New York, an area where abolitionism and women's rights had long been popular and where she had bought a home. She raised money for schools for freed slaves and worked to care for the elderly. She bought twenty-five acres of land near her own house and formally opened the Harriet Tubman Home for the Aged and Indigent Colored People in 1908. She died there of pneumonia in 1913.

"And Ar'n't I a Woman?"

"Nobody eber helps me into carriages, or ober mud-puddles, or give me any best place," said [Sojourner] Truth, and, raising herself to her full height, and her voice to a pitch like rolling thunder, she asked, "And Ar'n't I a woman? Look at me. Look at my arm," and she bared her right arm to the shoulder, showing its tremendous muscular power. "I have plowed and planted and gathered into barns, and no man could head me—and Ar'n't I a woman? I could work as much and eat as much as a man (when I could get it) and bear de lash as well—and Ar'n't I a woman? I have borne thirteen chillen, and seen 'em mos' all sold off into slavery, and when I cried out with a mother's grief, none but Jesus heard—and Ar'n't I a woman?"

—Sojourner Truth, 1851,
as recorded by Frances Dana Gage
and published in *Narrative of Sojourner Truth*, 1875

How did Sojourner Truth get her name?

Isabella Van Wagenen, as **Sojourner Truth** (1797?–1883) was known until she took up her evangelical calling, was born a slave in upstate New York. After deciding to become a traveling evangelist in middle age, she told author **Harriet Beecher Stowe** that she asked the Lord for a new name. "And the Lord gave me Sojourner, because I was to travel up an' down the land, showin' the people their sins." Then she told the Lord she wanted two names because everybody else had two, "and the Lord gave me Truth, because I was to declare the truth to the people."

Isabella had seen the brutality of the slave system firsthand. Her second owner sold her away from her mother when she was about nine, and her third owner beat her because she could not speak English, only Dutch. As she grew older and attached to a slave named Robert from a nearby farm, she had to watch as he was beaten by his owner and the owner's son for coming to see her. Treating Robert like an animal, his owners wanted to mate him with a woman on their own farm.

She married a man named Tom who lived on the same farm. They had five children. Brought up to be honest in all ways, Isabella said she knew it was mean to run away from her owners, but she could *walk* away—and she did. A year later, her son Peter was sold into continued slavery in Alabama even though New York's law freeing the slaves barred such actions. Isabella went to court repeatedly and eventually won her son's release. While she was doing domestic work in Kingston, New York, to support herself during this period, she attended church for the first time.

Deciding to broaden her horizons, she moved to New York City. Through one of her employers, she came into contact with **Robert Matthias,** who called himself "the last of the Apostles" and preached that he had come to set up the Kingdom on Earth. Isabella went to live with a community of about twenty of his followers who shared homes near Sing Sing along the Hudson River and in New York City. This chapter was not the prettiest part of her life, and she ended up accused by several disenchanted followers of helping Matthias poison another of their colleagues, who had probably died of epilepsy. Isabella was never formally charged and Matthias was acquitted, so she successfully brought slander charges against her accuser.

One of her biographers, Carleton Mabee, who wrote *Sojourner Truth: Slave, Prophet, Legend,* has pointed out that she remained illiterate throughout her lifetime although she had opportunities to learn to read and write. True, he wrote, masters rarely taught slaves to read, but Sojourner Truth was only about thirty years old when she became a free woman. Several people tried to teach her to read; she said the letters were jumbled for her. Mabee speculated that she might have had a vision or learning disorder that today could have been treated but in the nineteenth century would not have been. Or, like others trying to learn to read once they reach adulthood, she may simply have been too intimidated by the task. Later she began to boast that she had achieved what she had achieved without ever learning to read or write. As Mabee put it, she had turned illiteracy from a handicap "into a significant element of her charm."

After she became an evangelist and took her new name, Truth focused on several causes over her public years, often in conjunction with selling the book *Narrative of Sojourner Truth,* written down for her by her friend, abolitionist **Olive Gilbert.** Truth's first documented reform speech occurred in October 1850 at a women's rights convention in Worcester, Massachusetts. She said women should become active in the world because "woman set the world wrong by eating the forbidden fruit, and now she was going to set it right." The following month she spoke out at a meeting in Providence, Rhode Island, against the law that required the return of escaped slaves to their owners.

She continued to speak out against slavery and then, near the end of the Civil War, went to Washington to work for a relief association to help freed slaves learn about their rights and obtain jobs. By example, she helped them assert their right to ride on Washington's segregated public transportation, having encountered segregation herself when she was forced to ride in smoking cars on trains or outside on stagecoaches. On several occasions in Washington, she insisted on riding with the rest of the passengers, one time riding farther than she intended because she was so pleased at having been successful. Another time she was dragged several yards while clinging to a railing when a horse-car conductor started the car quickly so that she could not get aboard. She complained to the president of the company and the conductor was dismissed. When another conductor tried to put Truth off one of the horse cars and slammed her into a door, bruising her shoulder, she charged him with assault. The man was brought to trial, and he also lost his job.

Best known today for her feminist speeches, Truth was in her day one of the few black women allied in that cause. She constantly goaded women to assert themselves, saying in one speech in 1869, "If you want any t'ing, ask for it. If it ain't worth asking for, it ain't worth having." Having grown up a slave, she was especially conscious of working-class women's need for fair pay. She echoed many a more modern woman's urging for women to have money of their own when she said, "We do as much, we eat as much, we want as much. . . . What we want is a little money. You men know that you get as much again as women when you write, or for what[ever] you do. When we get our rights, we shall not have to come to you for money, for then we shall have money enough of our own."

Her constant theme was that women worked as hard, or harder, than men and deserved equality. It was in that vein that she gave her most famous speech in Akron, Ohio, in 1851, in which she said that she had as much strength as any man and that she had plowed and chopped and mowed and that she deserved equal rights. Carleton Mabee has argued that the rhythm of that speech—especially the repetition of the now-famous phrase, "And Ar'n't I a woman?"—came more likely from Frances Dana Gage, the woman who was presiding at the Akron meeting and who recorded the speech twelve years later, than from Sojourner Truth herself.

Historian Nell Painter also found no contemporary documentation for Truth's most famous words. For the substance, yes, in the *Anti-Slavery Bugle* of Salem, Ohio, but for the exact style, no. She has argued that Truth's marketing technique—"selling her shadow to support her substance"—helped provide the link between Truth and the "Ar'n't I a woman?" lines. Truth dictated her narrative to Olive Gilbert and sold the small volume to help support herself. Accustomed to having others tell her story in writing, she never contradicted Gage's account of the speech in which the famous lines first appeared. Those words certainly conveyed Truth's meaning. "It may seem ironic," Painter concluded, "that Sojourner Truth is known for words she did not utter, but American history is full of symbols that do their work without a basis in life. . . . Like other invented greats, Truth is consumed as a signifier and beloved for what we need her to have said."

Who were the first Southern white women to speak out against slavery?

Angelina Grimké (1805–1879), raised in a slave-owning family in South Carolina, argued that no person could be considered a *thing,* and that God gave all mankind a natural right to freedom. Even though women did not make laws, she addressed her 1836 manifesto, *Appeal to the Christian Women of the South,* to them to encourage study, prayer, and speeches on the subject. "Try to persuade your husband, father, brothers and sons that slavery is a crime *against God and man,* " she wrote, urging the women to petition their legislatures for an end to slavery. Her message, the first by a Southern woman to Southern women and published by the American Anti-Slavery Society of New York, resulted in a warning from Charleston authorities that she would be subject to arrest if she returned to her hometown. The Charleston postmaster publicly burned copies of the *Appeal.*

Angelina and her older sister **Sarah** (1792–1873) had moved from Charleston to Philadelphia because of their increasing discomfort with slavery but more immediately because they sought compatible surroundings in which to practice the Quakerism to which they had both converted.

Sarah, who would also become an abolitionist agent like her sister, had shown signs of restiveness as a child. The Grimké sisters' father, a judge and prominent planter, had encouraged education for Sarah similar to that of her brother Thomas—up to a point. Sarah, who had studied world history, Greek, and science and participated with her brothers in family debates, was told no when she asked to join her brother in studying Latin. But Sarah's education was hardly the only one that was stunted. The laws of South Carolina forbade teaching slaves to read or write. Sarah wrote later that she took "almost malicious satisfaction" in teaching the slave girl who waited on her to read. "The light was put out, the keyhole screened, and flat on our stomachs, with the spelling-book under our eyes, we defied the laws of South Carolina." Found out in her efforts, she received a severe lecture and began to realize that not only did the slave have no freedom but she herself had far less than her brothers.

After their father died, Sarah became increasingly interested in the Quaker teachings and moved to Philadelphia in 1821. Angelina, whom Sarah had helped raise, followed in converting to Quakerism and then left Charleston herself late in 1829. The sisters remained relatively uninformed about political issues until Angelina started attending antislavery lectures in 1835. That summer she wrote a personal letter to abolitionist leader **William Lloyd Garrison** supporting his outspoken devotion to emancipation. Garrison printed the letter in his paper, *The Liberator,* and Angelina was publicly launched in the cause as one of the few white abolitionists who had lived with slavery and knew its consequences firsthand.

Not long after Angelina's *Appeal* was published the following year, the sisters went to work as antislavery agents in a day when women rarely spoke in public. They spoke in churches and other public forums—at first to women only, then to mixed audiences—about the evils of slavery that they had seen. Some of their own supporters worried that they would harm the cause because their lecturing might be labeled "a Fanny Wright affair" after the outspoken woman who had gone on the lecture circuit a decade earlier. That concern did not deter the Grimké sisters.

Sarah also appealed to her former compatriots in an *Epistle to the Clergy of the Southern States,* writing about the incompatibility of slavery and Christianity. Facing attack from the nation's pulpits, Sarah later would assert women's rights and defend their free speech in *Letters on the Equality of the Sexes.* She compared women's condition with that of slaves and condemned mistreatment of slave women. Women must assert themselves to be free, she said. "All I ask our brethren is, that they will take their feet from our necks, and permit us to stand upright on that ground which God designed us to occupy."

In 1838, Angelina became the first woman ever to address a state legislative committee in Boston. She urged the lawmakers to act on the antislavery petitions signed by twenty thousand

Massachusetts women, and she defended women's political activity as citizens. That same year, she married **Theodore Weld,** who had helped school her in abolitionist thought and organizing methods. After their marriage in Philadelphia, the Welds were soon back at antislavery meetings in the new Pennsylvania Hall, built expressly so abolitionists could have a hall of their own in the face of rising hostility toward them. No sooner was the hall dedicated than mobs formed. Angelina Grimké Weld—married two days—calmed the group inside the hall as bricks hurled from outside shattered the windows. The mob continued its agitation as she spoke for an hour—her last public speech for many years as she would soon begin raising a family. The next day women walked arm in arm, black with white, away from the hall amid a rain of curses and stones. That night the mob burned the new hall to the ground.

After the Civil War, the sisters discovered that one of their brothers had fathered three children by the slave woman who was his children's nurse. They helped support two of the young men through college. **Francis Grimké** became a Presbyterian minister and Howard University trustee. **Archibald Grimké** graduated from Harvard Law School in 1874 and was a writer and political figure, serving as U.S. consul to Santo Domingo and also as an NAACP vice president. In their later years, the Grimké sisters were educators and raised Angelina's children.

Why was medical school especially tough for Elizabeth Blackwell?

Elizabeth Blackwell (1821–1910) applied to twenty-nine medical schools before she was admitted to one. There, the students and faculty seemed to treat her arrival as a joke. As the sole female medical student, she had to endure the scorn and loneliness of being an oddity; later she was also unable to rent office space, was shunned by male doctors, not allowed access to city hospital wards, and cut off from chances for professional growth and stimulation. The indignities made her more determined to succeed. She not only established a clinic run by female doctors but also eventually started a medical school for women.

Born in England, Blackwell came to the United States when she was eleven years old. The daughter of an outspoken abolitionist, Elizabeth had to go to work as a teacher when her father died of a fever when she was seventeen. But teaching bored her, and the prospects of the lifelong association involved in marriage repelled her. When the idea of studying medicine was suggested to her, she was, as she said later, disgusted by "the physical structure of the body and its various ailments." But she seems to have decided that studying medicine might enable her to avoid marriage; once she drew rebuffs in her academic efforts, the "great moral struggle" appealed to her. She may also have felt drawn to medicine after a friend confided that her suffering—from what likely was uterine cancer—might have been reduced had she been treated by a female doctor.

At Geneva College, Blackwell attended dissection classes that no woman had attended before and had to fight for her rights and for the respect of her fellow students. Yet so torn was she about the role she should play that when she graduated in 1849 at the head of her class—the first woman to earn a medical degree in the United States—she chose not to walk in the procession because it would be unladylike.

She traveled to Europe for further instruction after graduation and was influenced by **Florence Nightingale** to focus on the importance of hygiene to good health. Women were gaining some acceptance in medicine because of the general movement toward prevention instead of "heroic" measures such as surgery. There was still great resistance within the public and the profession; men praised women for their nursing skills but were not willing to open medical schools to them or conduct clinical practice with those women who proved able to obtain an education.

On her return to the United States, unable to find patients or places to treat them, Blackwell prepared lectures on hygiene and physical education for girls. The lectures attracted an audience among Quaker women, who in turn steered patients toward her and provided moral support. She opened a small dispensary to treat poor women on East 7th Street in New York in 1853. Later, she enlarged it into the New York Infirmary for Women and Children on Bleecker Street in 1857. Working with her were her younger sister, Dr. **Emily Blackwell,** who had graduated with honors from Western Reserve in 1854, and a Polish-born doctor, **Marie E. Zakrzewska.**

Elizabeth and Emily Blackwell did not want to remain lonely pioneers as women in medicine, and in 1860 they wrote strong arguments for training more women. Female physicians, they said, might better treat women patients and could help spread to other women a knowledge of hygiene and physiology that would enable them to raise healthier families. Increasingly, people were learning that health was a science; the Blackwells argued that its principles needed to be taught to women as well as men. They also considered that the medical profession was too far removed from the daily lives of women, who were, after all, half its patients. And they disputed the notion that medical education would harm women in their family roles, believing instead that it would help them to a "wider view of their work."

Blackwell opened the Woman's Medical College of the New York Infirmary in 1868. She set high standards so that the college's female students could withstand the scrutiny they would doubtless receive from the men in the profession and from potential patients. There were entrance examinations, chances for clinical experience, and an outside examining board of physicians. Blackwell's college was one of four founded for women that matched in standards the best medical schools for men. In fact, the high caliber of training these women's medical schools provided was then used by opponents of coeducational training as an argument that women didn't need admission to Harvard and other male-only schools.

In 1871, having returned to England to live permanently, Blackwell started the National Health Society, whose motto in many ways summed up her credo: "Prevention is better than cure." She died in 1910 after a fall downstairs.

Could the Blackwells be called the "First Family of Women's Rights"?

The Blackwell clan included two of the first female physicians in the United States, an early female journalist, and two male family members who supported their wives in their own groundbreaking reform work. **Samuel Blackwell** exposed his daughters and sons to progressive opinions. Four maiden aunts, plus a grandmother who railed against marriage, held different views than were espoused in many families in the first half of the nineteenth century. None of the Blackwell girls ever married.

The women born into the Blackwell family were at their most active in opening the professions to women. The oldest Blackwell, **Anna,** became a journalist; one of the younger sisters, **Ellen,** was an artist. **Elizabeth** was the first woman to graduate from medical school in the United States, and her sister **Emily** took that path as well. Rejected by eleven medical schools, Emily was accepted at Rush Medical College in Chicago, but the state medical society blocked her enrollment there after the first year. She graduated from Western Reserve University. She worked with her sister at an infirmary and medical school for women in New York and, once Elizabeth moved to England, Emily ran the school for thirty years, serving as dean and professor of obstetrics and diseases of women. When Cornell University's medical school admitted women, Emily Blackwell transferred her students to Cornell because she and her sisters were firm believers in coeducation.

The women who married into the Blackwell family focused on social reforms. **Lucy Stone** campaigned for the abolition of slavery and votes for women. **Antoinette Brown Blackwell** was active in the suffrage movement after becoming the first woman ordained as a minister in 1853. While a senior at Oberlin College, Antoinette wrote an essay arguing that the Greek version of Paul's biblical warning that women should keep silent in church was being misinterpreted. Inconsequential babbling, not serious talk, was Paul's intended target, she wrote. Antoinette joined with sister-in-law Lucy Stone in working with the American Woman Suffrage Association (AWSA) and writing for its *Woman's Journal.*

Finally, there is **Alice Stone Blackwell,** who was an adolescent when her mother, Lucy, organized the AWSA in 1869. Elected class president while at Boston University, she worked at the *Woman's Journal* after graduation and undertook the bulk of its preparation for the next thirty-five years. She was a prime mover in reunifying the rival suffrage groups—her mother's AWSA and the National Woman Suffrage Association headed by **Susan B. Anthony** and **Elizabeth Cady Stanton.** Alice remained active in the new organization until the Nineteenth Amendment giving women the right to vote became part of the Constitution in 1920, then helped found the Massachusetts League of Women Voters. She died at ninety-three in 1950.

CHAPTER 3

~

America at
Mid-Nineteenth Century:
Stirrings of Change

Why did a man preside over the first women's rights meeting at Seneca Falls, New York?

Who was Elizabeth Cady Stanton's mentor?

What did the women's declaration of independence seek?

Why did feminist Elizabeth Cady Stanton argue that she had to stay home with her children instead of attending women's rights conventions or making speeches?

What were the last public words of Susan B. Anthony? Since women didn't have the vote by the time she died, had her lifelong mission been for nothing?

What were bloomers, and who wore them?

What was a "Lucy Stoner"?

Milestones: Landmarks on Women's Road to the Ballot Box

~

Why did a man preside over the first women's rights meeting at Seneca Falls, New York?

Upset as they may have been about inequities women faced, the founding mothers of feminism didn't have the nerve to preside over a public meeting of women and men in 1848. Proper women didn't even speak in public in those days, let alone run the show. So the women who called the first women's rights convention at Seneca Falls asked a man who supported their cause, **Lucretia Mott**'s husband, **James,** to chair the session. Even at a follow-up session held two weeks later in Rochester, **Elizabeth Cady Stanton** objected to naming a woman, **Abigail Bush,** to chair the session, calling it "a hazardous experiment." She explained later that she felt women were so unused to public activity that they might be uncertain what to do.

The Seneca Falls convention grew out of the experiences Elizabeth Cady Stanton and Lucretia Mott had shared when female delegates were excluded from participating in an international antislavery meeting in London in 1840. Eight years later, when Mott and her sister **Martha Coffin Wright** were visiting in New York State, they had tea with Stanton, **Jane Hunt,** and **Mary Ann McClintock**. The women did more than talk about their frustrations at home, in their churches, and in their legal standing in the community; they decided to call a convention "to discuss the social, civil and religious condition and rights of women" on July 19 and 20 at the Wesleyan Methodist Chapel in Seneca Falls.

Uncertain how to frame their grievances, they "felt as helpless and hopeless as if they had suddenly been asked to construct a steam engine." After examining various models of masculine organization, they finally took the Declaration of Independence as their example. Stanton drafted and read aloud at the meeting the Declaration of Sentiments in which the women talked not only about their political concerns but also about economic and social issues.

Lucretia Mott, accustomed to appearing in public as a Quaker minister, gave a lengthy address. She also proposed a resolution that passed that women seek to "overthrow the monopoly of the pulpit" and work for equality with men in business and the professions. Former slave and abolitionist publisher **Frederick Douglass** attended and supported the women's ambitions, especially the call for the right to vote. But, as the feminists later recorded in their *History of Woman Suffrage,* the women's efforts were "unsparingly ridiculed by the press, and denounced by the pulpit." The women said they had been "wholly unprepared to find themselves the target for the jibes and jeers of the nation."

Decades would pass before real progress materialized in the fight for women's rights. But the process had been begun in a little village as five discontented women took tea together.

Who was Elizabeth Cady Stanton's mentor?

Lucretia Mott (1793–1880) came from a background that helped mold her as a women's rights leader. In the whaling community in which she grew up, the men were often away, thus leaving the women in charge of business as well as the home. She also worshiped in a Quaker sect that held that men and women were equal before God. She became a teacher and early on saw that female teachers earned less than half the money that men made, which she considered unfair.

Mott became a Quaker minister after the death of her first son. Later she was a leading abolitionist who decried the use of any products, such as cotton cloth, made by slave labor. She helped form antislavery societies and faced down mobs opposing her position. In 1840, she and her husband **James Mott** traveled to London, where she was to be a delegate to the World's Anti-Slavery Convention. A faction of the antislavery movement that opposed women's participation in public life controlled that convention and excluded the female delegates. Present with her husband, Henry, a delegate, was **Elizabeth Cady Stanton,** who talked with Mott about the treatment women received at this meeting and in life in general. Stanton allied herself with Mott's group, considering that most of the abolitionist present were hypocrites, "pretending to be teachers and leaders of men" while subjecting half the human race to their will.

The two women spent much time together in London. Mott, twenty-two years older than Stanton, encouraged her inquiries into philosophy and religion. From Mott, Stanton realized, "I had the same right to think for myself that Luther, Calvin and John Knox had." After women were excluded, Mott and Stanton decided that when they returned home, they would "form a society to advocate the rights of women." It took several years, but they did it, convening the historic Seneca Falls, New York, meeting in 1848. In 1850, Mott wrote *Discourse on Woman* in which she outlined the discrimination women faced in political rights, education, and employment. She remained a firm advocate of women's rights for the remaining thirty years of her life.

In January 1881, Stanton delivered the eulogy at a memorial ceremony for Mott, who had died the preceding November. She extolled this woman who was both mother and independent thinker as "a woman who had sufficient confidence in herself to frame and hold an opinion in the face of opposition." Stanton also finally heeded Mott's frequent urging to write a history of the women's suffrage movement, taking up the task along with **Matilda Joslyn Gage** and **Susan B. Anthony.**

What did the women's declaration of independence seek?

The Declaration of Sentiments, debated and adopted at the first women's rights convention at Seneca Falls, New York, July 19 and 20, 1848, proclaimed in words parallel to the American colonists' Declaration of Independence from Britain: "We hold these truths to be self evident: that all men and women are created equal." Because their treatment by men and government had been inequitable, the women declared that they were demanding "the equal station to which they are entitled."

To support the argument that "the history of mankind is a history of repeated injuries and usurpations on the part of man toward woman, having in direct object the establishment of an absolute tyranny over her," the declaration offered the facts that women could not vote, were subject to laws made without their representation, were considered civilly dead once married, and could not own property or earn wages independently of their husbands. They also could not attend college or become teachers of law or medicine, the women stated in their declaration, and they were excluded from the ministry and from most church participation. On top of all those grievances, they said that they were also denied self-respect and independence.

The principal resolutions debated and passed at this women's rights convention included:

- That any laws that conflicted with women's "true and substantial happiness" should be considered invalid.
- That any laws that placed woman "in a position inferior to man were contrary to the great precept of nature" and therefore had no authority.
- "That woman is man's equal—was intended to be so by the Creator, and the highest good of the race demands that she should be recognized as such."
- That men should encourage women to speak and teach at religious assemblies.

- That men and women be treated the same for their transgressions of behavior.
- That women had been satisfied too long with the reduced role prescribed for them in the Bible, that is, the "corrupt customs and a perverted application of the Scriptures," and should move into an enlarged sphere of activity.
- That women should secure "their sacred right to the elective franchise."
- And that the success of the women's cause "depends upon the zealous and untiring efforts of both men and women, for the overthrow of the monopoly of the pulpit and for the securing to woman an equal participation with men in the various trades, professions and commerce."

The document was debated, adopted, and signed by sixty-eight women and thirty-two men after the group voted to allow the men to join in signing. The closest vote came on the resolution urging women to secure the right to vote. **Elizabeth Cady Stanton** saved some of her toughest language for this debate, saying that if "drunkards, idiots, horse-racing rum-selling rowdies, ignorant foreigners and silly boys" had the vote, women should be insulted that they did not. "Have it we must," she added. "Use it we will."

Why did feminist Elizabeth Cady Stanton argue that she had to stay home with her children instead of attending women's rights conventions or making speeches?

Sheer numbers, for starters. **Elizabeth Cady Stanton** (1815–1902) had seven children. While she was outspoken and vigorous in her support for women's rights, she was well aware that society would discredit her views if she neglected her children. There were few if any women, especially mothers, that she could use as models for a life in the public sphere. Her husband was on the road constantly, on either legal or political business. As much as Stanton complained about changing diapers and stirring the pudding, she indeed loved her children and apparently took no steps to prevent pregnancy. Stanton often became pregnant when her husband did come home.

Elizabeth Cady was born into a family that was comfortably situated in Johnstown, New York, where she studied Greek at home and read widely in her lawyer father's library. There is a story, perhaps true, that when her older brother Eleazar died at twenty and her father was disconsolate, ten-year-old Elizabeth climbed onto his knee and tried to think what she could possibly say that might make him feel less gloomy. Then he said to her, "Oh, my daughter, I wish you were a boy." She replied that she would try to be all her brother had been. She alternated between trying to please her father and being annoyed that the same public activities that he criticized when she undertook them would have been praised if they had been engaged in by a brother.

Elizabeth graduated from Troy Female Seminary in 1832. Her next few years were spent mainly in visiting relatives and friends. In 1840, she married **Henry Stanton,** a journalist who was also an agent for abolitionist groups. They took their honeymoon in England, where Stanton was a delegate to an antislavery convention. Women were excluded from participation, and amid the discussion about this discrimination, Elizabeth Cady Stanton fell into more general conversation with **Lucretia Mott,** a Quaker from Philadelphia, about the injustices women faced.

Back home, Stanton had three children by 1845—with four more to follow between 1851 and 1859. During visits with family members in Albany, the state capital, in the middle 1840s, Stanton did help distribute petitions and lobby the legislature for increased protection so that married women could hold property and not have to surrender its control to their husbands. In 1848, Lucretia Mott went with her husband to a Quaker meeting, and Stanton visited her in Waterloo, New York, pouring out her frustrations. The pair, along with several other Quaker women, decided at last to have the meeting they had pledged to convene when they first met in London. Stanton drafted their Declaration of Sentiments, which called for women to have the right to vote, the first time that demand was made publicly.

Confined to home because of the care of her children, Stanton wrote articles for *The New York Tribune* as well as *The Lily,* the temperance newspaper published by **Amelia Bloomer,** who also lived in Seneca Falls. She insisted on being called Elizabeth Cady Stanton—not the customary Mrs. Henry Stanton—so that she would not feel submerged behind a man's identity.

Stanton met **Susan B. Anthony** in 1851, embarking on their remarkable political partnership and deep friendship that affected the course of feminism until Stanton's death. Stanton frequently called upon Anthony to rescue her from her household drudgery (even though she had servants and one particularly faithful housekeeper) so that she could write the speeches and letters that Anthony was always urging on her. As Stanton became more confident in her later years, she saw less of Anthony, whom she often considered increasingly sanctimonious and whose nagging about her weight clearly bothered her, although not enough to do much about it. At times, as happens even in the most solid of friendships, one would leave the other virtually alone to withstand criticism, resulting in wounded feelings. For example, Anthony took the brunt of fire from local press during a trip the pair made to California—even though both had spoken out on the sexual hypocrisy of a murder case involving a prostitute. Anthony may also have resented the fact that even though they started the newspaper *The Revolution* together, it was Anthony who paid off ten thousand dollars in debts when the paper was sold, even though Stanton had a family inheritance that might have helped.

Nonetheless, the collaboration worked remarkably. Anthony encouraged Stanton to write a keynote speech and deliver it herself at a women's temperance meeting—Stanton's first public speech since her appearances at the Seneca Falls meeting and a follow-up session in Rochester. She spoke about divorce, saying that drunkenness should be grounds for dissolving marriages and that women who had been married to drunkards should have custody of their children.

In 1854, Stanton and Anthony took to the New York legislature the case for the rights of women to vote, to be educated, to own property, to earn and inherit money, and to serve, when widows, as executors of their husbands' estates. Stanton made a stirring speech, but it would be her last for six years as she again felt the need to stay home with her family. In 1860, she was back in Albany, speaking to a legislative committee considering action on married women's property rights. She compared women to slaves, telling the lawmakers that women's ultimate protection would be the right to vote.

Women's rights agitators shut down their activities during the Civil War on grounds that the nation was too distracted to focus on their concerns. Many of the women gathered signatures on petitions for the Thirteenth Amendment, which would free the slaves. Stanton thought devotion to that cause alone would earn reciprocal backing from abolitionists for women's voting rights; Anthony disagreed, and Anthony was right. After the war, the Republicans backed voting rights for black men, not black women or white women. With wicked pen, Stanton attacked by criticizing the qualifications of newly freed slaves as voters. Her antiblack rhetoric stunned her former abolitionist colleagues, contributing to the wedge that divided and retarded women's suffrage activities in the latter decades of the nineteenth century. While the well-born Stanton sympathized with the plight of women in many walks of life, she still wrote from an elitist point of view and also often attacked immigrant men, who she felt opposed women's rights.

By fifty, Stanton could be more independent and focused intently for five years on the reemerging drive for women's rights. She and Anthony, who opposed the Fourteenth and Fifteenth Amendments because women would be excluded from citizenship and voting, became increasingly isolated from their former abolitionist allies. During these years, the allies also petitioned the New York constitutional convention for women's right to vote. They lost—but among the signers of the petitions were Stanton's mother and the wife of suffrage opponent **Horace Greeley.** Greeley was presiding at the subcommittee session before which Stanton and Anthony appeared. They campaigned unsuccessfully for a women's suffrage referendum in Kansas, started the National Woman Suffrage Association, and advocated a constitutional amendment giving women the right to vote. In 1866, Stanton also ran for Congress in New York City, independent of any party affiliation; she received only twenty-four votes and said with her characteristic wit that she wished she had pictures of her "two dozen unknown friends."

Throughout her life, whether an occasion dealt with temperance, abolition of slavery, or specifically on women's rights, Stanton usually used it to talk about how women should be allowed to vote, should refuse to pay taxes on any property they owned until they did have the vote, should be educated, and should be aware that clergymen were women's "most violent enemies." Her feminism deepened, and her perspective on the problems women faced was broader than that of Anthony, who focused more narrowly on tactics needed to win women the right to vote.

Stanton spent most of the 1870s on the lyceum circuit, lecturing for months each year across the country. By 1870, she was for all intents separated from her husband. Henry Stanton later lived in New York while his wife kept her home in Tenafly, New Jersey, where the Stantons had moved in 1868.

Always concerned that religion suppressed women, Stanton delved increasingly into that subject in her later years, to the concern of Anthony, who wanted to keep her focused on political rights. Anthony succeeded for a time, and between 1881 and 1886 the pair published the first three volumes of *History of Woman Suffrage.* (The work was later completed with three more volumes by **Ida Husted Harper,** taking the story through passage of the Nineteenth Amendment.) Finally, Stanton returned to her studies of the way the Bible and organized religion treated women, publishing *The Woman's Bible* in 1895 and a second volume three years later. The next year, her more conservative younger colleagues in the suffrage movement attempted to distance their organization from her work. Anthony tried unsuccessfully to talk them out of their censure, and Stanton became more convinced that the second generation of feminists was too tame.

Stanton, long the more popular speaker than Anthony because of her humor and her warmth, found in her last years that Anthony had become the beloved suffrage leader. Even as new leaders came along, Anthony controlled the major suffrage organization and worked with its younger members, who knew Stanton only as an unpredictable, unorthodox radical thinker. But without Stanton's liberating ideas to couple with Anthony's tireless campaigning, the stage would not have been set for the suffrage amendment that would pass within less than two decades after their deaths. In 1898, Stanton published an autobiography, *Eighty Years and More.* She died in 1902, not long after writing President **Theodore Roosevelt,** asking him to endorse women's right to vote.

What were the last public words of Susan B. Anthony? Since women didn't have the vote by the time she died, had her lifelong mission been for nothing?

"With such women consecrating their lives, failure is impossible!" the suffragist and feminist leader **Susan B. Anthony** (1820–1906) told a crowd gathered for her eighty-sixth birthday celebration. Those were her most famous words, and her last ones in public, for she died less than a month later, on March 13, 1906. Weakened by a severe cold that she caught during a blizzard, Anthony struggled through her birthday festivities, showing her feistiness when President **Theodore Roosevelt** sent greetings; she replied that she would rather have a constitutional amendment giving women the vote than congratulations for another birthday. Then she looked off into the middle distance and said the words that became a rallying cry for feminists for years thereafter.

Anthony was born into a Quaker household in the Berkshires of western Massachusetts and had, as biographer Kathleen Barry wrote, a common enough childhood. Her father allowed no singing or dancing but the children played in the fields and the woods and worked hard with household chores. Young Susan watched, however, as her mother, who was not born a Quaker, repressed some of her own feelings as a result of her husband's church's reaction to his marriage outside his faith.

At four, Susan began learning to read intently—so intently that her eyes crossed. After a few weeks of rest, one eye returned to normal but the other remained crossed the rest of her life. Susan later attended a Quaker school in Pennsylvania, where she heard a lecture by abolitionist **Lucretia Mott,** with whom she later worked on women's issues. When her father's cotton mills failed during the late 1830s, Susan and her sister sought teaching jobs. Susan first worked at a Quaker school in New Rochelle, New York, and later at the Canajoharie Academy near the Mohawk River.

Her first overt political activity came in the cause of temperance, that is, abstinence from alcohol. Nineteenth-century reformers saw alcohol abuse as the cause of many of the ills besetting families—wife-beating, child abuse, desertion, or lack of financial support. Anthony joined the Daughters of Temperance in Canajoharie and made her first public speech in 1849. She especially urged women—the principal victims of "the foul destroyer's inroads"—to unite in action outside the home to curb abuses. She quit her teaching job and moved home to her family's farm in Rochester. For the rest of her life, she remained an activist, supported emotionally and sometimes financially by her family as well as by those working for her causes. She did not make a home for herself until late in life when she bought a house in Rochester, where she lived with her sister Mary.

Working in the temperance movement led to working against slavery; Anthony saw that women were oppressed by being owned and often cruelly treated just as they were oppressed when husbands or fathers drank and abused them. In educating herself on antislavery issues, she traveled to Syracuse in 1851 to hear the famous abolitionist **William Lloyd Garrison** speak and then visited in Seneca Falls, New York, with her friend **Amelia Bloomer**. She had heard about Bloomer's neighbor there, **Elizabeth Cady Stanton,** who had helped call the women's rights meeting in 1848 in her hometown. Anthony met Stanton, and so began a singular political and personal partnership that lasted fifty years.

It is hard to know which was the more remarkable of the pair—Anthony for defying the norm of marriage and family or Stanton for writing and working as she did despite a marriage and family. The common perception is that Stanton was the theorist and Anthony the practical implementer, but it is clear that each fed ideas and strength to the other. Stanton was the radical writer, but Anthony led the more radical life. Both women withstood frequent criticism by the public and the press, but that directed at Anthony was often more personal because she was unmarried, outwardly dour, and often domineering.

Anthony campaigned in Maine for a law tightening controls over traffic in alcohol, her first effort to seek legal changes. She realized that while men might say they voted in women's interests, women could not really have their interests represented unless they themselves had the vote. Her emerging voice was a rare one among women, who were supposed to hold domain at home but not in public. Next, in 1854, she took on the issue in New York State of married women's rights to control their own property. Anthony, Stanton, and their allies lost that crusade but kept at it for the rest of the century, gradually winning some changes. In 1855, for example, Anthony took her petition drive to every county in the state in attempts to organize women on the issue; it would be a pattern of travel and organizing, renting halls, and speaking with local women, politicians, and preachers that she followed across the country and even into Europe for the rest of her life.

Nineteenth-century reformers divided over several fundamental issues: whether abolition of slavery should be immediate or gradual, whether women should get the vote when black males did after the Civil War, and whether the campaign for women's right to vote should be conducted at the national level or state by state. Anthony played key roles in each of these debates.

For example, Anthony and Stanton split with many other abolitionists who considered the time during and immediately after the Civil War as "the Negroes' hour," in that it was essential to protect former slaves by giving them the vote. The Republicans essentially said they lacked the strength to support two reforms—Negro suffrage and women's suffrage—at the same time. Historians have argued that was not the case, that they were instead seeking only the black vote because it would probably go Republican and help keep them in office, whereas the women's vote was less predictable. Anthony and Stanton shot back that black women, as well as black men, had been slaves and were being left out of the Fourteenth and Fifteenth Amendments to the Constitution that guaranteed equal rights of citizenship and suffrage. They had worked in tandem with abolitionists in seeking the end of slavery and felt betrayed when the antislavery forces abandoned their drive for women's equality. They left themselves open to charges of racial bias with their argument that white women were better educated and therefore capable of more informed political participation than the newly freed male slaves.

The women had to go it alone with the exception of brief help from Democrat **George Francis Train,** who helped pay for their losing women's suffrage campaign in Kansas in 1867. Train's anti-Negro opinions further weakened the support Anthony and Stanton had had among the former abolitionists, but he did help finance *The Revolution,* a paper edited by Stanton and **Parker Pillsbury,** with Anthony as publisher. The paper, which opposed the Fourteenth and Fifteenth Amendments and supported equal pay and fairer laws for women, first appeared in 1868 and lasted under Anthony's control only until 1870.

In 1872, Anthony and three of her sisters registered to vote even though local authorities weren't sure they should let them sign up. The voting inspectors who registered the sisters were arrested. Anthony then showed up to vote, along with thirteen other women. Other women had tried to vote over the previous four years in various states, most unsuccessfully, but the arrival of a national figure like Anthony at the polling place made headlines. She was arrested and, after her preliminary hearing in January 1873, wanted to go to jail, but her lawyer paid her bail. Indicted, she voted in a local election in March—this time the only woman who dared do so. When her trial finally started that June, Anthony could not be a witness in her own defense. The reason: she was female. The judge directed that the jury find Anthony guilty in an opinion that he had obviously written before the day's hearing even began. She was fined one hundred dollars and court costs. Anthony refused to pay the fine and the judge refused to jail her until the fine was paid, thus preventing her from appealing the decision to the Supreme Court. Permitted to speak at the end of the trial, Anthony said defiantly that she had not been convicted by a jury of her peers and had been tried under laws "all made by men, interpreted by men, administered by men, in favor of men and against women." She added that she would continue "to urge all women to the practical recognition of the old Revolutionary maxim, 'Resistance to tyranny is obedience to God.' "

Stanton and Anthony worked together despite differing emphases. Anthony felt that without the vote, women would lack the clout to achieve other goals. Stanton leaned more toward achieving some measure of economic independence that would then allow women the freedom to participate in politics. Anthony was not only the on-the-road organizer but also the frequent goad who encouraged—sometimes even browbeat— Stanton into putting her theories into speeches and other documents. Anthony stayed for lengthy visits with Stanton, taking care of her children and becoming part of the family. That neither lived to see women get the vote takes nothing away from their premier leadership in outlining the issue, campaigning for it relentlessly, and paving the way for its eventual accomplishment.

In her last years, Anthony compromised her waning strength with a crusade culminating in the admission of women to the University of Rochester in 1900. Anthony not only spearheaded the drive to raise money for the additional buildings the university said it would need to admit women, she pledged her own life insurance for the last two thousand dollars needed. A few days after the deadline for raising the money, she suffered a small stroke. But well into her eighties, she never stopped her work. For her, there was no way to divide the political from the personal.

What were bloomers, and who wore them?

Radical changes in women's fashion can draw even more attention than radical changes in women's thoughts, but when the two come together, they drive men wild. In the early 1850s, women's rights leaders started wearing a Turkish-looking pantaloon buttoned at the ankles in place of cumbersome long skirts. They still had a skirt over the pants—a skirt that reached slightly below the knees—but this practical clothing reform drew instant derision, even though it made climbing stairs or performing chores easier.

The pantaloons were dubbed bloomers because **Amelia Bloomer,** editor of a temperance newspaper, *The Lily*, championed this dress reform. The name stuck because it sounded a bit silly to the men and women who wanted to put down the reformers, who preferred to call their new outfits simply short dresses or "the American costume."

This new style actually first was worn by **Elizabeth Smith Miller,** who convinced her cousin, women's rights advocate **Elizabeth Cady Stanton,** of its practicality during a visit at her Seneca Falls, New York, home. Stanton not only wore the new costume to speak at the Women's State Temperance Convention in Rochester in 1852, at a time when simply speaking out in public was an assertive act for women, but she also bobbed her hair in a day when respectable women wore their hair long. Furthermore, her message was a radical one—calling for women to unite behind legislation allowing women to divorce their husbands if the men were drunkards and giving women in such situations custody of their children. Later, her adoption of bloomers figured in her husband Henry's campaign for the New York State senate when a wag in the opponent's camp penned these lines: "Twenty tailors take the stitches, Mrs. Stanton wears the breeches."

Stanton's ally **Susan B. Anthony** resisted the new fashion, but by December 1852 she, too, reported that she was "in short skirts and trousers." She had also had her hair cut short. But she found that bloomers drew such hostility when crowds of men would follow her and taunt her as she moved about town, whether renting a hall for a meeting or going to the printer's office, that she began to doubt the wisdom of wearing what she wanted. Ministers preached against the new look, and some people even threw sticks at women who wore bloomers. But Anthony was stubborn and didn't want to cave in to the harassment. "The cup of ridicule is greater than you can bear," Stanton eventually told her friend. "It is not wise, Susan, to use up so much energy" on that question. So Susan B. Anthony let down the hems of her dresses and decided to concentrate on one issue at a time.

What was a "Lucy Stoner"?

When **Lucy Stone** (1818–1893), the first Massachusetts woman to earn a college degree, married **Henry Blackwell** in 1855, she kept her own name, which wasn't done in those days. So any women who followed her example became known as "Lucy Stoners."

Given the inequities that Stone saw in her own life as she was growing up, it was inevitable that she would become a campaigner for women's rights. She felt that her brother had more opportunities and attention even though she could run faster— even learn faster. She didn't like the hard labor that many women, including her mother, had to do, and she didn't appreciate the fact that she could not vote in the affairs of her Congregational church. Later, she also discovered that she earned less as a teacher than men did.

At Oberlin College, Stone studied Greek and read the Bible

in the original to learn if the texts concerning the rights of women had been correctly translated. Many had not been. She became an early abolitionist and women's rights advocate. Later, she and her husband split with **Susan B. Anthony** and **Elizabeth Cady Stanton** over the tactics that should be used to win the right to vote for women. Stone and Blackwell, the more conservative pair, questioned some of the allies chosen by Anthony and Stanton, such as free-love advocate **Victoria Woodhull** and anti-Negro Democrat **George Train**. Stone and Blackwell supported the Fifteenth Amendment giving black males the vote while Stanton and Anthony adamantly opposed it because women were excluded.

To advance their views, Stone and Blackwell started the *Woman's Journal,* a rival publication to Anthony and Stanton's *The Revolution,* in 1870. Historians considered that the paper, edited by daughter **Alice Stone Blackwell** in later years, provided the best reporting on the women's movement, serving in essence as its voice for decades. The paper was not as progressive on issues involving workers as it was about women, however.

By 1890, the rival suffragists reunited in the National American Woman Suffrage Association although antagonisms remained. Lucy Stone died three years later.

Milestones: Landmarks on Women's Road to the Ballot Box

1848—The women's rights convention at Seneca Falls, New York, heard the first public resolution that women should have the right to vote. It passed narrowly. **Lucretia Mott** and **Elizabeth Cady Stanton** led the call for the meeting.

1850—The first national women's convention, attended by Lucretia Mott, **Sojourner Truth,** and **Angelina Grimké,** among others, was held in Worcester, Massachusetts.

1851—Elizabeth Cady Stanton and **Susan B. Anthony**

met, initiating an alliance that led the campaign for women's rights for more than fifty years.

—At an Akron, Ohio, women's convention, Sojourner Truth rose and mesmerized the audience with her argument against the contentions that women were weak and deserved special protection rather than equal rights. To each such argument, she would respond with the burdens she had borne and add, "And ar'n't I a woman?"

1854—Susan B. Anthony led women in a petition drive in New York State for the right to vote as well as for the right for women to control their own earnings and to receive custody of their children in case of divorce. Elizabeth Cady Stanton spoke before the state legislature, which rejected the women's arguments.

1861–1865—Women's rights organizing was suspended during the Civil War. The Woman's National Loyalty League, including Susan B. Anthony and Elizabeth Cady Stanton, circulated petitions to support the Thirteenth Amendment ending slavery.

1866—The American Equal Rights Association was formed to promote the vote for the freed slaves and for women.

—The proposed Fourteenth Amendment for the first time tied citizenship to sex, and was opposed by Stanton and Anthony. It was ratified in 1868.

1867—Kansas voters defeated referenda on both Negro and women's suffrage despite a campaign involving many of the women's rights leaders, including **Lucy Stone** and **Henry Blackwell** as well as Anthony and Stanton.

1868—The first edition of *The Revolution* appeared, edited by Stanton and **Parker Pillsbury** with Anthony as publisher. In its short life span, the newspaper covered the women's movement and editorialized about suffrage, economic equality and opportunity, divorce, women's health, and the discriminatory treatment of women in organized religion.

—Refused the opportunity to vote in the regular election, 172 women in Vineland, New Jersey, cast ballots in boxes set aside for them, demonstrating that they would vote if given the opportunity.

—Senator **S. C. Pomeroy** of Kansas introduced the first federal woman suffrage amendment. A joint resolution for both houses of Congress was submitted in 1869.

1869—Suffrage advocates split over whether they should crusade for their cause on a national level, as Anthony and Stanton wanted, or state by state, as advocated by Lucy Stone and Henry Blackwell. Separate organizations were formed.

1870—The Fifteenth Amendment to the Constitution was ratified. It gave the vote to black males but not to black or white women.

—Women voted in Wyoming Territory, which did not crumble as a result. Because they could register, they also served on juries. Utah Territory enacted women's suffrage.

—Angelina Grimké Weld and her sister **Sarah Grimké** walked through a blizzard to cast ballots into a separate box along with thirty-eight other women in Hyde Park, Massachusetts.

—Between 1870 and 1910, there would be seventeen referenda on women's suffrage in eleven states, most of them west of the Mississippi River. Only two were successful. In all, there were 480 campaigns in thirty-three states to try to get the issue on the ballot.

1872—The notorious **Victoria Woodhull** attempted to become a candidate for president. Susan B. Anthony voted, and was later convicted of doing so illegally.

1876—As the United States observed its centennial, no women were scheduled to speak at the Fourth of July celebrations in Philadelphia. Women asked to present a new Declaration of Rights for Women but were turned down. So, led by Anthony, five women marched into Independence Hall and handed their document to the chairman and marched out again.

1878—Senator **A. A. Sargent** of California introduced the "Anthony Amendment" for women's suffrage, which would be the text debated until it became the Nineteenth Amendment in 1920.

1882—Both houses of Congress named select committees on woman suffrage, and both reported the measure favorably.

1887—The U.S. Senate voted, 16–34, with 26 absent, against women's suffrage. Southern senators were overwhelmingly opposed. One orator's final argument reminded his colleagues that it was shricking women who led bloodthirsty mobs during the French Revolution.

1890—The schism between the two major groups advocating the vote for women ended with formation of the National American Woman Suffrage Association.

—Wyoming was admitted as a state with women's suffrage.

1893—Women's suffrage won in a Colorado referendum.

1900—Susan B. Anthony turned the presidency of the National American Woman Suffrage Association over to **Carrie Chapman Catt**.

1910—Washington became the first state in fourteen years to give women the right to vote. Utah, new to the Union in 1896, had last given women suffrage.

1911—Despite the opposition of liquor interests, which feared that enfranchised women would enact temperance reforms, women won the vote in a closely fought contest in California, bringing to six the number of western states with female suffrage.

1913—**Alice Paul** organized a suffrage parade to compete with President **Woodrow Wilson**'s inauguration.

1917—**Jeannette Rankin** of Montana took her seat as the first woman elected to Congress.

—The National Woman's Party, led by Alice Paul, sent pickets to the White House for the first time in January. They carried signs asking how long women had to wait for liberty, and they marched silently at first. Arrests began in June amid war fever as the women's banners announced that America was a democracy in name only. The imprisoned women went on hunger strikes and officials tried to force-feed them.

1918—A federal appeals court overturned the arrests and sentences of the women who had picketed for suffrage.

—The U.S. House of Representatives passed the women's suffrage amendment, 274–136, with four members coming from their sickbeds to vote; one of them was even carried in on a stretcher.

1919—With far less drama, the U.S. Senate approved the suffrage amendment.

1920—The Nineteenth Amendment granting women the right to vote became law. Only **Charlotte Woodward,** of all the women present at Seneca Falls in 1848, lived to see the right to vote become a reality. She cast a ballot for president that year.

CHAPTER 4

❧

Sending the Girls
to School

Who was one of the first American women to argue that girls needed education for its own value and their own betterment?

Why was higher education considered harmful for women?

Why did African-American women face difficulty attending college?

How did the first women's colleges train their students?

What was the "girl question" in education at the beginning of the twentieth century?

When did women start moving in any numbers onto college and university faculties, and what triggered the advances?

What was significant about the University of Pennsylvania's appointment of a new president in 1993?

_____

❧

Who was one of the first American women to argue that girls needed education for its own value and their own betterment?

Judith Sargent Murray (1751–1820) first tackled the subject of education for girls in an article published in 1779 called "Desultory Thoughts upon the Utility of Encouraging a Degree of Self-Complacency, Especially in Female Bosoms." She addressed the subject again in essays in *Massachusetts Magazine* beginning in 1792.

Married for the first time at eighteen to a sea captain, Murray felt that young women needed more of a sense of themselves so that they wouldn't rush into marriage just to establish their status. Instead of directing young women solely toward marriage, Murray contended that they should become accustomed "to habits of industry and order. They should be taught with precision the art economical; they should be enabled to procure for themselves the necessaries of life; independence should be placed within their grasp." Murray, who had been widowed when her first husband died in 1786, argued that women should be "qualified to administer by their own efforts to their own wants." If women could do for themselves, she added, "The term, *helpless widow,* might be rendered as unfrequent and inapplicable as that of *helpless widower . . .* "

Why was higher education considered harmful for women?

In the eighteenth century, men—and most women—viewed women's role as exclusively that of wife and mother. In colonial society, few women needed more than a smattering of education; they could read and write but little more than that, and indeed many could not sign their own names. Higher education could harm women, the "weaker vessels"—or so the thinking went. Too much stimulation and mental exercise might harm their development. Besides, if women were educated, who would want to stay home and do chores? Many especially felt higher education would be wasted on women because they would only marry and not use their "book learning."

After the American Revolution, in which women had maintained not only the home but sometimes the farm or business as well, people began to see the wisdom of educating women more than minimally. If nothing else, they should know literature, history, and philosophy, as well as reading and writing, in order to bring up their sons to better serve the new republic. The religious revivals that swept the young country in the early nineteenth century also fueled a desire among more women to be missionaries or otherwise do the Lord's work—or at least be sufficiently educated to bring up their children in proper Christian fashion. Economics played a part as well. As young men moved west and some towns had a higher population of women than men, more families also saw that their daughters should be educated so that they could help financially at home or be self-supporting.

Primary schooling for girls originally was conducted in homes, either by the mother or by a neighbor woman who ran a "dame school." Wealthier families had tutors for their sons and sometimes their daughters. A few seminaries were opened for young women in the late eighteenth century but there were no colleges that would admit women while men had Harvard, Yale, and William and Mary.

Threats to the status quo motivated some of the opposition. Educated women might become more than reactors to their families and their surroundings; they might even try to plan their lives. They might, if educated, question being shut out of political life, as they had been by the men who wrote the Constitution, and being rendered dead under the law when they married. And, educated, they could earn their own money and not have to rely on father or brother or husband for bread or roof. The founders of women's colleges sought to assuage these fears by educating women for their domestic and spiritual roles. But they also gave women, initially a few and then thousands, an independence of mind and a sense of community that they had not had. The opposition's concern was justified; the feared questioning came to pass.

While there were some men who helped advance the cause of education for women, it was women themselves who took the major steps toward both quantity and quality of female schooling. **Mary Lyon** (1797–1849) worked hard for her own education and wanted to ensure that women of little means could attend school if they were diligent. By having students perform much of the cleaning, cooking, and sewing at Mount Holyoke, opened as a female seminary in 1837, Lyon was able to keep tuition comparatively low. There was no such thing as student aid in those days; families either financed a young woman's education or she worked her way through school, frequently dropping out to teach or find other employment to earn tuition money.

Despite advances in the nineteenth century, carping critics endured. As late as 1873, retired Harvard Medical School professor **Edward Clarke** questioned women's stamina for higher education and said that young women could not study without risking "neuralgia, uterine disease, hysteria and other derangements of the nervous system." Many educated young women did experience depression after they left school, but from today's perspective it seems more likely that any problems they faced resulted from the lack of opportunity to use their educations rather than the fact that they had gotten them in the first place.

Why did African-American women face difficulty attending college?

Few schools would admit African-Americans even if they had the money—and few had jobs that earned enough to pay tuition or families able to help them financially. Oberlin College in Ohio was the first to admit black and white, male and female. One of its first black female graduates was **Fannie Jackson Coppin** (1837–1913), who had been born a slave in the District of Columbia and later was allowed schooling when she worked as a servant in Newport, Rhode Island. After her graduation in 1865, she taught at the Institute for Colored Youth in Philadelphia and soon became the school's principal; it later moved and became Cheyney State College. Another early Oberlin graduate was **Anna Julia Cooper** (1858?–1964), a teacher and principal who had earned her bachelor's degree in 1884 and a master's degree in 1887. Cooper estimated that in 1891 there were only thirty black women in American colleges.

Education for Southern black women was an even less likely prospect, although by 1881, white missionaries **Sophia Packard** and **Harriet Giles** had opened the Atlanta Baptist Female Seminary. They had raised one hundred dollars at a Baptist church in Medford, Massachusetts, then parlayed that backing into support from the Woman's American Baptist Home Mission Society. With the help of an influential black Baptist pastor in Atlanta, the women also won the support of local ministers and were able to recruit their first eleven students, many of whom walked miles to attend classes and worked to support themselves. The school, named Spelman Seminary soon after its founding in honor of **Mrs. John D. Rockefeller**'s parents (her husband was a major donor), stressed practical skills that black women could use in jobs available to them or in their own homes. There was also a highly moralistic tone, as the founders stressed "right ideas of Christian living" and temperance. Many of Spelman's first graduates became teachers, who were in great demand in the South because blacks had been denied literacy under slavery. In 1900, Rockefeller gave two hundred thousand dollars for new buildings; the school became Spelman College in 1924 and started building toward its goal of providing an excellent liberal arts education. It was not until 1987, however, that Spelman named its first African-American female president, **Johnnetta Cole,** who had been professor and director of Latin American and Caribbean studies at Hunter College in New York City.

How did the first women's colleges train their students?

Mount Holyoke, located in South Hadley, Massachusetts, was the first of the so-called Seven Sisters women's colleges that were created by the close of the nineteenth century. Mount Holyoke started a four-year college curriculum in 1861; a new charter changed the school's name to Mount Holyoke College in 1893. The first school established from the outset as a full-fledged college for women was endowed by a wealthy brewer named **Matthew Vassar** in Poughkeepsie, New York, in 1865.

The earliest women's colleges were designed to offer classes and accommodations under one roof, partly to build a community among faculty and students, partly to protect the female students from the world outside. In *Alma Mater,* Helen Lefkowitz Horowitz examined the original buildings at Mount Holyoke and Vassar, for example, and concluded that, "in each case, the plan of the campus serves as a text that illustrated the hopes and fears that accompanied the bold act of offering the higher learning to women." Men might board out around their campuses and take classes in scattered buildings, but **Mary Lyon** wanted her school housed in one gigantic building. The young women would not only study there but be constantly exposed to the discipline and the example of their teachers, who could become their mentors. Vassar College may have begun with no questions about the quality of women's minds, but the men who planned it followed Lyon's model because, as Horowitz wrote, "Male promoters of women's colleges feared unladylike behavior and scandal above all."

More than 80 percent of the women who graduated from Mount Holyoke in its first dozen years became teachers, a path followed by many of the earliest female college students. Demand for their services developed as new frontier communities established schools; few other jobs were open to educated young women. Women might teach in grade schools and high schools, but few taught at the college level. Few could obtain the graduate degrees that were increasingly necessary. Bryn

Mawr offered graduate degrees from the outset, but many of the men's colleges refused for decades to admit women to graduate-level courses.

That Bryn Mawr should be a leader in graduate education for women should be no surprise, given the selection of **Martha Carey Thomas** (1857–1935) as its first dean. Thomas, who had been in the first Cornell University class to admit women, receiving her bachelor's degree in 1877, later was admitted to graduate study—but not to classes—at Johns Hopkins University. She worked with a private tutor but ultimately received her doctorate *summa cum laude* from the University of Zurich in 1882. After receiving her appointment as Bryn Mawr's dean, Carey Thomas set up a school with high standards employing many German-trained male scholars. She also established a graduate school so that faculty could stay current in their fields by doing research.

What was the "girl question" in education at the beginning of the twentieth century?

What were women supposed to be? Should they learn domestic-science skills so they could better manage their homes? Since some women did find themselves in the wage workforce, should they be trained for trades? Or should they be taught clerical skills to fulfill the expanding business needs? This was the "girl question" in American education in the Progressive Era, 1900 to 1930, a logical extension of the national debate occurring over the broader "woman question." Women's roles, and thus women's needs for education, remained unsettled, and the debate would affect American education for young women for decades.

As policy makers shaped the school curriculum in the early twentieth century, politics and the relative strength of various women's lobbying groups dictated the outcome. Girls' secondary schooling had been much like that of boys. However, as more girls attended public school and more immigrants sought education, it became clear that many young people would not be attending college and might drop out of school. Teachers and reformers sought ways to help them.

In 1914, Congress created a Commission on National Aid to Vocational Education to decide what federal aid should be given to schooling for girls. Initially, the commission gave short shrift to home economics and commercial education programs because advocates of training for trades—many of them from the Women's Trade Union League—dominated the commission. But when the Smith-Hughes legislation that incorporated the commission's findings was being cobbled together in Congress, home economics proponents in the General Federation of Women's Clubs and the American Home Economics Association moved into gear. Allied with male legislators who felt women's place was indeed in the home, they carried the day.

But people's preferences defeated the policies. The public school population, which was growing larger and more diverse, sought education for better jobs. That meant factory or office work, not cooking and domestic science. So, as Jane Bernard Powers wrote in *The "Girl Question,"* girls voted with their feet, rebelling against the home economics classes, which remained a course without a constituency. Home economists promised that girls would be taught what science and math they needed to run their homes, so little encouragement was given young women to take these courses as part of the academic program. Meantime, education for the trades was stinted; commercial education took off as girls sought careers in office work. Business courses in high schools enrolled 519,000 in 1900 and 4,497,000 by 1934. By the 1920s, two-thirds of these students were young women. Once educated much the same as young men, they had been segregated by sex into programs purportedly designed to help them.

When did women start moving in any numbers onto college and university faculties, and what triggered the advances?

Women attended college in record numbers as the nation moved into the early decades of the twentieth century, but they did not show the same progress at the faculty level. In fact, the highest proportion of women on college faculties—36 percent—occurred in 1880. The percentage of women on college faculties dropped to 19.8 percent by 1900 and had reached only 27.6 percent by 1940. The boom in university expansion occurred after World War II, in the 1940s and 1950s, when women were discouraged from seeking jobs and so they did not benefit by increases in faculty hiring. So despite this expansion—or more accurately, because of it—the percentage of women on college faculties actually dropped back to 22 percent by 1960. By 1991, women made up 31.7 percent of faculties.

The women's movement of the 1960s and 1970s helped open doors to increased faculty employment generally but, as in so many other fields, it took specific action to move colleges and universities off the dime. In 1970, **Bernice Sandler** of the Women's Equity Action League filed a class-action complaint against institutions of higher learning, charging sex discrimination against faculty women. Individual women and groups brought similar charges on their own campuses, and they lobbied for federal enforcement of the laws against sex discrimination specifically directed at universities. The lobbying effort led the Department of Health, Education, and Welfare to issue higher-education guidelines in 1972; Congress also passed Title IX, which for the first time extended the prohibition against discrimination to students. Even though universities started hiring women as a result of the requirement for affirmative action plans and more regular record-keeping, that did not mean they had to keep the women. Obtaining tenure—that is, job security—remained difficult for women because the process is subjective and secret. For example, by 1991, 70.1 percent of male faculty members had tenure while only 49.1 percent of women did. Women continued to be concentrated in the lower-paying faculty ranks—and teaching more courses.

One of the most poignant examples of discrimination against women on college campuses was the story of **Alice Hamilton,** a pioneering specialist in industrial medicine who discovered that fumes and lead poisoned workers. Hamilton joined the Harvard University medical school faculty at age fifty in 1919 on condition that she not join the academic processions. Despite her obvious distinction, she remained an assistant professor when she retired. But times change. In 1973, she was honored with membership in the National Women's Hall of Fame at Seneca Falls, New York.

What was significant about the University of Pennsylvania's appointment of a new president in 1993?

Judith Rodin's selection at the University of Pennsylvania made her the first woman to be president of an Ivy League institution. Rodin, a behavioral psychologist, served as provost at Yale University in a difficult period after Yale's president had resigned and faculty and students were anxious about possible cuts because of a budget deficit. Her appointment followed shortly after the inauguration of **Nannerl O. Keohane,** a former Stanford University professor and president of Wellesley College, as president of Duke University. Keohane, trained as a political scientist, figured most prominently in the news when she handled with diplomacy the protest by some Wellesley students over the selection of First Lady Barbara Bush as graduation speaker.

Other women heading major academic institutions were **W. Ann Reynolds,** chancellor of the City University of New York, and **Katherine Lyall,** president of the University of Wisconsin. Their most prominent predecessors among women heading key research institutions were **Hannah H. Gray,** who had retired earlier as president of the University of Chicago, and **Donna E. Shalala,** who left the University of Wisconsin to become Secretary of Health and Human Services in the Clinton administration.

CHAPTER 5

❦

Unsettled Lives: From the Fallen Woman to Frontier Women

Who were "fallen women," and how were they treated?

Why did cowgirls, and other frontier women, sometimes get the blues?

What truth is there to the notion of women as the "great civilizers" of the West?

Were frontier women all "saints in sunbonnets"?

What could Sarah Winnemucca do about the loss of land by her Paiute Indian people?

How Indian were the Indian schools, and how did their training affect girls' lives?

"What," an archeologist asked, "could this awl mean?"

❦

Who were "fallen women," and how were they treated?

Few women went to prison in the early days of the American republic because their sphere was in the home, the social controls on them were many, and the liberties they had to violate were few. By the 1860s, the old order was changing, more people lived in cities with fewer family ties as stabilizers, and more women were going to prison. Prostitution was a frequent charge. Prisons were not designed for women, and female prisoners drew little attention from male reformers, often because the women had been promiscuous and were thus considered pariahs.

The Great Awakening, the religious revival of the 1820s and 1830s, prompted discussions of the possibility of redeeming souls, even those of degraded sinners. So it is not surprising that women's religious groups were the first interested in prison reform. In America, it was the Philadelphia Quakers who first visited the Arch Street Prison in 1823 to offer religious instruction, provide libraries, and teach sewing and writing. In New York, a group of women who formed a female auxiliary of the Prison Association wanted to set up a halfway house for women leaving prison so that they could have a place for shelter, training, and prayer. Feminist **Margaret Fuller** helped the crusade with articles appearing in the *New York Tribune* about institutions so gloomy and conditions so deplorable that women leaving them needed help. She argued, however, that these victims were redeemable, wanting "only good influences and steady aid to raise them from the pit of infamy into which they have fallen." The home was established in 1845 and in almost twenty years provided shelter for nearly three thousand women.

The Civil War created a new corps of women who had worked as nurses and in social services. Some of these women became interested in prison reform. They also started looking at the causes of women's crimes, focusing increasingly on the limited economic opportunities that might push women into prostitution or shoplifting. As women outside prison started seeing more of the conditions facing women inside prison, they recognized the sexual exploitation that often occurred because women were not jailed in separate institutions and had male jailers. Many of the reform efforts of the late nineteenth century centered on creating separate women's prisons, with the first such institution opening in 1874 in Indianapolis. The women's training in prison generally prepared them only for jobs as domestic help. These separate prisons did, however, give rise to a new profession for the women who staffed them.

The next generation of prison reformers "did not have to argue for the right to work in prisons for they had inherited these institutions from the previous generation," wrote historian Estelle Freedman in *Their Sisters' Keepers: Women's Prison Reform in America, 1830–1930*. Less motivated by religion and better educated than their predecessors, they treated prisoners more like social service clients and objects for research. These women of the Progressive era wanted to head off crime before it happened and to rely more on probation than imprisonment. Change the environment for the woman, ran their thinking, and you may change the causes of crime. Change the economic opportunities for women as well, and you may change their motivation for turning to crime. Despite the Progressive-era reformers' goal of providing preparation for jobs beyond domestic service, training for employable skills remained "wholly inadequate," according to a 1927 survey. Even the authors of that report on prisons and prison labor rejected training women for jobs like printing and making pottery, recommending instead farming, sewing, and laundering.

By World War I, there was also a different approach to prostitutes. Where woman had been the victim, by wartime she became the threat to soldiers and thus society. Soldiers who got venereal diseases couldn't fight for democracy, so prostitutes, not the men who frequented them, had to be punished. Barbed wire went up, treatment was harsher, and the nature of prison inmates changed. "Instead of young girls and first offenders," Freedman wrote, "women with serious medical and social problems now filled the institutions. . . . Thus the reformatories increasingly housed those women perceived by the society as the most dangerous, not the most hopeful, cases."

Why did cowgirls, and other frontier women, sometimes get the blues?

Life on America's frontier was harsh, lonely, and dangerous. So why leave home and hearth in New England or Ohio to head for Kansas or Colorado or California? Most families went to better themselves economically; many rejoiced in the open land and the freedom they found but also faced isolation and living conditions far less comfortable than those they had left. Women sometimes were reluctant pioneers, traveling west because their husbands wanted the change. In many cases, however, they found a hard equality that they might not have had in the more settled East.

Joanna Stratton's great-grandmother collected reminiscences of women who had helped settle Kansas when it was still a frontier. Those recollections, published in *Pioneer Women,* have provided a rich day-to-day look at their lives in a way most histories overlook. The chance to till their own soil and build their own communities lured these pioneers to Kansas; the beauty they found held them even through adversity. One woman described how she had resisted leaving her home but that "the characteristic disposition of the male prevailed" and so they left, she weeping bitterly as they did. They arrived in Winfield, Kansas, one Sunday morning and, with the sound of church bells ringing, drove through town to a "beautiful valley, encircled by a fine stream of water," and so "felt that instead of the wild West, we had found God's own country, and were quite content to accept it as our future home."

But homes were unlike those they had left, especially in western Kansas, where there was little wood or stone with which to build. Many pioneers spent their first years in Kansas in sod houses—if they were fortunate—or dugout caves that leaked during the winter rains. Housecleaning was virtually impossible, as dirt constantly filtered down on all the furnishings. Little light could get into the homes, but they were cool in the blistering summer and could be kept warm in winter if a family could find enough cow or buffalo chips (essential, again, because of the scarcity of kindling wood).

Beyond housing, the next task was breaking the thick prairie sod and plowing the fields. Women generally worked on the home chores, but if there were few sons or when weeding or harvesting demanded extra hands, the women were in the fields. Growing crops in Kansas required particular fortitude: if hail storms didn't flatten the corn, bugs would. "August 1, 1874, is a day that will always be remembered by the then inhabitants of Kansas," one woman said, describing a plague of grasshoppers that swept over the land. "For several days there had been quite a few hoppers around, but this day there was a haze in the air and the sun was veiled almost like Indian summer. They began, toward night, dropping to earth, and it seemed as if we were in a big snowstorm where the air was filled with enormous-size flakes." Fields of vegetables or wheat were devoured and trees stripped. If that weren't enough, grass fires could also roar seemingly out of nowhere and destroy crops or homes.

Pioneer women's chores never ended. Before they could even start the washing or the cooking, women often had to walk a mile or more to haul water in buckets hung on yokes across their shoulders. In addition to doing the cooking and laundry—for which they would use washboards and soap that they had made—they also produced everything the family needed, from clothing to candles. "Fruit, when it could be obtained, was preserved, dried and canned," one pioneer woman recalled. "Vegetables were stored and meat preserved and smoked, and all the bread and pastries were made in the kitchen." Women made sausage and smoked meat as well. To make their clothing, they often had to produce the yarn and the wool cloth, as well as find berries or bark to make dye. Women often doctored their families—and sewed up injured farm animals as well. Some women even gave birth at home alone, although midwives could sometimes be found in time to help with the delivery.

Cultures clashed in Kansas as the white settlers moved onto what had been Indian lands. Initially, at least, whites and Indians coexisted peacefully, with whites usually avoiding much contact with people whose habits they neither understood nor tried to understand. Indians frequently would simply stroll into a settler's home. Why shouldn't they? They felt it was their land. "I still recall how scared I was in my first experience," said one woman. "It was warm and my windows were open and I was combing my hair. My hair was then very long, thick and even, and as I drew the comb through it and looked up to the mirror before me, which was opposite the window, I saw reflected two big Indians, one had just gotten inside and the other was climbing over the window sill. Well, I thought of course they were after my scalp and I screamed and ran out the door," nearly knocking over a guest. The man went inside and found the Indians laughing. They had only wanted to see her hair. Later, relations turned violent as more and more Eastern tribes were pushed west, more whites moved in, and the federal government failed to keep many of its promises to the Indians.

Women often proved themselves side by side with men in enduring the prairie hardships. Soon they sought to have that equality written into law. In 1859, **Clarina Nichols, Mother Armstrong,** and **Mary Tenney Gray** attended the state's constitutional convention seeking the right to vote for women. They didn't get it, but the constitution did give women the right to own property and maintain custody of their children equally with men. By 1861, women had the right to vote in school elections, and by 1887, the right to vote and run for city offices. That April, **Susannah Medora Salter** was elected mayor of Argonia—the nation's first female mayor.

What truth is there to the notion of women as the "great civilizers" of the West?

The saloons, gambling, and prostitution in frontier cities offended Victorian women, and some of them set out to civilize the West. They not only engaged in civic reform but also tried to help Indian women, who they felt were in distress on reservations, or immigrant women who had been lured into prostitution. Often these reformers were opposed every step of the way. Almost as often, they were condescending to the people they were trying to "rescue," having little idea that each culture might have its own benefits as well as its disadvantages. In that era, white was right. So was Christianity.

For example, mission society members saw Indian women working hard physically and felt they were treated as drudges. They did not realize that these women's power came from sources other than being wives and mothers—that it often came from their work in the fields, from their religion, and from their knowledge of medicine.

Peggy Pascoe, writing in *Relations of Rescue: The Search for Female Moral Authority in the American West, 1874–1939,* explored the successes and drawbacks of this movement. For example, the Connecticut Indian Association sent a medical mission to the reservation of the Omaha Indians after one of them, **Susette La Flesche,** had toured with tribal leader **Standing Bear** to talk about the injustices they faced in Nebraska. The organization put Susette's sister, **Susan,** through medical school after she graduated from Hampton Institute in 1889. She returned to the reservation to practice medicine and became active in temperance work. She had seen the devastation wrought by alcohol; her husband, Henry Picotte, a Sioux, died of an alcohol-related illness. She was opposed by many of her fellow Omahas who felt "Indians had as much right to drink as white men did."

Another frontier rescue effort provided refuge for Chinese prostitutes. Many young women had been sold from China into slavery in California. In 1874, the San Francisco Chinese Mission Home was founded despite widespread anti-immigrant feeling resulting from economic problems and racism. Pascoe reported that when the founders of the home went to look at one potential building for their headquarters, the landlady discovered that Chinese would live there and spit in the face of one of the committee members. The mission home gave women who wanted to escape mistreatment a place to go and a chance to learn skills they might need to marry respectably. The organizations also hired many women and encouraged the professionalism of their social service work. They also employed "native helpers," who were invaluable in helping translate for women who spoke little or no English and in otherwise running the program. But the very name indicates that the helpers never could rise far from those jobs.

Were frontier women all "saints in sunbonnets"?

Pioneers on the prairie and the plains came in all ages, several races, many religions and nationalities. Not all were married. And they didn't fit the stereotype of "saints in sunbonnets." One woman went so far as to say those garments were "an obstruction to sight and an impediment to hearing." Historian Glenda Riley found that her study, *The Female Frontier,* had to center on their homemaking, often a more than full-time task, but she also recorded that many women of the prairies and plains produced income, either by selling products they made at home or by holding jobs. Teaching the growing population offered women one of their best chances for employment—especially once men discovered that they could make more money on farms or in factories than in teaching. By 1880, Riley found, Illinois had more than 10,000 female teachers and 6,148 male teachers; Iowa had 10,157 women and 4,380 men in its classrooms. Teachers often had little more than a building—no chairs, no blackboard, and only what books their pupils' parents might have brought with them or ordered from the East. The most acceptable jobs for women on the frontier, as in the East at that time, were those associated with their domestic roles—such as making clothing, serving food, keeping an inn, or teaching the young.

Despite the initial hardships for women on both prairie and plains, Riley concluded, their lives soon improved with the arrival of more family members and the establishment of churches, schools, and community organizations devoted to everything from dispensing charity to developing culture. Women saved their money to buy books, formed literary clubs, and worked hard to develop higher education for themselves or their children. In 1866, for example, following a strenuous lobbying campaign by women, the new University of Kansas became the nation's first state university to accept women and men on equal terms.

What could Sarah Winnemucca do about the loss of land by her Paiute Indian people?

As a child, **Sarah Winnemucca** (1844?–1891) feared the whites who increasingly were moving into the Northern Paiute homelands of western Nevada, northeastern California, and southern Oregon. Whites killed her uncle as he fished in the Humboldt River; later, Sarah and a cousin were buried in sand by relatives for one entire hot day to hide the two from approaching whites. The fear and distrust existed even though Sarah's grandfather had guided whites crossing the Great Basin and fought with General John Frémont in California's Bear Flag Rebellion against Mexico.

Sarah—her Paiute name was Thocmetony, or Shell Flower— probably received her Christian name around 1857, when she and a younger sister lived with the family of Major **William Ormsby,** a stagecoach company agent. She learned English and worked for her keep in the Ormsbys' house. Her knowledge of English would help her later as she repeatedly sought land or food for the Paiutes; she was also able to earn a living as an army interpreter.

The life of hunting and gathering pine nuts that her grandfather and her father, **Chief Winnemucca,** had known was fast changing as prospectors and ranchers moved onto their land. The ranchers refused to pay Chief Winnemucca for the land because they said Indians had stolen some of their cattle. In May 1860, a party of volunteers, led reluctantly by Ormsby, headed for the Paiute base at Pyramid Lake, where they were attacked. Many were killed, including Ormsby. Four companies of U.S. troops and about five hundred volunteers then marched on Pyramid Lake and were unable to capture the main body of Paiute. A peace treaty was negotiated and a reservation established. That only led to more problems.

Food and blankets promised the Paiutes rarely were delivered, nor was a sawmill constructed to make lumber for housing. Sporadic fighting occurred in the period and Sarah's mother, sister, and a baby brother died in brutal army raids. There was one bright moment when the Malheur Reservation was set up in Oregon with **Samuel Parrish** as agent. He kept his promises as well as he could, which could not be said for his successor, Major **William Rinehart,** with whom Sarah Winnemucca tangled repeatedly because she felt the Paiutes were being cheated.

In 1878, Chief Winnemucca was forced to join a warring party of Bannock Indians. Learning of her father's situation, Sarah and two Paiutes rode 223 miles round trip through Idaho and into Oregon in two days and brought out her father and many others from the hostile camp. She herself went into the camp, unrecognized by the Bannocks among the other Paiutes, and helped her father and others sneak away.

Sarah Winnemucca frequently lectured about the shabby treatment the Paiutes were receiving and also appealed for whites "to send teachers and books among us." She petitioned the Interior Department to return Samuel Parrish or someone equally honest as agent at Malheur. She and her father went to Washington in 1880 to try to convince the federal government to give the Paiutes decent land. Interior Secretary **Carl Schurz** wrote a letter promising 160 acres to each family head and each adult male; he also pledged to send 100 tents that Sarah would distribute. She was optimistic, but returned to the West to find no tents, no land, and little food.

On a lecture tour, Sarah met sisters **Elizabeth Peabody** and **Mary Peabody Mann,** widow of educator Horace Mann, and they helped finance and edit her book, *Life Among the Piutes* [sic]. It enhanced her credibility as a spokesperson for the Paiutes. With the financial support of Elizabeth Peabody, Sarah Winnemucca started a school for Indians in Nevada. The school was significant because it was run *by* Indians *for* Indians. The children learned English and other skills Sarah felt they needed to avoid living on reservations. She was disappointed when the Dawes Act of 1887 required that Indian children be educated at English-speaking schools away from home, whether their parents agreed or not. Sarah Winnemucca died in 1891.

How Indian were the Indian schools, and how did their training affect girls' lives?

American missionaries had advocated educating Indian children—presumably to better enjoy "the benefits of civilization"—for several decades before the U.S. government officially entered the field in the late 1870s. Across the country, Indians were being driven off their traditional land and onto reservations. The move toward education of Indian children was in fact a move to make them more like the European-descended settlers who were heading west. The schools, then, were Indian only in the sense that Indians attended them, as opposed to any concept of education in things Indian by Indians. Girls, especially, were targets of attempts to mold them into ideal American womanhood by teaching them domestic skills and removing them from tribal cultures that whites felt, often erroneously, exploited their physical labor.

Hampton Normal Institute in Virginia, a school that had educated only black students, enrolled its first Indian students— all male—in 1878. Then Captain and Mrs. **Richard Henry Pratt** traveled along the Missouri River to recruit Indian girls for the school, but many parents did not want to send their daughters. A few did, and the girls started learning about cooking, sewing, and laundering with diminishing time for academic instruction. Pratt soon started a separate school, Carlisle, for

Indians—although there had been no racial problems (except in the minds of the white administrators) at Hampton. In keeping with their operation by military men, both Hampton and Carlisle, as well as later schools, stressed strict discipline.

Indian girls were often placed in private homes to learn household skills. The girls often were used as cheap household labor, however. When the Indian schools faced severe budget problems in the 1880s, they started using the girls to help run the schools instead of concentrating on book-learning. Girls made the bedding and curtains at Hampton Institute, cleaned the teachers' rooms, and scrubbed much of the building. Because of the lack of academic training and because of discrimination within the broader society, Indian girls educated at these schools faced limited job opportunities, mostly menial work, or employment with the Indian Bureau itself. They rarely were hired as teachers, though, being more likely to work as cooks or matrons' assistants. When girls returned to their reservations from this schooling, they found that their new ways, however reluctantly learned, clashed with those of the people left behind. Thus, they were not accepted in the world they had entered nor completely at home in the one into which they had been born. Indian education may have made the educators feel virtuous, but it did little for their charges except make them ill-prepared for whichever world they chose.

"What," an archeologist asked, "could this awl mean?"

The archeologist wasn't just making a pun but asking a research question about an awl found during a dig at the site of a Dakota Indian village in Minnesota.

Women of the Eastern Dakota, or Sioux, Indians performed a variety of economic tasks for their people as they lived and worked around a settlement at Little Rapids along the Minnesota River near Jordan, Minnesota. In the early to mid-nineteenth century, they not only planted, harvested, and stored corn, they gathered berries, repaired their housing, and also converted animal hides into material for tents as well as moccasins and clothing. To poke holes in the hides they were working, they used a metal-tipped tool called an awl, with a handle made from an antler.

Reconstructing fragments dug from the earth and aided by travelers' accounts and the stories of descendants of a branch of the Dakota, University of Minnesota archeologist Janet D. Spector told how a girl from that tribe may have worked hides and recorded her accomplishments with the help of the awl found at Little Rapids. When the girl finished beading a pair of moccasins, for example, she would make a dot on her awl handle, coloring it by using dye made from a sumac plant; when she completed a more complex project, like a dress, she would make a pattern of dots on the awl handle. The more dots and clusters, presumably the more work she had completed for the good of the group. One young woman who had doubtless used such an awl was **Mazaokiyewin,** daughter of a prominent man in the Dakota settlement.

Missionaries and other white settlers who encountered the Dakota at Little Rapids often encouraged the men in the group to switch from hunting to agriculture, not realizing that farming was the women's task. The women also built the living quarters—except for putting on the roofs—when Dakota work parties shifted from place to place. They moved often, depending on whether it was the season to fish, gather wild rices, or collect maple sugar. Women also did much of that work—from building the birch troughs in which to collect the sap to tapping the trees with axes to storing the end product so that it could be used throughout the year.

CHAPTER 6

❧

Women at Work

When did American women first go to work?

Who were the "mill girls"?

While waiting for Johnny to come marching home, how did women see their lives change in wartime?

Who was "Rosie the Riveter"?

What was life like for minority women workers well into the twentieth century?

If the first secretaries were men, why did that change?

Why was teaching one of the few professions open to women in the nineteenth century?

Did women suffer double discrimination during the Great Depression?

When did nurses start receiving professional education, and what innovations have they contributed to health care?

Why do women still earn only seventy cents to every dollar a man makes, and can't they do something about it?

Why couldn't girls "do science"?

Who was America's pioneer scientist?

Who first made a lifelong career of science?

~

When did American women first go to work?

Americans, like many other nationalities, have practiced massive denial about the role of women in their workforce. Indian women have always worked. Black women worked. And since colonial times, white women have always worked—on the farm and in the kitchen, and later in the factory or in the office—yet America wanted an idealized picture: Dad plowing in the fields or heading for the factory with his lunchpail or coming home, briefcase in hand, to Mom in her apron preparing a nutritious meal for their 2.2 beautiful children. That image never squared with reality, but it shaped the way in which women were allowed to enter the world of work and how much (not much) they were paid.

The first settlers came to the American colonies of the European empires in the seventeenth century to escape economic as well as political and religious repression. Fewer women than men made the crossing originally, and some of those women had comparative independence—owning land, running print shops, operating small businesses. In the main, women and men worked together on their farms in the country or in shops in villages and towns. The women hauled the water for cooking and laundry, preserved fruits and vegetables, cured meat, wove flax and stitched shirts and shoes, and made soap and candles—but it was not rare for a woman also to help clear the land, build the house, or plow the field. Work was equally shared by families that ran tailoring, boot-making, and print shops in urban areas.

Rough as this work often was, there were many American women who had to work even harder. The country's Native American women raised food, made clothing, pitched tents, or helped transport them. Many women came to America as servants and, after 1691, as slaves from Africa, and they did much of the heavy work in homes and in cotton fields. Servant and slave alike depended on their masters for meager food and clothing; the servant could lose her wages and have her time of service lengthened for the slightest infraction, while the black slave had no wages and little or no prospect of freedom.

Who were the "mill girls"?

In the young United States, women's jobs centered around the home or domestic skills, such as hat-making or cooking. But widows, women abandoned by their husbands, and unmarried women from large families in which their labor might not be required at home often needed to support themselves. The textile industry developing in New England at the end of the eighteenth century attracted many of these women. Initially, whatever they earned was more than they had dared dream, so there were few complaints. Mill operators ran boardinghouses with strict rules to try to avoid scandals, and there was little competition from men for the jobs because men were involved in farming or commerce. The jobs originally went to native-born whites. IRISH NEED NOT APPLY, the factory want ads in many a newspaper read, as immigrants moved to America to escape the potato famine. Free black women knew better than to even try to obtain mill jobs because they would not be hired. They could usually find work only cooking or cleaning.

When the economy became depressed between 1837 and 1839, manufacturers discovered the "speed up." If millhands worked faster and longer, they could produce more goods for no more pay. Where once millworkers tended two looms, said the *Voice of Industry* newspaper, now they tended three or four, "making nearly twice the number of yards of cloth (although the pay is not increased to them, while the increase to the owners is very great)." If a worker didn't like the conditions, other women and, by then, even men waited eagerly for the jobs. As the nation turned from agriculture to a more wage-oriented economy, more men applied for mill and other factory jobs, pushing women out.

Some women resisted the poor conditions. For example, three hundred to four hundred female cotton millworkers went on strike in December 1828 in Dover, New Hampshire, protesting the "shocking fate of slaves" that they felt they shared. Eight hundred struck in Dover over reduced pay in 1834. In 1844, factory workers struck over reduced pay in Allegheny, Pennsylvania, and in 1845 for shorter working hours. The Lowell Female Labor Reform Association was organized to fight for the ten-hour workday in January 1845. But the wave of immigration from Ireland late in that decade undercut the organizing efforts. These men and women, desperate after enduring hunger in the potato famine, would work for less money.

Labor unions often proved little better than mill owners in their dealings with women. Why encourage women to work when their presence on the job pulled salaries down, and when they should stay at home anyway? The National Labor Union, a federation of reformers and trade unionists, was an exception. Although it admitted women as members and its leader, **William H. Sylvis,** advocated better treatment, even he felt women's proper sphere was the home and that anyone who sought to turn her from her role as "presiding deity" was robbing her virtue.

While waiting for Johnny to come marching home, how did women see their lives change in wartime?

War has always changed the roles of women in the American workplace. During the Revolutionary War, women made uniforms and some took up arms themselves, usually by disguising themselves as men. During the Civil War, women again made the uniforms, tended farms for absent men, and sought to enter the paid workforce in even greater numbers. Some were hired for government clerical jobs. The violence of war created a need for people to nurse wounded soldiers, and **Clara Barton** and others stepped in, despite the outspoken critics who felt women should not be exposed to the sights of battlefields and amputation wards. Those who felt women would be too squeamish ignored the fact that women had birthed babies as midwives, helped with deliveries of farm animals, tended sick children, and cared for dying parents for centuries.

World War I spurred the entry of more women into the wage workforce. This time they drove ambulances, worked in weapons factories, typed and filed in offices, and ran streetcars; many of the jobs ended when the war did. Black women migrated north in greater numbers than men did during this period because they could get jobs. Many worked as maids, cooks, or seamstresses, hoping their children would have a better life. By 1922, two million black women worked in three occupations—domestic service, farming, and manufacturing or mechanical industries.

Who was "Rosie the Riveter"?

To free men for military service during World War II, American munitions, shipbuilding, and airplane plants recruited "Rosie the Riveter" and her sisters to jobs that had been closed to them only a few short years before. Newsreels demonstrated how homemaking tasks resembled riveting or welding, and blared the warning that it would be unpatriotic for women not to tie back their hair and roll up their sleeves. Black women remained among the last hired and entrusted with major craft positions, but they, too, made it into the shipyards and factories. Although President **Franklin D. Roosevelt** set aside federal money to construct day-care centers for mothers working in war-related industries, the projects were slow to be built and often run by poorly trained and underpaid staff. They frequently charged too much and stayed open too few hours. Virtually all pretense at providing safe and adequate child care financed by government or industry ended when the war itself ended.

So did many of the women's jobs. When the war ended and men returned, many women were fired from the jobs for which so big a sales pitch had been mounted for so long. But some men did not return for the jobs and some women did not leave willingly. Said **Lola Weixel,** who had been a welder during the war and could only get a job running office machines afterward, American women had hoped to rebuild the cities and do "beautiful things" because there were so many more trained workers then. Instead, men and women became competitors for jobs. "There was a lot of money around but it wasn't in our pockets," Weixel told documentary filmmakers in *Rosie the Riveter.* Laughed at when she tried to find a job in an ornamental ironwork shop, she said, "Being a woman, it was over for us. . . . All I really wanted was one day to make a very beautiful ornamental gate. . . . I still think of it. When I pass a beautiful gate, I say, 'Was that too much to want?' "

Again, the propaganda guns fired forth their message that a woman's place was in the suburban home with all the appliances that were being created to make her a happy consumer. But those appliances, and other elements of a middle-class lifestyle, cost money, so many women remained in the workforce. Never again would the trend line of women's participation in paid labor turn down for long: in 1940, 25.3 percent of American women worked outside the home; in 1950, 29 percent; in 1960, 34.5 percent; in 1970, 40 percent. For the first time, half of American women were employed outside the home in 1978.

What was life like for minority women workers well into the twentieth century?

Despite Emancipation, black women still faced limited job prospects after the Civil War, especially in the South. With their husbands, many became sharecroppers. They planted cotton on white men's land, weeded the cotton, and then picked the crop in the fall, only to find that the landowner kept most of the profits. It was slavery under another name because share-croppers could not protest their treatment without facing violent reprisals; they could only move on to the next plantation with little likelihood of economic improvement. There were pockets of independent black farms in the South where wives and husbands worked on the margins of existence to maintain a precarious independence, but they faced constant threats to their land and their lives from jealous white neighbors. Black women who didn't want to pick crops or clean other people's bathrooms usually could find only hot, hard work in laundries or tobacco-processing plants in the South.

A different form of slavery had developed on the West Coast in the nineteenth century, where Chinese women were imported and sold into prostitution in mining camps. Some escaped that fate and worked as servants, often treated little better than their sisters in the camps. On both coasts, women of Asian and African descent who migrated to the cities or smaller towns could occasionally survive and prosper by making clothing or hats or becoming beauticians.

And while a few Mexican-American women in old, established land-grant families in California—known as the Californios—might live in luxurious haciendas, many worked in canneries or in the fields by the late nineteenth century. For example, the first fruit cannery in Santa Barbara County, established in 1880, employed 100 to 150 girls and women during the peak season, along with a few boys and men. When Chinese almond pickers and shellers left the Hollister Ranch near Santa Barbara, Chicanas and their children were hired to replace them. In some areas of California's San Joaquin Valley, men kept the women out of the fields and canneries but by the 1930s those practices were changing. Women started joining unions and played key roles in the Southern California berry strike in El Monte in 1931 and in the strike of orange pickers in Santa Ana in 1936.

If the first secretaries were men, why did that change?

Just as the American economy underwent one revolution when factories took over producing goods that had been made at home, it faced another as commerce, banks, and government started keeping records and generating massive amounts of correspondence. Secretarial jobs were held at first by men, but employers soon found they could pay women less. Women were effectively barred by custom or law from higher-wage jobs and the professions; many worked only a few years before they married and raised families. Wide use of the typewriter toward the end of the nineteenth century cemented the change because, like the millworkers who ran the looms, women were considered better for jobs requiring precision and the proverbial "nimble fingers."

Why was teaching one of the few professions open to women in the nineteenth century?

As the American population grew and jobs called for more workers who could read and write, there was a corresponding expansion of public schools and demand for more teachers. Women had frequently taught their own children at home and, during the nineteenth century, some held small classes for the daughters of the middle class. For example, **Margaret Fuller,** well educated by her father and most celebrated as editor of the Transcendental movement's journal, *The Dial,* taught at

Bronson Alcott's progressive school in New England in the 1830s.

Teaching, at least of children below university age, was considered an extension of women's role in the family, and so on the eve of the Civil War, 25 percent of the nation's teachers were women. Female teachers were paid less than men. That inequity occurred with the blessing of some female leaders such as **Catharine Beecher,** who had founded the Hartford Female Seminary in 1823. Asking Congress for money to train women as teachers, Beecher said that "women can afford to teach for one-half, or even less, the salary which men would ask, because the female teacher has only to sustain herself; she does not look forward to the duty of supporting a family, should she marry, nor has she the ambition to mass a fortune."

Did women suffer double discrimination during the Great Depression?

Both men and women lost their jobs during the Great Depression in the 1930s. But with that Depression came a debate over whether women should be working at all when thousands of men were unemployed. Schoolteachers had long understood that they must quit their jobs when they became pregnant, and they were often at risk of being fired when they got married. During the Depression, that risk of dismissal became a more frequent reality as half the nation's school systems routinely fired women who married. Women were losing ground in one of the few fields that had consistently welcomed them: They were 85 percent of the teaching profession in 1920 but by 1940 they were 78 percent. Yet despite loud campaigns to keep women at home, more started working for wages, especially older married women. Their families needed the income and, as Alice Kessler-Harris indicated in *Out to Work: A History of Wage-Earning Women in the United States,* they benefited because jobs open to women had not been concentrated in the heavy industries hardest hit by the economic slide. As plants were

forced to modernize to compete, the new jobs that they produced often were those that women could perform. Still, 20
percent of women who worked in 1940 were domestics, and 50
percent of those were black or Hispanic.

When did nurses start receiving professional education, and what innovations have they contributed to health care?

Women have nursed others almost since time began, but it
was not until after the Civil War that American women started
receiving professional education for the work. The name of
Florence Nightingale, a British woman, is virtually synonomous
with the beginning of the modern nursing profession; she improved the level of care for the wounded during the Crimean
War from 1854 to 1856 and was the foremost hospital reformer
of her time. In the United States, many women worked as
nurses for troops of both sides during the Civil War. Those min-
istering to Northern soldiers were directed by **Dorothea Dix,**
who had already spearheaded reform in care of the mentally ill.
Although controversial as an administrator, she tried to recruit
competent women and force hospitals to raise their standards
of care. It was not until 1873, however, that the first nursing
schools were founded at hospitals in Boston, New York, and
New Haven, Connecticut.

Nursing school superintendents began setting training
standards for nurses in the 1890s. By 1909, there were more
than one thousand hospital-based nursing schools. That year,
the University of Minnesota initiated the first baccalaureate
program in nursing.

At the turn of the century, nurses were delivering health
care to rural areas and immigrant communities in the cities. After her own graduation from nursing school, **Lillian Wald** pio-
neered in public health nursing from the Henry Street
settlement that she established in 1895 in New York after she

saw the conditions in which tenement dwellers lived. The Henry Street Visiting Nurses Service provided thousands of home-care visits to people not sick enough to be hospitalized but in need of medical attention.

The Henry Street settlement attracted many of the women who were leaders in public health and social work. For example, **Lavinia Dock,** whose research led to the founding in 1896 of what is now the American Nurses Association, lived there for twenty years. Dock was a frequent contributor to the *American Journal of Nursing* and also wrote much of the first history of nursing, published in 1907. Later, she crusaded against venereal disease and then for voting rights for women, going to jail frequently in 1917 and 1918 as she allied herself with **Alice Paul** and the National Women's Party.

Nursing grew as a profession for women in the twentieth century, and the demand for nurses during World War II created one of a series of shortages. Despite this demand, the Army set exceptionally low quotas for black nurses and the Navy would accept none. **Mabel Staupers,** a graduate of Freedmen's Hospital School of Nursing in Washington, D.C., and one of the founders of the National Council of Negro Women, knew discrimination firsthand already because black nurses could find few jobs in hospitals, settlement houses, or public health work. She led the fight to integrate military nursing services and later helped break down racial barriers within the American Nurses Association in 1948.

By 1993, there were approximately 2,240,000 registered nurses in the United States, more than 96 percent of them women. Nurses are not only the health care system's largest profession but also its backbone. People aren't in hospitals unless they need nursing care, and therefore nurses have broad responsibility for monitoring patients, providing prompt diagnoses, and educating patients and their families on dealing with illnesses. They have been leaders in improving intensive care and establishing hospices so that people may die with dignity.

Congress created a National Center for Nursing Research in 1986 after 75 organizations lobbied for more study of nurses' roles in such fields as disease prevention, nutrition, caring for the elderly, and other health needs. In 1993, the center became the National Institute for Nursing Research, but still with a miniscule budget compared with the other groups within the parent National Institutes of Health.

Why do women still earn only seventy cents to every dollar a man makes, and can't they do something about it?

Seventy cents on the dollar is better than fifty-nine cents, which was the figure in the 1960s when the modern women's movement started paying increasing attention to women's wages. And it's also better than the three-fifths of a man's worth prescribed for women in the Bible (Leviticus 27:3–4). But that still won't buy you a cup of coffee in many places.

Women have almost always been paid less than men because employers knew they needed the work and had to settle for less because they had few options—or felt their work was similar to what they did at home so that they didn't need to be paid much. Women have also organized unions and coalitions, gone on strike, picketed, sued, won legislation—but many still are confined to a low-paying job ghetto.

Despite women's steady progress into the workforce, white women earned only 59.5 percent of what white men made in 1960 while black and other minority women made 38.8 percent of white men's pay. By 1992, the gap had closed between white and black women and between all women and men, but women still earned only 70.6 cents to each dollar a man received. During the 1960s, politically active women took their quest for pay equity into the legislative and union arenas, where they fought first for equal pay for equal work. That was necessary because employers still felt that they could pay women less because they would only remain as employees for a short time before raising families. As more women, especially those with children, started working outside the home, they insisted that their pay be comparable to that of men doing the same jobs. Congress passed the Equal Pay Act in 1963 and the Civil Rights Act in 1964, both of which affected discriminatory pay scales. That still left many women in jobs that had been historically underpaid and undervalued because women performed them. Secretaries, for example, might earn less than, say, forklift operators even though the skills and educational levels needed for each job might be comparable or even higher for the women's jobs.

In the 1970s and early 1980s, women and their allies in public employee unions, which had been highly successful in organizing government workers, started to push for pay equity. They wanted jobs filled predominantly by women to be reevaluated, and they wanted higher pay when skill levels matched those in better-paying jobs held predominantly by men. They got action first in Washington, Minnesota, and California, bargaining for studies of state or city pay practices.

The unionized public sector proved more fertile ground for these agreements than did private business, and collective bargaining and legislative lobbying was more successful than lawsuits in the increasingly conservative federal courts. Although comparable-worth legislation was introduced in Congress and some Democratic presidential candidates backed the concept during the 1984 primaries, the climate engendered during the Reagan–Bush years was hostile to national action. The Reagan Justice Department sided with the state of Washington in its appeal of a successful suit by the American Federation of State, County and Municipal Employees. The Supreme Court overturned the lower court decision that had given the union a victory. Civil Rights Commission chairman **Clarence Pendleton,** a conservative African-American, weighed in against comparable worth, likening it to the foolishness of the popular "Looney Tunes" cartoons.

The state and city governments where the movement had moved the farthest the fastest—including the state of California and the city of Los Angeles—made pay equity adjustments until the nation's economic downturn left governments increasingly strapped for funds. As of April 1993, twenty states had made payroll adjustments to correct sex or race bias, up from five in

1984. Six of those states had completed a full implementation of a pay equity plan.

Why couldn't girls "do science"?

Women had to jump through many hoops to make careers in science. First, men said women were not sufficiently educated to be scientists. So they went to college. Once they did, it was said they had the skills best suited for scientific clerks' jobs. The Harvard College Observatory hired women as assistants to keep records and sort photographs in 1881, a trend that spread to many other observatories. Outside of faculty positions at women's colleges, many women trained in science could find only assistants' jobs in government or industry for many decades.

Once women performed capably in these assistantships, it was said they showed no ambition. When they demonstrated ambition, it was said they would distract the male scientists if they were allowed to study for doctorates or participate in scientific societies. Elite schools refused to admit them, so women turned to other universities that were starting to grant graduate degrees: Syracuse, Boston University, University of Wooster, the University of Michigan, and Cornell University. Then in the early 1890s, Yale, Penn, Columbia, Brown, Stanford, and Chicago opened their graduate schools to women. Yale was the key. As historian Margaret W. Rossiter wrote in *Women Scientists in America: Struggles and Strategies to 1940,* Yale came to its decision not only because women had already been doing good work as special students but also because its president **Timothy Dwight** took particular interest in women's education. "His mother had been highly intelligent and convinced him that women deserved a full education," Rossiter added.

Harvard remained a holdout. The new Association of Collegiate Alumnae raised money to send women overseas for graduate study, the idea being that if women could succeed in foreign universities, that would be an "entering wedge" into U.S. schools. Once women did win acceptance at German universities, one of their mentors alerted Harvard psychology professor **William James,** who, Rossiter wrote, "understood the implied comparison" with Harvard. Liberal professors at Harvard had been admitting some women to classes and decided to make a test case in 1895. **Mary Whiton Calkins** had passed her examinations brilliantly but still was refused a Harvard degree. In 1902, Harvard formed the Radcliffe Graduate School for women and offered its doctorate to Calkins. She refused and never received that degree, although she became a professor at Wellesley and was elected president of the American Psychological Association and the American Philosophical Association.

Once women won acceptance at many graduate schools, they were not hired except for jobs in fields considered womanly, such as home economics or botany. Once they began to get teaching jobs in any numbers, their fields were "professionalized" and standards of educational preparation raised. "The concepts of prestige, status and professionalism," wrote Rossiter, were in the late 1800s "closely intertwined with that of masculinity," and so the requirements for new members to join professional associations also were raised. To be sure, some of the groups admitted women, but often only as associate members, or they required women—but not men—who sought membership to have doctorates. Some even had social events identified as "smokers" at their association meetings. Since respectable women did not smoke in that era, the signal was clear. Women formed their own societies, but this segregation meant less opportunity to present their ideas at professional societies and to learn from their scientific peers who were men.

Wartime brought advances for women in science. In the government, women's contribution was greatest in the area of home economics. During World War I, the federal government was trying to increase food production and decrease consumption, and toward that end, hired home economists to get the message across to housewives. Although two home economists, **Sarah Field Splint** and **Martha Van Rensselaer,** were the highest-ranking female government scientists with the wartime Home Conservation Division, they worked for a man, Stanford

University President **Ray Lyman Wilbur,** head of the Food Conservation Division.

Chemists were especially needed in industry, which was ill-prepared for war and making munitions. Illinois Steel Company hired seven female chemists, who learned quickly, performed well, and were sick less often than the men, their boss reported. However, Rossiter found that two months after the chief chemist's article, entitled "The Woman Chemist Has Come to Stay," appeared in the *Journal of Industrial and Engineering Chemistry,* Illinois Steel added this note in the same publication: "The women chemists of the Illinois Steel Company not only made good as chemists but showed their fine spirit by resigning in order to make places for the men returning from war work."

By the early 1920s, women had the vote and were poised for new gains after their loyal wartime service. The number of women in science was increasing, as was the percentage receiving doctoral degrees. Anthropologists **Ruth Benedict** and **Margaret Mead** were achieving prominence. Nonetheless, Rossiter reported, women were still channeled into secondary roles. Even as they documented discrimination against them, their statistical reports had little effect because they had no power to change the sex segregation they faced. By 1940, women were as marginal in science as they had been in 1920. Women tried various strategies to break out of this lowly position—working harder, proving themselves "exceptional," accepting the slights and the channeling into jobs as assistants or home economists, forming their own organizations and awarding their own prizes. But until World War II and well afterward, women doing science were often overqualified and underutilized.

Who was America's pioneer scientist?

Jane Colden (1724–1766) was the daughter of a well-educated Scot who moved to New York State and was active in politics all his life there while also pursuing his interests in science. Jane was interested in the garden at their home, and her father ordered a small library of books from England to help with her education. She cataloged three hundred local plants in the Hudson River valley, naming one of her discoveries *gardenia* after the American naturalist **Alexander Garden,** with whom she corresponded. Colden married in 1759, apparently did no further science, and died at forty-one in 1766.

Who first made a lifelong career of science?

Maria Mitchell (1818–1889) grew up watching the heavens in the seafaring community of Nantucket Island, Massachusetts. Her father was interested in astronomy and his daughter followed his example. She furthered her own education when she became a librarian on Nantucket and worked in the evenings with her father, whose lookout post had become a station for the U.S. Coast Survey. In 1847, she discovered a new comet and the following year became the first woman elected to the American Academy of Arts and Sciences in Boston.

Matthew Vassar, founder of the college that bears his name, recruited Mitchell to join the faculty, and she moved to Poughkeepsie, New York, with her father for the opening of the school in 1865. She was a founder of the Association for the Advancement of Women, which held annual congresses for women's reports on their progress in employment, suffrage, and other concerns. An early president of that organization, Mitchell regularly reported on women in science. Writing in *Women Scientists in America: Struggles and Strategies to 1940,* historian Margaret W. Rossiter said Mitchell was especially concerned with educated women's attempts to gain employment other than as teachers. Mitchell also worked to change women's reception in major scientific societies, which often barred them or grudgingly admitted them only to associate-member status without voting privileges. Mitchell may have been one of those so-called "exceptional women" that the men in her field occasionally allowed to come to prominence, but she also believed in the future of women in science. She trained a number of them who carried her determination into the next century.

CHAPTER 7

❧

Teamwork: From Book Groups to Unions

How do book groups fit into history?

Who founded the American Red Cross?

Why did Jane Addams found Hull House?

What did Jane Addams and author Leo Tolstoy have to talk about when they met at Tolstoy's estate in 1896?

Why was Jane Addams drummed out of the Daughters of the American Revolution and denounced by the American Legion?

What was somebody named "Mother Jones" doing in miners' camps at the beginning of the twentieth century?

Who was "Red Emma"?

Milestones: The Law and the Politics of Reproduction

When did the Blondes have more fun?

What was a "Boston marriage"?

If romantic friendships between women had been generally accepted, what changed for lesbians in twentieth-century America?

What was a shirtwaist, and how did it figure in history?

How did the Triangle Fire help direct the career of Frances Perkins, the first woman in a president's cabinet?

Who founded the Girl Scouts?

How did women help to curb lynching?

Why were so many of the Latinas who are remembered in American history activists in the labor movement?

What obstacles did these unions that represented Latinas face?

Who was America's most noted crusader for the handicapped?

～

How do book groups fit into history?

American women have been organizing for self-improvement or community betterment since the Revolutionary War. Seeing a need and wanting to do something about it seems as basic a part of the American heritage as the Boston Tea Party. The earliest literary societies were a form of mutual aid set up by black women. The Female Literary Association of Philadelphia, started in 1831, sought to combat prejudice by developing its members' talents. Historian Anne Firor Scott recorded that a Ladies Literary Society for book discussions existed in Kalamazoo, Michigan, in 1852, and a Minerva Society in New Harmony, Indiana, in 1859. Although colleges for women were established by the middle of the nineteenth century, women who could not afford college—or who married instead of continuing their schooling—started literary societies for their own advancement in the 1870s. The women who joined these groups echoed many a member of a contemporary book club. Said one who joined a reading circle in 1884 in North Carolina, "I consider [it] as a mild form of compulsory education and that is why I joined it. So I would feel obligated to read books which otherwise I would neglect."

But women didn't stop with literary societies. Helping others was considered a natural connection to women's sphere of interest in the home. Among the earliest of women's benevolent societies on which Scott reported in *Natural Allies: Women's Associations in American History* was the Female Association for the Relief of Women and Children in Reduced Circumstances, founded in Philadelphia; the Colored Female Religious and Moral Society of Salem was established in Massachusetts in 1818. Women also set up missionary societies, either to finance work overseas or among the Indians. These organizations also affected the women who established them. Throughout the nineteenth century, women had only the most subservient roles in associations established by men. In their own societies, however, women had a chance to exercise leadership and think about redefining their own status.

Women soon looked beyond the effects of poverty to the causes. In some cases, they set up employment training and placement so that women might earn better wages or not turn to prostitution. The reformers moved into temperance work as well because they felt that drunkenness helped keep poor people in dire economic straits. In both temperance and antislavery agitation, women were challenging the notion that they should not speak in public, let alone tackle controversial issues. Black women led in opposing slavery, forming societies in Salem, Massachusetts, and Rochester, New York, in 1832.

The United States Sanitary Commission, which recruited nurses during the Civil War and worked on other matters pertaining to public health, was established after women, especially in New York State, had gotten organized on their own to do war work. In the South, Scott wrote in *Natural Allies,* a considerable amount of the spinning and knitting needed for uniforms may have been done by slaves "for the benefit of an army fighting to keep them enslaved." Scott noted another irony: "If women on both sides had kept closer to their assigned sphere and let the two governments muddle on without their labor, the short war which so many had predicted might indeed have occurred, and nearly everybody would have been better off."

In their Civil War work, women learned about record-keeping and consensus building as well as other organizational skills. They also became less tolerant of the patronizing manner of the men with whom they worked in missionary societies, men who denied them the opportunity to participate in church leadership. "By opposing what might easily have been interpreted as the natural right of women members who, after all, had founded many churches and supported the practical side of church life from the beginning," Scott noted, "church men created the very thing they feared"—a movement for women's full rights.

Religious enthusiasm in the 1870s buoyed the temperance movement, especially the strength of the Women's Christian Temperance Union (WCTU). And WCTU members did more than smash saloons and encourage drinkers to "take the pledge" of abstinence. In Michigan, WCTU members lobbied for a girls' reformatory under an 1879 law that said women should be in the majority of its board. It was on that board that women first held public office in Michigan. Members of the Young Women's Christian Association (YWCA) also worked on a variety of issues. Originally interested in "saving souls," the Y on college campuses became by the 1920s an organization whose members preached "a more radical version of the social gospel" than that which guided its community-based organizations, Scott wrote.

In the South, however, many YWCA members insisted on separate branches for black and white. Few other groups did even that much. "It rarely occurred to white women, as they began to link their own clubs in city and regional federations, that it would have made sense to include the black clubs as well," Scott said. The National Association of Colored Women's Clubs, set up in 1896, brought together groups around the country that were working to provide aid to widows and orphans, the unemployed, and those in need of education. It also supported churches and other institutions. These groups also were consciously trying to change the prejudiced images of black women held by many whites.

The communities in which colleges had been established to educate African-American students provided a core of middle-class women who were working "for the advancement of the race" locally. These women identified local problems and worked not only to improve the conditions they found but also to enhance their own spiritual and economic development. Historian Cynthia Neverdon-Morton, author of *Afro-American Women of the South and the Advancement of the Race, 1895–1925,* wrote that in Virginia, for example, women established a home for destitute black women who had no family to care for them as they aged. In Atlanta, kindergartens were started in 1905 for black children whose parents could not send them to private schools, and in Maryland an organization called the Baltimore Colored Empty Stocking and Fresh Air Circle was set up in 1904 to provide food and clothing for poor children.

With the establishment of Hull House in Chicago and its support by the Chicago Women's Club, women's associations moved into an era of "municipal housekeeping." They made the case that women's social responsibility didn't stop at their front doors but extended into their communities. They tackled sweatshops, child labor, impure food and drugs, and a variety of other consumer or health-related issues. By 1912, Anne Scott wrote, the platform of former President **Theodore Roosevelt**'s insurgent Progressive Party was "a summary of the causes women had developed over the preceding forty years." By the time women got the vote, their associations had proved "miniature republics in which to learn about politics," historian Scott concluded. They not only aided their own communities (although sometimes with great condescension, despite noble motives) but also helped themselves. They learned subject matter and skills on a scale that might never have been accomplished if the men had simply let them join their groups in the first place.

Who founded the American Red Cross?

Clara Barton (1821–1912) had gained nursing experience as a child during the two years in which she cared for her older brother David, seriously injured while helping build a barn. Although never formally trained as a nurse, she later cared for hundreds of young men wounded during the Civil War. She then turned her energies to providing an agency that was not part of the government that could respond to human needs during natural disasters and other emergencies—the Red Cross.

Barton faced discouragement time and again. Born in North Oxford, Massachusetts, she started teaching at eighteen and later founded a public school at Bordentown, New Jersey. The school was immediately successful, but the town would not tolerate a female principal, so a man was placed in charge. Barton resigned because of the school board's ingratitude to her and because of the petty way her new superior treated her. She moved to Washington, D.C., and obtained a job as a clerk at the patent office. She was thus probably the first woman hired permanently by the federal government, not an easy first because her male colleagues were frequently rude to her. They called her a "pest in petticoats" and spit tobacco juice or blew smoke at her.

When the Civil War began, Barton first helped Massachusetts soldiers serving in the Washington, D.C., area, then gathered medial supplies and food to take to field hospitals in Maryland and Virginia. "If I can't be a soldier, I'll help soldiers," she said. Brigade Surgeon **James L. Dunn** recalled that she arrived at the battle of Cedar Mountain in Virginia "while the shells were bursting in every direction" and helped first on the battlefield and later behind the lines at Culpeper. "I thought that night if heaven ever sent out a holy angel, she must be one, her assistance was so timely," said Dunn. In June 1864, Barton was named Superintendent of the Department of Nurses for the Union Army of the James, under General **Benjamin F. Butler.** Starting in 1865, she helped locate missing soldiers and then identified the dead and marked the graves of many men who perished at the Andersonville prison in Georgia.

Barton lectured widely after the war about her experiences, and during those tours she also spoke about women's rights. She met **Susan B. Anthony** and **Elizabeth Cady Stanton** in 1867, and Anthony backed the idea of the Red Cross in the feminist paper *The Revolution.* Barton was far more conservative than Anthony or Stanton, not wanting the cause of the Red Cross to be identified too closely with the women's movement for fear its establishment might be jeopardized. However, she bristled at an antifeminist placard she saw in Iowa before an 1867 lecture; it indicated that she was not "the class of woman" who spoke on women's rights "after the style of Susan B. Anthony and her clique . . ." Toward the end of her talk about the war, she read the offending sentences to the veterans she had been addressing and told them the words maligned her friend. It was people like Susan B. Anthony and Elizabeth Cady Stanton, she said, who opened the way for women to do the work they had done during the Civil War. And she concluded: "Boys, three cheers for Susan B. Anthony," and she noted in her journal that the windows shook.

Barton had become interested in the Red Cross movement while traveling in Europe for her health after the Civil War. She became a fervent backer of the Treaty of Geneva, which allowed those caring for the wounded in wartime to move under the neutral flag of a white field with a red cross. After five years' effort, she managed to convince the American government to ratify the treaty in 1882. A year earlier, Barton had helped organize the American Association for the Red Cross, of which she served as president for its first twenty-three years. Then as now, the Red Cross answered the call for relief in forest fires, hurricanes, and floods. And when the Red Cross answered the call, Barton was often there herself. Well into her sixties, she set to work to bring relief supplies to victims of the Johnstown, Pennsylvania, flood of 1889 and, nearing eighty, she personally led the relief efforts for the hurricane and flood in Galveston, Texas, in 1900. Even she confessed to needing a helping hand at the end of three months of work amid the destruction and the stench of bodies being burned. She died at ninety-one in 1912.

Why did Jane Addams found Hull House?

The daughter of a successful businessman who served eight terms in the Illinois legislature, **Jane Addams** (1860–1935) was educated at the Rockford Female Seminary. Women were just starting to attend college in any numbers in that era—Addams received her degree in 1882—and they discussed the life ahead for them with a freedom that previous generations had not envisioned. But once they left the intellectual stimulation of the campus, their families frequently had traditional plans for them. Addams's stepmother, for example, wanted her to marry her stepbrother. Young women in that day were often frustrated as they sought the useful and satisfying roles for which they had been educated. They found few such opportunities.

Addams, who had done some volunteer work among Baltimore's black population while living there with her stepmother, traveled in Europe in 1887 and 1888, visiting a settlement started by Oxford University men in London's East End. Using Toynbee Hall as a model, she and **Ellen Gates Starr** opened Hull House in Chicago in September 1889. Addams would live there for the rest of her life when not traveling (although she and **Mary Rozet Smith** bought a house together at Bar Harbor, Maine, for summer vacations).

Hull House was not only a residence for young working women but also a home for clubs, community meetings, sewing and cooking courses, a dispensary, concerts, and plays. Addams and her co-workers began investigating sweatshop labor, living conditions for immigrants, juvenile justice, and the welfare system and lobbied the legislature for improvements. Addams recognized that recreation was vital for the poor and worked with the Playground Association of America to provide places for children to play. She was also an educational reformer, developing a kindergarten at Hull House within weeks of its opening.

Addams later served on the Chicago Board of Education —an experience that taught her how difficult winning acceptance of new ideas would be. So she returned to private action, helping found the National Child Labor Committee and the National Society for the Promotion of Industrial Education. She wasn't so much interested in having young people learn trades, as that association's title might indicate, but rather was concerned that all people learn how industry worked. A great deal of American ingenuity had gone into the development of manufacturing processes and yet when individual workers started their factory jobs, they came to the machinery as though it had just been invented. They knew little or nothing about its history. She felt that if workers knew "the big picture," they might see the social and historic connections of their work. Toward that end, Hull House established a series of exhibits at what it called its Industrial Museum. "I am not willing to agree that industrial education is one thing, and cultural education is of necessity quite another."

As Addams moved more and more into the political arena, she became more firmly convinced that women must have the vote. Her argument was not based on any natural *right* to vote, rather on the idea that the more government became concerned with social and economic life, the more women should be involved so that these issues would be addressed humanely. She equated civic housekeeping with domestic housekeeping. At the 1912 Republican convention, Addams, by then a vice president of the National American Woman Suffrage Association, urged the party's platform committee to include a plank on woman suffrage. Her request received only cursory consideration. She was soon asked to join former President **Theodore Roosevelt**'s new Progressive political party, which she did. (Many said that Roosevelt had finally endorsed votes for women after a visit with Addams in Chicago.) While she did not agree with some of the national defense provisions in the Progressive platform nor with the exclusion of blacks from party activities in the South, she nonetheless seconded Roosevelt's nomination and received almost as much applause as the candidate himself. She campaigned extensively for Roosevelt, arguing that women had helped bring about many reforms only to see them falter in government hands. There would be, she said, infinite benefits "if women were taking a natural and legitimate share in the development and in the administration of governmental activities."

While some of her biographers have skittered over this point, it was clear to author Lillian Faderman, who has written a history of lesbian life in America, that Jane Addams and Mary Rozet Smith had a lasting and loving relationship, no matter what one called it, for forty years. They "always slept in the same room and the same bed, and when they traveled Jane even wired ahead to be sure they would get a hotel room with a double bed," Faderman wrote. Historians have readily acknowledged that, absent any models for her action, Addams created a public life as a social and educational reformer for herself personally and as an example for educated women in general. What Faderman would have them acknowledge is that Jane Addams also "devoted her entire emotional life to women, . . . considered herself married to a woman, and . . . believed that she was 'delivered' by their shared love."

What did Jane Addams and author Leo Tolstoy have to talk about when they met at Tolstoy's estate in 1896?

During the depression of 1893–1894, **Jane Addams** felt profoundly distressed that she was living comfortably while the poor around her were not. She remembered reading **Leo Tolstoy**'s account in *What to Do* of his attempts to help the poor during the severe Russian winter of 1881. Tolstoy had decided that only those who shared their own food and shelter with the poor could be said to have truly helped them. Addams wanted to learn whether Tolstoy's undertaking to do the same physical work as the poor "had brought him peace," as she wrote in her autobiography *Twenty Years at Hull House*. While on a trip to Europe in 1896, she went to Russia expressly to meet Tolstoy. He was working the fields of Yasnaya Polyana with the peasants and dressed in their simple clothing. At dinner, Tolstoy ate only porridge and black bread while his guests ate a more elaborate meal.

Addams noticed that Tolstoy was looking distrustfully "at the sleeves of my traveling gown which unfortunately at that season were monstrous in size." He pulled out one sleeve "to an interminable breadth [and] said quite simply that 'there was enough stuff on one arm to make a frock for a little girl' " and then asked her directly if she didn't find " 'such a dress' a 'barrier to the people.' " Understandably disconcerted, Addams recalled that she did not make a clear explanation except to say that working girls wore sleeves even more monstrous and that if she tried to wear simple peasant garb as he did, she would have to pick among thirty-six nationalities recently counted at Hull House.

Later Tolstoy asked her, since she worked with the poor in Chicago, who fed her and how she afforded her shelter. As she answered that she lived on the income of a farm she owned about a hundred miles from Chicago, she knew what the next scathing question would be: "So you are an absentee landlord? Do you think you will help the people more by adding yourself to the crowded city than you would by tilling your own soil?" It is clear from Addams's autobiography that she didn't have an answer; she was made even more uncomfortable when one of Tolstoy's daughters appeared for five o'clock tea that afternoon after having worked in the fields since five o'clock that morning in place of an injured peasant.

Tolstoy stirred deep questions for Addams. After reading all of his work that had been translated into English, German, or French, she decided to try to spend two hours a day in the Hull House bakery, perhaps to assuage her aroused conscience. She was, after all, the daughter of a miller who was tested by her father on her twelfth birthday on her ability to produce "a satisfactory wheat loaf." She soon decided she could not keep her pledge because of letters to answer and actual human needs waiting her attention. "Were all these things to be pushed aside and asked to wait while I saved my soul by two hours' work at baking bread?"

Why was Jane Addams drummed out of the Daughters of the American Revolution and denounced by the American Legion?

Jane Addams was a pacifist. "She believed," wrote her intellectual biographer John C. Farrell, "that war destroyed democracy and culture." After her visit with Tolstoy, even though she had some misgivings about his ideas, she realized that she had to put her moral principles into action or it would be clear that she really didn't believe them. She joined peace organizations, telling an audience not long after the end of the Spanish American War that she opposed war because she believed in the worth of each human life and in the obligation to build up civilization. She wanted "a moral substitute for war," something that would appeal to courage and the capacity to nurture life.

Working with **Carrie Chapman Catt,** whom she had known through her suffrage activities, Addams invited delegates to help found the Woman's Peace Party in 1915 to try to rally antiwar sentiment in America. In April 1915, at a meeting at The Hague, Addams spoke of the solidarity of women even as internationalism seemed to be deteriorating. Addams and **Aletta Jacobs,** a Dutch woman and an international suffrage leader, presented the women's appeals for mediation of their conflicts to British, German, Austrian, Hungarian, French, and Italian leaders. Upon her return to the United States, she called upon President **Woodrow Wilson** in July and again later in the summer but with little success.

Once war was declared, Addams continued to speak out about pacifists' devotion to their country. Chicago, having undergone labor unrest and filled with immigrants, was particularly edgy during the war years. Newspapers attacked her position. Although she worked with **Herbert Hoover** in distributing food overseas, she was increasingly isolated. After the war, she was attacked by the American Legion because she had opposed military training in the schools; the charges, increasingly shrill, escalated into a contention by the commander of the American Legion in Illinois that Hull House was "a hotbed of communism."

Addams had been made an honorary member of the Daughters of the American Revolution (DAR) not long after serving as the only female juror at the Paris Exhibition of 1900 at which the DAR exhibit received a gold medal, yet she was expelled on spurious charges that she was unpatriotic. Of her membership, she said: "I supposed at the time that it had been for life, but it was apparently only for good behavior. . . ."

In 1919, Addams helped found the Women's International League for Peace and Freedom and became its first president. She worked actively for an end to wars and in 1931 shared the Nobel Peace Prize with Columbia University's **Nicholas Murray Butler.** She died in 1935 at the age of seventy-four.

What was somebody named "Mother Jones" doing in miners' camps at the beginning of the twentieth century?

Leading them in strikes. Encouraging their wives to join the picket lines. Trying to improve working conditions for their children. And going to jail with them.

Mary Harris Jones (1830–1930) left her native Ireland at eleven. Her grandfather had been hanged by the British for his insurgent activities on the side of the hired hands—or "cotters"—and against the landlords. Her father was on a "wanted" list for his own revolutionary activities. The first high school graduate in her family, Mary started teacher training in Canada, where her family had settled. But she liked sewing better and became an expert seamstress. She married **George Jones,** an iron molder in Memphis, Tennessee, where she had traveled looking for a job. Concerned about working conditions in the foundries, George helped establish a branch of the Iron Molders Union after the Civil War and became a union organizer in Tennessee. Through his experiences, his wife saw the value of collective action to help ease workers' grievances.

Forced to support herself after her husband and four children died in 1867 in one of the waves of yellow fever and cholera epidemics that swept the poor sections of Memphis, Jones went to Chicago, where she worked as a seamstress for rich families. She lived behind her shop on the city's west side and saw the disparity between what she described as the "tropical comfort" of the people for whom she worked and the "poor, shivering wretches" among whom she lived. In 1871, she lost what few possessions she had in the Great Chicago Fire. Soon after the fire, she joined the Knights of Labor as one of the union's few female organizers.

For more than fifty years, Mother Jones, as she soon was dubbed, worked with miners, textile workers, and others as they tried to improve their pay and working conditions. It was an era when mine and factory owners would as soon turn guns on strikers as negotiate with them. "Join the union, boys!" was her constant cry, whether in West Virginia in the 1890s or in Colorado with the metal miners in 1911 (when she was eighty-one years old). One judge labeled her "the most dangerous woman in America."

Working in Cottondale, Alabama, just before the turn of the century, she saw gray-faced children who worked long hours in the cotton mills to the detriment of their schooling and their health. Machinery maimed their hands; one little girl was killed when her hair caught in a machine and her scalp was pulled off. Later, in West Virginia coal mines she saw the "breaker boys" who sat hunched over all day sorting slate from coal as it passed by. Thousands of children were exploited for the low wages that their impoverished parents needed. In 1903, Mother Jones helped dramatize their plight. Pennsylvania had a law barring work by children under thirteen, but the Textile Workers Union had been unable to win any enforcement effort. When the union went on strike for shorter hours (fifty-five hours a week instead of sixty), Mother Jones went to help. Deciding the group needed to make some news to force publicity in newspapers owned by the mill owners and their friends, she led the children employed at the mill on a mile-long march within Philadelphia on June 17, 1903. "I put the little boys with their fingers off and hands crushed and maimed on a platform," she said. "I held up their mutilated hands and showed them to the crowd and made the statement that Philadelphia's mansions were built on the broken bones, the quivering hearts and drooping heads of these children. . . ."

That demonstration generated news stories, but only briefly, so she decided to lead the children on another, longer walk of 125 miles, this time to see President **Theodore Roosevelt** at his vacation home on Long Island, New York. She hoped he would care enough about the children's lack of education and their injuries to take federal action. The president refused to see the group, and it was years before federal laws were enacted. But the publicity generated contributed to the climate of opinion that eventually led to outlawing child labor.

Mother Jones, who had defiantly appeared at rallies despite injunctions against her speaking and had gone to jail for her organizing activities, nonetheless opposed women's voting and political involvement in her old age. "In a long life of study of these questions," she said, "I have learned that women are out of place in political work. There already is a great responsibility upon woman's shoulders—that of rearing rising generations. It has been part of their sad neglect of motherhood which has filled reform schools and which keeps the juvenile court busy." Perhaps she was reacting to her own inability to protect her children from death by disease; perhaps she so distrusted politics that she doubted women could have any impact. She represented another case of a woman who preached what she did not practice in terms of women's public roles. But when she raised her own voice, it had been unmistakably to champion a better life for those who did the nation's heaviest labor.

Mother Jones, in ill health, celebrated her one-hundredth birthday on May 1, 1930, with a party at the home of a retired miner and his wife. Paramount News cameras recorded the day as she characteristically attacked the "old fools" who had stuck the country with Prohibition (she felt working people needed the relief they could find at saloons) and criticized women who allowed capitalists to convince them that asserting their power wouldn't be ladylike. "Maybe it wouldn't but, hell, who wants to be a lady anyhow when women are what we want and they have a great mission to fulfill." She died on November 30, 1930.

Who was "Red Emma"?

Emma Goldman (1869–1940) advocated anarchy, free speech, birth control, and sexual freedom. Authorities from the Chicago police to **J. Edgar Hoover** sought to suppress her message, but her lectures drew thousands and many of her ideas, radical at the time, have become increasingly mainstream.

Born in a part of Russia that is today Lithuania, Goldman moved with her family in 1881 to St. Petersburg, where she saw firsthand the struggles of nihilist students and others against the power of the czar. Anxious to be free of her father's rages and strict control, she left for America, settling in Rochester,

New York, then in New York City. There she met two of the three men who would most affect her life—**Johann Most,** editor of the *Freiheit* newspaper, and **Alexander Berkman,** a young anarchist. Most's paper urged violence to speed up social revolution and at times even carried directions for making bombs.

Berkman and Goldman became lovers and lived together in a small commune in New York in the early 1890s. In 1892, they followed the events at the steel plant owned by **Andrew Carnegie** and managed by **Henry Clay Frick** in Homestead, Pennsylvania, as workers sought a new contract. Frick broke off negotiations in June, locked out the workers, and hired Pinkerton guards to protect strikebreakers. Workers fought the guards as they arrived and sixteen people were killed—seven Pinkertons and nine workers. Berkman traveled to Homestead, planning to kill Frick and blow himself up. Admitted to see Frick on a ruse, Berkman wounded but did not kill him. He was tried and sentenced to prison, where he remained for fourteen years. Not until forty years later did Goldman admit that she helped Berkman test explosives and plan the attack. Her position on violence had changed during the years after the assassination attempt, and she usually said that education was the better tool for anarchists.

By 1893, the United States was in the midst of the deepest economic depression it had yet known. Goldman spoke before a crowd of the unemployed on August 21 in New York's Union Square and was arrested for telling people that if they had no bread, they could take it. Before her trial, she was interviewed by journalist **Nellie Bly** of *The New York World*. Bly was clearly impressed with Goldman, who told her she worked for "masses against classes." She expected few gains so was "satisfied to agitate, to teach, and I only ask justice and freedom of speech." She was convicted in October and served ten months in prison.

Goldman was frequently arrested in the next decades as her speeches pushed local authorities beyond their limits of tolerance. Goldman's theories of anarchism were muddy; she advocated a mix of communalism and individual responsibility. She was most consistent in her resistance to even the most liberal forms of the state. She opposed the military draft, censorship, and votes for women; she felt voting created a false illusion of political participation. Goldman opposed marriage, saying, "If two people care for each other, they have a right to live together as long as that love exists. When it is dead, what base immorality for them still to keep together."

In 1901, Goldman became caught up in the assassination of President **William McKinley. Leon Czolgosz,** the disturbed young man who shot the chief executive, had paid a call on her and said he had been inspired by her. She was jailed for more than a week, but authorities could never prove any plot because there was none. Czolgosz was doubtless insane. Goldman disavowed any influence on him, but increasingly sympathized with his plight and was angered that no other anarchists would defend him.

Deeply depressed, Goldman withdrew for a time from speaking and organizing. When recovered, she launched the radical magazine *Mother Earth* in 1906. What really fired her passions, however, was her meeting in 1908 with a doctor and former hobo named **Benjamin L. Reitman.** Theirs was a torrid, sensual love affair—with jealousies and possessiveness that seemed out of keeping with Goldman's theories on love and sex. He became in effect her manager as well, helping arrange speaking engagements and ultimately helping edit *Mother Earth.* Goldman resisted Reitman's wishes for children and a settled life; finally in 1917 Reitman married another woman and became a doctor in Chicago.

Goldman's views received a wider and more tolerant hearing after the furor over the McKinley assassination abated and as the Progressive movement gathered steam. Knowing that she was violating the laws, Goldman started discussing birth control techniques in her speeches in 1915 and distributing pamphlets on birth control, including one by **Margaret Sanger.** Goldman served fifteen days in jail for her activities the following year.

As World War I began, the country's attitude toward radicals hardened. Goldman opposed the military draft and she helped organize the No-Conscription League in 1917. Arrested and tried on charges of conspiring to prevent draft registration, advocating violence, and taking German money, Goldman and

Berkman were convicted on July 9 by a jury that deliberated for thirty-nine minutes. But Goldman had had her brilliant say in court, speaking for two hours and arguing that if America wanted to make the world safe for democracy through war, "she must first make democracy safe in America." Goldman served two years in the penitentiary. Within a few months of her release, she and Berkman and others rounded up in the Red Scare were deported.

Goldman soon discovered that the Bolsheviks also suppressed dissenters and left Russia after two years. She wrote her autobiography, *Living My Life,* in 1931, and died in Toronto in 1940.

Milestones: The Law and the Politics of Reproduction

1821—Connecticut banned abortions after the stage of pregnancy when the fetus can be felt to move, known as the quickening. It was the first such law, and did not bar abortion by poisoning before quickening.

1860—By the eve of the Civil War, twenty states had enacted laws limiting abortion, in most cases to protect the life of the mother.

1873—Congress passed the Comstock laws banning distribution of birth control information through the postal service. The laws were named after morality crusader **Anthony Comstock.**

—"Voluntary motherhood"—that is, at women's discretion through periodic abstinence from sexual intercourse—was the theme of women's rights advocates. The First Congress of the Association for the Advancement of Women held a session devoted to what the group called "Enlightened Motherhood." Those who advocated voluntary motherhood, however, opposed contraception and abortion.

1876—Dr. **Edward B. Foote** was arrested for sending contraceptive information through the mails in violation of the Comstock laws. He was fined three thousand dollars, and his conviction led to a decline in birth control education.

1888—Many doctors opposed contraception within marriage in this time period. They thought it was bad for women's health and morals. A doctor wrote that couples who used contraceptives during intercourse were committing "marital masturbation."

1905—President **Theodore Roosevelt** criticized women who avoided having children as "criminal against the race." He thought the movement toward smaller families was a sign of moral decay.

1912—The American Medical Association elected as its president pediatrician **Abraham Jacobi,** who endorsed birth control. His presidential address is considered part of a move toward the control over birth control information by the medical community.

1915—**Margaret Sanger** began using the phrase "birth control" to describe attempts to regulate fertility.

1916—Sanger opened America's first birth control clinic in the Brownsville section of Brooklyn. Ten days later, she was arrested for violating laws against giving out birth control information. First her sister **Ethel Byrne,** who was working with her, was convicted and jailed, then Margaret spent thirty days in prison.

1921—Sanger convened the first American Birth Control Conference in New York. She sought attention for her issue, which the Catholic Church viewed with hostility and emerging feminists considered not their top priority. Over the next forty-five years, Sanger operated clinics, lobbied against the Comstock laws, raised money for research into new birth control methods, and educated people around the world on women's need to control their own fertility.

1929—Sanger's birth control clinic in New York was raided by police and medical records impounded, a mistake that led the medical community to rally behind her.

1920s and 1930s—The birth control movement became transformed from a set of local populist associations to a professional, staff-oriented organization.

1942—The American Birth Control League that Sanger had founded in 1921 changed its name to the Planned Parenthood Federation of America.

1951—Chemist **Carl Djerassi** led a Syntex Corp. research team that created the steroid that would become the basis for oral contraceptives.

1960—Dr. **John Rock** developed "the pill"—the oral contraceptive.

1965—The Supreme Court, in the case of *Griswold v. Connecticut*, struck down a state law that forbade giving birth control information to married couples. It cited privacy arguments.

1973—The Supreme Court ruled unconstitutional laws restricting abortion in Texas and Georgia in the cases of *Roe v. Wade* and *Doe v. Bolton*. States could intervene in the second trimester of a woman's pregnancy only to protect the woman's health and could prohibit abortion in the final trimester except when the woman's life or health was at stake.

1976—Representative **Henry Hyde** of Illinois successfully sponsored an amendment barring use of federal Medicaid money for abortions for poor women. Its constitutionality was upheld in 1980.

1984—President **Ronald Reagan** announced that family planning organizations in foreign countries could not receive U.S. aid if they provided abortion information or services.

1986—**Randall Terry** organized Operation Rescue, which blockaded clinics that performed abortions.

1989—The Supreme Court ruled in a Missouri case, *Webster v. Reproductive Health Services,* that states could regulate access to abortion.

1991—The Supreme Court ruled that the so-called "gag rule" issued by President Reagan was constitutional. That rule prohibited doctors and counselors at clinics that received federal money from providing any information about abortions or making abortion referrals.

1992—In a Pennsylvania case, the Supreme Court upheld *Roe v. Wade* but also allowed a series of restrictions passed by the state to stand.

1993—President **Bill Clinton** rescinded the "gag rule" on family-planning clinics and reversed the policy against U.S. aid to overseas organizations that provided abortion information or services. He also named to the Supreme Court Federal Judge **Ruth Bader Ginsburg,** who supported a woman's right to an abortion.

—Dr. **David Gunn,** a Pensacola, Florida, physician who performed abortions, was murdered at his clinic during a protest demonstration in March. In August, another doctor who performed abortions was shot but not seriously wounded outside his clinic in Wichita, Kansas.

—The House passed a slightly broadened Hyde Amendment, 255–178, but the fundamental principle that public money should not be spent for abortions for poor women was reinforced.

1994—In 1994, the Supreme Court ruled that abortion clinics could use a federal law designed to control racketeering to sue violent antiabortion groups for damages. It also upheld some restrictions to keep abortion protesters from blocking access to the clinics.

—Dr. **John B. Britton** and **James H. Barrett,** who were escorting a physician into an abortion clinic, were murdered in Pensacola, Florida. An abortion opponent faced state and federal charges in the case.

When did the Blondes have more fun?

The first time women ever played baseball for pay, a team named the Blondes beat the Brunettes, 42–38. According to Barbara Gregorich, a baseball historian, the women played six innings on September 11, 1875, in Springfield, Illinois. They wore long skirts and high-button shoes. The game was riddled with errors, the Blondes making thirteen miscues to the Brunettes' nine. The Brunettes won in their next meeting, 41–21, in Decatur, Illinois. Clearly, these were not pitchers' battles.

What was a "Boston marriage"?

In the nineteenth century, two women maintaining a common household were often said to have a Boston marriage, so named because the arrangements were especially common in New England, where many of the first women's colleges were established. These deep "romantic friendships," as they were also often called, may or may not have been sexual in nature, but they were definitely based on love. They offered college graduates of that era an alternative to marriage in which both partners might have equal say in money matters and other decisions plus the companionship and support that they sought.

If romantic friendships between women had been generally accepted, what changed for lesbians in twentieth-century America?

Women living without men over the greater course of their lives—except as widows—were rare until women went to college and could become economically self-sufficient. In *Odd Girls and Twilight Lovers: A History of Lesbian Life in Twentieth-Century America,* Lillian Faderman pointed to statistics that showed that generally only 10 percent of American women remained single between 1880 and 1900, but 50 percent of women who had gone to college did not marry. How many of these women lived alone or with their families, and how many chose not to marry because they preferred the company of women to that of men? There is no way to say. But the fact remains that middle-class women who had attended college were discovering their potential to contribute to society, especially as either teachers or settlement-house workers, as well as contemplating the prospect of lives not as wives or mothers. The relationships between women that grew out of this new independence were not viewed as particularly threatening to the community, however, because comparatively few women were involved.

As the writings of European sexologists became known in the United States, love between women began to be considered freakish. Feminists were often targets of criticism about their sexuality because, Faderman wrote, "they acted in ways inappropriate to their gender, desiring to get an education, for example, or to work in a challenging, lucrative profession." Women who a few years earlier had been more open about their orientation—such as **Willa Cather,** who in college called herself "Dr. William"—became more secretive. They were "cognizant of the fall from grace that love between women was beginning to suffer," according to Faderman. She pointed out, however, that by naming a type of behavior, the sexologists did tell women attracted to women that there might be others like themselves.

Then came World War I. Thousands of men went overseas, and as one blues song put it, "left the women at home to try out all their new stunts." After the war, sexual experimentation became popular in some circles. Even at the Harlem dives where whites and blacks alike went to try out this freedom, however, bisexuality was viewed more favorably than homosexuality. While there may have been attraction to a "lesbian chic" in Harlem or Greenwich Village, the vast American middle still would not tolerate what it considered deviation from sexual norms.

During the Depression, women increasingly were told they shouldn't compete for jobs with men who needed to support families. The bravado of the 1920s faded into the economic realities of the 1930s, only to be reawakened in the 1940s when World War II pulled more women into new roles. There were government campaigns to put women in blue-collar jobs (where they wore pants, attire that would have shocked the community only a few years earlier), and women joined the Army. "Like females in the women's colleges that only the privileged few attended in earlier decades, many now found themselves in an environment where women worked together in pursuits they could consider important, and where they could become heroes to one another without the constant distraction of male measuring sticks. It is not surprising that many of them discovered through their military experiences that they wanted to be lesbians," Faderman wrote.

The war ended, but not before a significant lesbian subculture developed. Repression was not long in coming to a society that had seen so much wartime upheaval. With the expansion of communism in Eastern Europe, the disciples of orthodoxy had a convenient banner to hide behind. The modern-day witch-hunts against dissenters rampantly violated civil liberties. Homosexuals were perceived as especially vulnerable to communist blackmail and thus to divulging military secrets. Faderman pointed out that between 1947 and 1950, nearly five thousand men and women were dismissed from military and civilian government service for homosexuality.

By presidential order, gays and lesbians were banned from

federal jobs in 1953. Police in many states cracked down on gay and lesbian bars. With the advent of the civil rights and women's movements, lesbians reasserted their own rights, either as feminists or even as separatists, seeking to establish complete independence from men. Feminists disagreed over lesbianism, and when the National Organization for Women (NOW) was established, it faced debates over the stress that should be given to lesbians' issues. As John D'Emilio and Estelle Freedman wrote in *Intimate Matters: A History of Sexuality in America,* feminists' opponents accused them of sexual deviance. " 'Dyke-baiting' became a vehicle for impugning the movement and trivializing female political grievances." But lesbians, who had confronted discrimination in employment for years, contributed energy and leadership to organizing against this bias. Eventually, NOW and other women's organizations included lesbian rights in their goals.

After police raided the Stonewall Inn in Greenwich Village in 1969 and gays and lesbians rioted, the media seemed slightly more willing to report homosexuals' concerns. Homosexuals also started organizing politically. By the 1972 election, the Democratic presidential contenders issued statements about homosexual rights. By 1976, the first openly lesbian delegate, **Jean O'Leary,** coordinator of the National Gay Task Force, was elected to the Democratic National Convention.

Even before the election of conservative Republican **Ronald Reagan,** the New Right began showing its political muscle to dampen the liberality of the late 1960s and early 1970s. In 1977, entertainer **Anita Bryant** campaigned successfully against a Dade County, Florida, ordinance that banned housing and job discrimination against homosexuals. That same year **Phyllis Schlafly** drew hundreds of conservative women to Houston to oppose the Equal Rights Amendment, abortion, homosexual rights, and other issues being favorably considered at the International Women's Year meeting also being held in Houston. In 1978, a conservative California legislator, **John Briggs,** placed on the state ballot a measure that would have barred homosexuals from working in any public school system. Gays and lesbians, together with many civil libertarians, defeated the proposition. Years later they were not as successful when Colorado voted that local communities could not pass gay rights ordinances.

By the 1992 election year, gay and lesbian leaders had developed more political and financial muscle, especially after organizing to push for more research into causes and possible cures for AIDS. Many supported the presidential candidacy of Arkansas Governor **Bill Clinton.** Gays and lesbians were named to several important jobs in the Clinton administration, joining in government service those who had been elected to federal, state, and local office in the late 1980s and early 1990s. The furor over gays and lesbians in the military in the first year of Clinton's presidency showed, however, that the nation was still far from fully accepting homosexuality.

What was a shirtwaist, and how did it figure in history?

A popular clothing style for women at the end of the nineteenth century and into the early twentieth, shirtwaists were blouses with crisp collars, an expanse of material across the bosom tucked down into a narrow, tapered waistline. They were usually worn with tailored skirts and became the outfit of the New Woman setting off to work. Shirtwaists were manufactured in factories that employed thousands of women in poor working conditions. During the winter of 1909–1910, women employed at the Triangle Shirtwaist Company in New York City went on strike seeking union recognition so that they could bargain for better wages and conditions. When the men involved in picketing dropped off the line, some ninety women continued. They were roughed up by the police and the company's guards and arrested. The Women's Trade Union League provided legal help, and its president, **Mary Dreier,** was arrested while picketing with the strikers.

Before the strike ended, the union and its supporters called for support from women working at other shirtwaist manufacturing plants. As the union secretary said: "I left the meeting and went out to Broadway near Bleecker Street. I shall never again see such a sight. Out of every shirtwaist factory, in answer to the call, the workers poured and the halls which had been engaged for them were quickly filled." As many as thirty thousand workers—three-quarters of the total—participated. Russians, Italians, and American workers were involved; many of the Americans walked out only in sympathy with the foreign workers, whose conditions they felt were worse than theirs. This difference in motivation—plus the Russian men's belief that no one else sufficiently shared their determination—led to division among those who had walked off their jobs. Some of the American women returned to work after a week or two of striking. However, in general, even though the women lacked trade union experience, they proved determined strikers. They went without food so that men they felt might need it more might eat, they picketed in bitter cold winter weather, and they endured rough treatment and arrest. The strike ended with mixed results after thirteen weeks. More than 350 shirtwaist-manufacturing shops signed union contracts for a fifty-two-hour workweek, better pay, and a limit on night work. But the women at the Triangle factory, who had started the walkouts, had to return to work with no union recognition and no contract, thus no improvement on conditions such as inadequate fire escapes.

A year later, on March 25, 1911, a fire began in the loft of the Triangle Shirtwaist Company. To try to prevent employees stealing goods or leaving work, the company had locked the doors to the stairs. Work spaces on the eighth, ninth, and tenth floors of the building were filled with bins of cotton scraps that were emptied only six times a year. Flammable paper patterns and oil for the sewing machines also contributed to the quickly spreading blaze. No fire extinguishers had been placed in the work area, no fire drills had been conducted, and none of the fire ladders reached high enough to help. As the fire spread, 47 people jumped from the eighth and ninth floors; in all, 146 women died in the blaze. Despite that fact that there had been eight fires in nine years, the company's operators were found not guilty of any wrongdoing and even collected almost $65,000 from their insurance company for property damage.

At a mass meeting a few days later, **Rose Schneiderman** of the Shirtwaist Makers Union refused to talk fellowship with those who only spoke platitudes about burned and maimed workers. Speaking intensely, she told the audience that "every time the workers come out in the only way they know to protest against conditions which are unbearable, the strong hand of the law is allowed to press down heavily upon us. . . . Too much blood has been spilled. I know from experience it is up to the working people to save themselves. And the only way is through a strong working-class movement." The Women's Trade Union League held a silent funeral procession for seven of the unidentified victims. One hundred thousand people marched in the April rain and another four hundred thousand lined the streets.

How did the Triangle Fire help direct the career of Frances Perkins, the first woman in a president's cabinet?

Frances Perkins (1882–1965), secretary for the New York City Consumers' League, lived near Washington Square and was having tea when she heard fire engines racing to the building that housed the Triangle Shirtwaist Company. She arrived at the scene just as women started to jump from the building's top floors. "I shall never forget the frozen horror which came over us as we stood with our hands on our throats watching that horrible sight, knowing that there was no help," she said.

Perkins, who had worked at settlement houses in Chicago and surveyed conditions in Hell's Kitchen in New York, was starting to investigate working conditions, especially in bakeries, for the consumers' league. In the aftermath of the Triangle Fire, she set up inspections to look for fire and other safety hazards at factories. Then, working with Assemblyman **Al Smith** and Senator **Robert Wagner,** key figures in her later public career, she helped push through legislation requiring fire drills, cause she felt mothers' primary duty was to home and children—although she had not placed those concerns uppermost herself.

After Roosevelt died, Perkins, one of only two people who served in his cabinet during his entire presidency (the other was Harold Ickes), was replaced as labor secretary. She served on the Civil Service Commission until 1953 and then lectured at colleges and was a visiting professor at Cornell University. Her students had not been born when much of the social change in which she had participated occurred and sometimes thought Social Security had always existed. "With her vivid memory for detail," her biographer George Martin wrote, "she could make real for others Chicago as it was before 1910, Jane Addams and the settlement houses, the Triangle fire, Smith and Wagner in the New York legislature and Roosevelt in the White House." Although nearly blind, Perkins remained active until slightly before she died in 1965.

Who founded the Girl Scouts?

Juliette Gordon Low (1860–1927), a financially independent woman from Georgia who was living in England, had worked with the Girl Guides there and decided America needed a scouting organization. She established the first Girl Guides in her hometown of Savannah in 1912. Her friend, Sir **Robert Baden-Powell,** who founded scouting, traveled in the United States promoting the Boy Scouts the same year, and his trip increased attention to the program. Low wrote a handbook, then helped organize Girl Scout troops nationwide "dedicated to helping girls develop as happy, resourceful individuals willing to share their abilities as citizens in their homes, their communities, their country and the world." With a new name, the Girl Scouts of America was organized in 1913. Low was president and dedicated herself to fostering scouting over the next decade until she died in 1927.

fire escapes, sprinkler systems, and limits on the number of workers in relation to the number of exits. "There was a stricken conscience of public guilt and we all felt that we had been wrong, that something was wrong with that building which we had accepted or the tragedy would never have happened," she said. "Moved by this sense of stricken guilt, we banded ourselves together to find a way by law to prevent this kind of disaster." This experience early in Perkins's career led her to believe that legislation protected workers better than unions did, important as unions were to workers' self-respect. As her biographer, George Martin, wrote in *Madam Secretary: Frances Perkins,* "She thought it was wrong that workers should have to strike in order to achieve safe conditions, reasonable hours and subsistence wages. These seemed to her the responsibility of society."

Educated at Mount Holyoke College, Perkins had majored in science but had been motivated to look at social problems after hearing a talk at her school by **Florence Kelley.** Kelley, then general secretary of the National Consumers' League, had worked at Hull House with **Jane Addams,** where she investigated working conditions and became Illinois's first inspector of factories.

Perkins had lobbied effectively in 1912 for state legislation to prevent women and children from working more than fifty-four hours a week. She was named as a member of the New York State Industrial Commission after Al Smith became governor of New York in 1918. Smith told her that since women had the vote (as they did by then in New York State), he thought he should bring women into his administration. "Why me?" she asked.

"I know a lot of women," Martin quoted Smith as saying. "Most of them in the Democratic party are the wives and sisters of political leaders. They're all right. They're nice women, but they don't know anything about things like this. They don't know anything about government. I didn't want to appoint somebody's sister or wife. That's kind of an insult to women, to appoint somebody just because she's related."

Franklin D. Roosevelt succeeded Smith as governor and told Perkins he wanted to name her to a top job to administer the state's labor department. Perkins told Roosevelt that she would take the job, but she wouldn't tell anyone about it so that he could change his mind. He didn't.

While serving in the New York State post, she began to question President **Herbert Hoover**'s optimistic predictions about economic recovery. In January 1930, she was particularly outraged and went to the press, telling reporters that Hoover was misleadingly citing improvements in employment from November to December, when stores normally hired more help for the holiday season. A more appropriate comparison, she said, would have been a previous December. That June the Hoover administration claimed unemployment was only 3 percent, but Perkins pointed out that the figures announced covered the entire population, not those people of working age. Thereafter, reporters frequently contacted her for comment on employment figures.

When Roosevelt was elected president, he asked Perkins to be his secretary of labor, a key post as the Depression deepened and government sought ways to put people back to work. As a measure of the emergency (and doubtless a sign of simpler times), the Senate confirmed all of Roosevelt's cabinet selections before he took office. Perkins, who had heard nothing from her Republican predecessor at the Labor Department, arrived to find him not packed to leave and the offices filthy with dirt, cigarette ashes, and even cockroaches. She diplomatically got him out of the office and tackled the problem of ridding the department of officials who had been shaking down immigrants. She caught several of them rifling the files one night, ordered them out of the building, posted a guard, and changed the locks on the cabinets.

Frances Perkins protected her privacy fiercely. Few knew that her husband, **Paul Wilson,** who had been an economist for the city of New York, was frequently hospitalized for depression. Perkins visited him every weekend from Washington; later he was able to live with her in Washington until he died in 1952. The couple had a daughter, Susanna. Perkins, a familiar figure in her trademark tricorn hat, used her own name professionally in an era when that was rarely done. To the chagrin of feminists, she

opposed the Equal Rights Amendment, preferring instead the legislative protections for women that she had helped enact.

Perkins's department supervised Depression-era work relief agencies such as the Civilian Conservation Corps. Roosevelt named her to head a cabinet committee to draft legislation to provide security for the unemployed and the elderly. The committee's purview was also to include health insurance, but the medical profession reacted so angrily to its mention in one of Perkins's radio speeches that that part of the package was dropped. Out of the committee's work came the federal unemployment insurance system and the Social Security Act of 1935.

Her defense of the rights of labor unions led to opposition by some rabidly conservative members of Congress. Their ire increased when she delayed a hearing on deporting **Harry Bridges,** the Australian who headed the longshoremen's union and whom some charged with being a communist. Perkins was waiting for a Supreme Court decision affecting deportation laws before acting. Representative **J. Parnell Thomas** introduced a resolution to impeach Perkins, and she received hate mail and bad publicity. The House Judiciary Committee held hearings and found no cause for impeachment.

Perkins resisted FBI Director **J. Edgar Hoover**'s attempts to fingerprint Americans in wartime—especially aliens, who were viewed as a particular threat—and to start dossiers on all Americans. She felt that the FBI was a police agency and, if allowed to take this step, would soon view all citizens as police viewed criminals. Hoover once suggested to her that fingerprinting people would enable the government to identify victims in train wrecks more quickly. "We could send cards to their families," he said, to which she replied: "Mr. Hoover, isn't it enough that his Maker would immediately recognize him?" In May 1940, Roosevelt transferred the immigration service into the Justice Department; there are those who think that had Perkins still had the president's ear on immigration in 1942, her concern with proper processes might have headed off the blatant violation of civil rights involved in interning Japanese-Americans as security risks. During the war, Perkins angered some women's groups when she opposed creation of child care centers be-

How did women help to curb lynching?

The word *lynching* came into use during the Revolutionary War when a Virginian named **Charles Lynch** formed a vigilante band to drive Tories loyal to Britain from his area. After the war, Lynch was exonerated; the state legislature said that sometimes imminent danger justified taking measures not strictly lawful. Through the latter part of the nineteenth century— once black slaves were freed after the Civil War—lynchings were concentrated in the South as whites killed black people to reassert the control they felt they had lost during Reconstruction. From 1889 to 1898, more than 1,600 people were lynched across the country, almost 1,400 of them in the South. More than 1,100 of those lynched were black.

Ida Wells-Barnett emerged in the early 1890s as one of the leading voices condemning lynching. A journalist, author, and lecturer, she branded as false the three excuses given for lynching. First, she wrote in 1895, Southerners who lynched contended that the violence was needed to prevent riots by blacks. When no insurrections occurred, despite murder of hundreds of people, lynchers then played on fears that blacks would gain political power. Again, Wells-Barnett wrote, "thousands of brave black men went to their graves" and the franchise became a barren promise. That threat gone, those who practiced the brutality turned to chivalry—they said that blacks had to be killed to avenge assaults on white women. White Southern men, who fathered mixed-race children in unions (frequently coerced) with black women, could not, or would not, envision that white women would willingly have sexual relations with black men. These relationships thus were automatically considered rape by the white men. With such charges, the men were controlling not only black men, but also patronizing white women.

Black women like Ida Wells-Barnett, **Mary Church Terrell,** and others started investigating lynchings and publicizing their findings. "It is easy to prove that rape is simply the pretext and not the cause for lynching," Terrell wrote in 1904. "Statistics show that, out of every 100 negroes who are lynched, from

75–85 are not even accused of this crime, and many who are accused of it are innocent. . . ." Lynching was about power.

The crusade that Wells-Barnett led, which also took her on a lecture tour to Britain, helped curb the number of lynchings, which decreased after 1893. However, in the four years after World War I, nearly three hundred people, most of them black, were killed in the South. In 1922, the NAACP established the Anti-Lynching Crusaders, a women's group headed by **Mary B. Talbert,** to lobby for an antilynching bill. The organization tried to win the support of Southern white women but was unsuccessful. By 1930, the number of lynchings was down to twenty—but in a South that was trying to modernize, twenty started to look like too many. **Mary McLeod Bethune,** a former president of the National Association of Colored Women and a leader in trying to promote interracial solutions to discrimination, decided the time had come to challenge white women to fight lynching. She did so in October 1930 in a statement released to the press. **Jessie Daniel Ames,** a Texan who had worked in suffrage campaigns and interracial activities, called a meeting in Atlanta the next month, which resulted in the founding of the Association of Southern Women for the Prevention of Lynching.

Southern white women did not need the protection of violence for their virtue, Ames and her organization argued; the courts could handle legitimate cases. She, too, pointed out that of 204 lynchings in the eight years before the association was formed, only 29 percent of the victims had been accused of crimes against white women. Lynching really was a violent means of keeping blacks from making economic or political gains.

As Jacquelyn Dowd Hall has written in her history of this antilynching campaign, *Revolt Against Chivalry,* the association concentrated first on signing up members—white women willing to declare their opposition to lynching. The group's principal goal was to educate women about the realities of lynching—that it was vigilante justice designed for social control, not to protect anyone's virtue—and to show Southern white men that women did not need or want that kind of protection. The women issued hundreds of leaflets about the nature of lynching, appeared before groups of church women, and spoke with local law officers to urge them to protect their prisoners when lynchings were threatened. They apparently headed off some killings. In 1934, for example, an Associated Press reporter called Ames with news that a black man had killed a police officer in Georgia and a mob was gathering. Ames telephoned a local Georgia contact who interrupted her Christmas dinner to call local law officers to urge them to prevent a lynching. None occurred.

Ames kept the organization all-white because in her eyes that increased its legitimacy, although some black women resented the patronizing attitude that exclusion represented to them. Ames also opposed proposed federal antilynching laws, thinking education was better than coercion, a stand that caused a rupture between her work and that of the NAACP. Lynchings decreased in the South after 1933. In May 1940, Ames issued a press statement that the South had undergone its first "lynchless year." In 1942, the association was disbanded, with Ames feeling that the public was finally aware that lynching could no longer be justified as a protection for white women.

Why were so many of the Latinas who are remembered in American history activists in the labor movement?

The majority of jobs that Latinas could obtain in the United States until well into the twentieth century were low-paying jobs picking crops, making clothing, or processing and packing food. In organizing to improve their pay and working conditions, Latinas found their unions were one of the few places they could assert leadership.

Women who emigrated from Mexico, Guatemala, and other Latin American countries or were the children of immigrants have been concentrated chiefly in the Southwest—Texas, New Mexico, Arizona, and California. They often worked to supplement the low wages their husbands were paid or as the principal support of their families. Barred from many professional or clerical jobs by both discrimination and lack of education, these women were concentrated in jobs that not only paid poorly but also involved hard or hazardous physical labor.

Among the earliest labor activists was **Lucia Gonzalez Parsons** (1852?–1942), who worked with her husband, **Albert Parsons,** on *The Alarm,* the weekly paper of the International Working People's Association in Chicago in the mid-1880s. Albert was arrested in May 1886 in connection with the bomb deaths of several policemen after officers shot into a crowd protesting the killing of five people at an employees' meeting at the McCormick Reaper Work. Although Parsons had not even been at the scene, he was convicted and sentenced to death because of the articles his newspaper had been running. Lucy Gonzalez Parsons led the unsuccessful fight to reverse the conviction while working as a dressmaker to support the family. Later she helped found the International Workers of the World (IWW) and spoke at its opening convention in 1905. She traveled to mining and lumber camps and union halls as an IWW representative and was repeatedly arrested as she led demonstrations of workers seeking higher wages.

More Mexicans came to the United States after the Mexican Revolution, arriving just as World War I and then the postwar business expansion created new demand for labor. Almost the same proportion of Latinas went to work in blue-collar jobs in this period as did European immigrant women on the East Coast. By 1930, 25 percent of the Mexican-American women wage earners in the Southwest were in industrial jobs. Vicki Ruiz, author of *Cannery Women, Cannery Lives: Mexican Women, Unionization and the California Food Processing Industry, 1930–1950,* estimated that about 70 percent of these women were single—the young, unmarried daughters—but the rest were married, widowed, or divorced. The women worked to supplement the family income and also to buy clothes or perhaps a radio or records. Women worked in the cotton fields of the San Joaquin Valley and in canneries throughout California.

With the 1930s came the Depression, and with the Depression came economic pressures on growers in California who sought to hold down labor costs. In 1933, cotton pickers in the San Joaquin Valley went on strike against what was then a major staple in the state's agricultural economy. By October, eighteen thousand workers, many of them Mexican-American, were on strike, camping on empty land. Women were involved in distributing food and clothing, often going into the fields to confront strikebreakers, mainly men.

Unions had relatively little success in the fields of California in the 1930s because of the strength of the growers, because strikebreakers always seemed readily available to pick the crops, and because the itinerant labor force was too difficult to organize. Union organizers turned their attention to the food-processing factory workers, hoping to build a base to return later to the fields. Disillusioned by the lack of attention they received from national union executives, a small group of organizers founded the United Cannery, Agricultural, Packing and Allied Workers of America (UCAPAWA). The group included **Luisa Moreno** (1906–1992), who had organized a Latina garment workers' union in Spanish Harlem and then worked for the American Federation of Labor (AFL) in Florida cigar factories. **Emma Tenayucca** was another key organizer. She had been arrested during a cigar workers' strike in San Antonio, Texas, and led pecan shellers in a thirty-seven-day strike there in 1938 as well as helping form two locals of the International Ladies Garment Workers Union (ILGWU) in the mid-1930s.

UCAPAWA represented black sharecroppers, Filipino lettuce packers, and Mexican field hands in its day. Much of its leadership was female because so many of the workers represented were women. Ruiz estimated that 44 percent of the principal offices in UCAPAWA locals were held by women and that women were 65 percent of the shop stewards. "Although the material benefits achieved in California canneries lasted only a few years," Ruiz wrote, "the skills and self-esteem that these women developed as a result of their UCAPAWA experience have had lasting value."

UCAPAWA's local 75 struck on August 31, 1939, at the California Sanitary Canning Company in Los Angeles. Virtually all of the company's 430 workers walked out to try to win higher wages, better working conditions, and recognition of their union. The women had to work with hazardous machines, on slippery floors, in poor ventilation, and with nasty supervisors who often belittled them for speaking Spanish. Women who nicked themselves while peeling fruit often could not take the time to bandage the cuts because of the quotas they had to meet, so the wounds would become infected.

Dorothy Healey, then twenty-four, was a principal organizer for local 75. She talked with workers in their homes, handed out leaflets at the plant gate, and recruited workers to organize others within the plant. Once the strike was called—at the height of the peach season—Healey organized food committees among the workers, which persuaded grocers in the area to contribute flour, sugar, and other staples to the union members, who were their customers. The union also launched a secondary boycott against stores that wouldn't take Cal San products off their shelves. At one point, Teamsters were unloading trucks at one store and some of the female union members became so angry "that they climbed onto the loading platform and quickly 'depantsed' a group of surprised and embarrassed Teamsters," Ruiz wrote.

The owners of the cannery still wouldn't negotiate. After two and a half months, workers went to the owners' neighborhoods and picketed with their children, who were carrying signs with slogans such as "Shapiro is starving my Mama" or "I'm underfed because my Mama is underpaid." Within a few days, the owners started negotiating. The workers won a small wage increase, dismissal of many of the supervisors and a closed-shop contract. Luisa Moreno took over in 1940 and helped consolidate the strength of the union.

The prevalence of women in union leadership yielded gains for women. By 1946, 66 percent of the contracts that UCAPAWA negotiated contained equal-pay-for-equal-work clauses and 75 percent of them provided for leaves without loss of seniority.

What obstacles did these unions that represented Latinas face?

Turf wars between unions, government hostility, and their organizing target's strength on the local political scene challenged Latina organizers. For example, the Teamsters Union muscled in on United Cannery, Agricultural, Packing and Allied Workers of America (UCAPAWA) territory after being given jurisdiction over food-processing locals in 1945 by American Federation of Labor President **William Green,** who acted without consulting the workers involved. **Luisa Moreno** tried to organize Northern California workers to resist this change of jurisdiction and, after a successful campaign gathering workers' signatures, the National Labor Relations Board (NLRB) granted their request for a representation election. The Food, Tobacco, Agricultural and Allied Workers of America (FTA), an outgrowth of UCAPAWA, won the election in October 1945, but the Teamsters counterattacked by refusing to haul goods to any canners under an FTA contract. The NLRB ultimately dismissed the election results. FTA lost a second election held in August 1946 and continued to lose ground to the Teamsters.

Throughout this period, the House Un-American Activities Committee sought to link UCAPAWA with the Communist Party. Historian Vicki Ruiz found that there were some Marxists involved, but mainly those active in the union described themselves as "just good liberals." Moreno herself said: "UCAPAWA was a *left* union, not a Communist union." Moreno, who had become the first Mexican-American vice president of a major trade union, married another organizer and retired in 1947. Nonetheless, she became a target of the red-baiters who gained the upper hand after World War II. She had emigrated from Guatemala to the United States in 1928 and was deported in 1950. Journalists **Carey McWilliams** and **Ignacio Lopez** organized her defense committee. The government offered her her citizenship if she would testify against San Francisco union leader **Harry Bridges** but she refused, saying she would not be "a free woman with a mortgaged soul." She died in Guatemala in 1992.

The next major attempt to organize field-workers came in 1962 when **Cesar Chavez** and **Dolores Huerta** (b. 1930) co-founded the United Farm Workers. Huerta, who had been a teacher in Stockton, California, began her career as a community organizer in the 1950s. She lobbied in the state capital for insurance and welfare benefits for farmworkers but realized that the workers would never make real gains until they had a union. She quit as a teacher, she said, "because I couldn't stand seeing kids come to class hungry and needing shoes. I thought I could do more by organizing farm workers than by trying to teach their hungry children." Huerta, who raised her own eleven children, was active with Chavez in negotiating with growers and organizing strikes and boycotts. She was elected the first vice president of the union at its first national convention in 1973.

Women also played key roles in the Amalgamated Clothing Workers of America strike against the Farah Manufacturing Co. in El Paso, Texas, which lasted from May 1972 until March 1974. Chicanas who worked at Farah never were promoted into supervisory posts, worked under quota systems that pitted one woman against another, and suffered from poor ventilation and neglect of their safety. Although there had been attempts to organize Farah workers earlier, the trigger for the 1972 strike came when several dozen workers were fired for union activity. Five hundred workers walked out of the plant in San Antonio in protest and soon others did in El Paso as well, even though they were threatened with losing their jobs. About 85 percent of the strikers were women, many of whom would never have thought of walking off their jobs. Management broadcast "La Golondrina," a song of farewell, as they left.

"When I started walking outside," one woman told researchers, "all of the strikers that were out there, yelling, they saw me, and golly, I felt so proud, 'cause they all went and they hugged me. And they said, 'We never thought you were one of us.' And I said, 'What do you think? Just because I'm a quiet person?' But it was beautiful! I really knew we were going to do something. That we were really going to fight for our rights."

Quite apart from the success or failure of the strike—and

the record was mixed—the women involved assumed many new responsibilities. They worked for the union, distributed goods sent in by supporters outside the area, and traveled to talk to people about the strike. They became more aware of politics and social movements that they had thought had no meaning for their own lives. And they spent time outside their homes and, learning of their own abilities, sometimes began to question their husbands' judgment. Most marriages survived and many were strengthened, according to Laurie Coyle, Gail Hershatter, and Emily Honig, the authors of "Women at Farah: An Unfinished Story," a study of the strike. However, some men, threatened by their wives' assertiveness, walked out. The authors quoted one teenager who said, "Mom used to be a slave. But since the strike she thinks for herself. It's a lot better."

After the initial settlement, which had resulted in higher wages and union recognition, a number of women were fired, however. They had not met production quotas, which had been increased arbitrarily after the strike. The union leadership would not file grievances and some of the workplace gains dissolved as time passed.

Who was America's most noted crusader for the handicapped?

Helen Keller (1880–1968), deaf, blind, and unable to speak after an illness early in childhood, learned through the perceptive teaching of **Anne Sullivan** how to connect with her world as well as how to communicate with it. Early on, she became a symbol to others of the ability of the handicapped to learn and to lead independent lives. She spent much of her life writing and traveling to educate others about helping the blind and deaf as well as raising money for such efforts.

How did Anne Sullivan reach this six-year-old child, whom one writer described as a "furious little termagant"? Helen had almost knocked down her teacher on first meeting and was carried upstairs, screaming, for her first lesson. How did Sullivan penetrate what Keller later called her "state of anarchy," her sense of drifting in a dense fog without sounding board or compass, lacking knowledge even that there were safe harbors?

The child did not know words existed or that they were connected to things. But clearly there was a deep well of intelligence. One day, while the pair was out for a walk, Sullivan held Keller's hand under a spout from a water pump and the child made the connection between the cool liquid and the word *water* spelled out in her hand. Then she learned Sullivan's name— she became "Teacher" to Keller almost ever after—and she learned dozens of words in hours and hundreds within a few months. She saw with her hands as teacher and pupil walked through the woods. She felt the breezes and smelled the changes of season. With her keen senses, those that had not been denied her, she could "feel" her friend **Mark Twain**'s words by holding her fingers on his lips as he read, or discern music by laying her hands on a radio. She knew when her train was passing St. Louis because she smelled its breweries miles away, she could tell by smell whether she was walking by a Catholic or a Protestant church, and she could even tell when a house painter was on the bus on which she was riding. Her voice remained a lifelong disappointment to her, and indeed Anne Sullivan had tried to discourage her from learning to talk, thinking it would be too frustrating. But Keller kept at it, and eventually people could understand most of what she said, if not especially clearly. The story of the collaboration between teacher Sullivan and student Keller has been dramatized in *The Miracle Worker*.

People constantly suggested to Keller that she should take this path or the other, but she remained her own person. She did not want pity or protection. "A person who is severely impaired never knows his hidden sources of strength until he is treated like a normal human being and encouraged to shape his own life," she wrote.

Keller was clearly a prodigy—able to recognize large groups of people from their handshakes, attending college despite formidable obstacles to winning admission, and reading Greek,

Latin, German, and French by the time she left college. Author Van Wyck Brooks reported that when **Woodrow Wilson** asked Keller why she had chosen to go to Radcliffe instead of one of the other prestigious women's colleges, she replied: "Because they didn't want me at Radcliffe, and, being stubborn, I chose to override their objections." She started college in 1900. With Anne Sullivan beside her to relay the lectures by spelling them into her hand, she completed her studies and received a bachelor of arts degree, graduating cum laude in 1904. She also received a citation for excellence in English letters. One of her professors encouraged her to write her autobiography, which became the classic *The Story of My Life,* first published in 1902.

Keller and Sullivan settled on seven acres of land at Wrentham, not far from Boston, where Helen continued her reading and writing. She also did various chores, pricking out the laundry list in Braille and checking it over when the laundry was returned, gathering flowers, and making beds. In 1905, Anne Sullivan married **John Macy,** who had helped Keller write her first book. Keller fell in love with her young secretary, **Peter Fagan,** and wanted to marry him in 1916. He took out a marriage license, but when the papers got hold of the story, Keller's mother spirited her off to her home in Alabama.

Concerned about making a living—and worried about how Sullivan, increasingly in ill health and separated from Macy, would survive without her as the magnet for income—Keller decided to go on the road. For several years in the early 1920s she appeared on the vaudeville circuit, answering questions in noisy tents, much to the dismay of some of her friends. Once again her stubborn streak emerged as she made it clear she had her own life to live, that her act was dignified, and that it paid better than writing.

Keller had visited poverty-ridden neighborhoods with Sullivan and never forgot the conditions in which people had to live. She became a dedicated socialist, especially concerned that poverty contributed heavily to blindness for many people. Not only did she want the blind to have the doors opened to their minds and be trained for jobs, she also worked to prevent blindness among newborns. Venereal disease often caused blindness in infants in those days, but no one would talk about sex-related ailments. Keller did, writing a clear-cut discussion for a women's magazine in 1907. She organized a concert at the Metropolitan Opera House to raise funds for the American Foundation for the Blind in 1921, and traveled widely to raise money and direct attention to the needs of the blind.

She never stopped learning, exploring works of art with her hands, sensing the stillness of the Egyptian desert, picturing the Parthenon in her mind as she ran her fingers along the columns. She knew she ran the risk of being preachy, but she never wanted to slip into the tranquillity of a Pollyanna, accepting her lot. She knew she had many blessings, described by Van Wyck Brooks in *Helen Keller: Sketch for a Portrait:* "She never had to handle money, she did not have to cross streets alone, she had always been able to count on personal kindness, and she had been spared the pain of many sights and sounds that afflicted those who heard and saw too much." She was tough-minded and able to laugh at herself. "True faith abhors preaching," she often said. The study of philosophy remained important to her, and she called it "a star in lonely hours and dark passages." Living a life in one's mind helped overcome the bonds of the body and its condition. Handicapped people especially realized that not all they saw and heard was reality, she said, and once wrote that "philosophy is the history of a deaf-blind person writ large."

Helen Keller outlived her teacher, Anne Sullivan, and her faithful secretary of later years, **Polly Thomson.** She died of heart disease in 1968 less than a month before her eighty-eighth birthday. Her ashes rest next to Sullivan's and Thomson's at the National Cathedral in Washington.

CHAPTER 8

∼

The Twentieth Century: Women Soar and Women Fight

Milestones: Twenty American Athletes for the Twentieth Century

Why did the name Angel Island not summon up heavenly memories for many Chinese women?

Who was the First Lady of the Air?

Why was First Lady Eleanor Roosevelt ridiculed—or revered?

Who organized the Black Cabinet?

What was a "picture bride"?

Is "Annie, Get Your Gun" and go to war a prospect for today's military women?

Had military policy toward women changed by the mid-twentieth century?

How did the Vietnam War affect U.S. military women?

Why did the military shift from resisting women's entry into the service academies to sending women to the Persian Gulf War?

What did the Persian Gulf War reveal about women's status?

From Tailhook to Tomcat Follies, what was the Navy doing about attitudes toward women in the military and in leadership?

How did a black singer from East St. Louis end up working for the French Resistance in World War II?

How did a woman become an official in the 1940s with a union that represented brawny autoworkers?

How did the internment of Japanese-Americans during World War II affect the women?

Whose work helped launch the modern environmental movement?

Why did the expression "Ride, Sally, Ride" describe history in the making?

Where is "mankiller" a term of respect?

∿

Milestones: Twenty American Athletes for the Twentieth Century

Mildred "Babe" Didrikson Zaharias—An Olympic gold medal winner in javelin and hurdles competition in 1932, she toured on basketball and baseball teams in the 1930s before helping found the Ladies Professional Golf Association in 1948. The Associated Press named her the Woman Athlete of the Half-Century in 1950.

Gertrude Ederle—After winning a gold medal and two bronze medals at the 1924 Olympics, she became the first woman to swim the English Channel, completing the distance in fourteen hours, thirty-one minutes in the summer of 1926.

Helen Wills Moody—While still a teenager, she started winning U.S. tennis championships, capturing seven national singles titles between 1923 and 1931 and eight Wimbledon singles championships between 1927 and 1938. She also helped modernize tennis clothing for women—away from the long-sleeved, long dresses and toward sleeveless, short dresses.

Helen Stephens—Running in what she described as "floppy tennis shoes," she went from a Missouri high school with no sports program for girls to win track titles at her first national Amateur Athletic Union (AAU) meet in St. Louis in 1935. The following year, she won the 100 meters in a record-setting 11.5 seconds for the gold medal at the Olympics in Berlin. She won a second gold medal anchoring the 400-meter relay. In 1938, she managed the Helen Stephens Olympic Co-eds, a barnstorming semiprofessional basketball team. She remained active in senior track events.

Alice Marble—A four-time U.S. Open tennis singles champion from 1936 to 1940, Marble won at Wimbledon in 1940 and shared a dozen doubles titles at those two tournaments. Toward the end of World War II, she conducted a spying mission against a Swiss banker to obtain his records of Nazi business dealings. Later, she coached **Billie Jean King** briefly and even nine-year-old **Sally Ride.**

Virne "Jackie" Mitchell—She struck out baseball greats **Babe Ruth** and **Lou Gehrig** in 1931 in an exhibition game between the New York Yankees and the minor league Chattanooga Lookouts, which had signed her to a contract. Mitchell, seventeen, had been taught to pitch by her neighbor, **Dazzy Vance,** later a big-league player.

Andrea Mead Lawrence—She won gold medals in both the giant slalom and slalom at the 1952 Olympics in Oslo. She was the only American woman to win two skiing gold medals in one Olympics.

Maureen Connolly—For decades, she held the record as the youngest winner of the U.S. Open, which she captured at sixteen in 1951. She also became the first woman to win the tennis Grand Slam—Wimbledon and the U.S., French, and Australian titles—in 1953, having also won Wimbledon on her first try in 1952. Injury in a horseback riding accident curtailed her career in 1954, and she died of cancer at thirty-four in 1969.

Althea Gibson—In 1957, she became the first black athlete to win the Wimbledon singles tennis title. She also won the doubles that year and captured both titles again the next year. In 1957 and 1958, she also won the singles competition at the U.S. Open.

Wilma Rudolph—Winning a bronze medal in the relays at the 1956 Olympics as the youngest member of the U.S. team, she won three gold medals in the 1960 games in the 100 meters, 200 meters, and the 400-meter relay, for which she was the anchor runner.

Tenley Albright—She won the gold medal in women's figure skating at the 1956 Winter Olympics at Cortina d'Ampezzo in Italy. She later became a noted surgeon.

Billie Jean King—A winner of the world's major tennis tournaments starting with her 1966 victory at Wimbledon, she not only dominated play (twenty singles, women's doubles, and mixed doubles titles at Wimbledon alone) but also pressed for women to be awarded prize money equal to that of men. She helped organize the Virginia Slims professional tour.

Jackie Joyner-Kersee—She won the gold medal in the demanding heptathalon at the 1988 Olympic games in Seoul and the 1992 games at Barcelona. Heptathalon consists of a 200-meter dash, 100-meter hurdles, 800-meter run, high jump, shotput, long jump, and javelin, spread over two days. Joyner-Kersee, who had also won the silver medal in the heptathalon in the 1984 Olympics, received the Sullivan Award as the best athlete in the United States in 1986.

Chris Evert—Popularizer of a two-handed backhand, she won scores of major tennis titles in the 1970s and 1980s, including six U.S. Opens and three Wimbledon singles championships. When she retired in 1989 at thirty-four, she held the record for most singles championships—157—until her friend but on-court rival, Czech-born **Martina Navratilova,** surpassed that total in 1992.

Florence Griffith-Joyner—A three-time gold medal winner (in the 100 meters, 200 meters, and relay) and silver medalist in the 1,600-meter relay at the 1988 games, Flo-Jo, as she was nicknamed, also made a fashion statement with her track suits and long, glowing fingernails. As a college athlete, she held the NCAA championship in the 200 meters in 1982 and 400 meters in 1983.

Janet Evans—Victorious in the 400-meter medley, 400-meter freestyle, and 800-meter freestyle races, she won the only gold medals not captured by Eastern European female swimmers at the 1988 Olympics. At the 1992 Olympics in Barcelona, Evans finished first in the 800 meters and second in the 400-meter freestyle.

Nancy Lopez—Near the top on the list of all-time women's golf money winners, Lopez won the Ladies Professional Golf Association (LPGA) tournament in 1978, 1985, and 1989. She was the tour's leading money winner in 1978, 1979, and 1985 and LPGA Player of the Year in 1978, 1979, 1985, and 1988. She holds records for the most consecutive victories—five—in 1987, and for the lowest seventy-two-hole score, 268, when she shot twenty under par in 1985.

Joan Benoit—She won the first women's Olympic marathon, at the 1984 games in Los Angeles, in two hours, twenty-four minutes, and fifty-two seconds. She finished 400 meters ahead of Norway's **Grete Waitz,** who had beaten her ten times. Moving ahead early, Benoit found that the only quiet reminiscent of her training runs at home in Maine was on the blocked-off Marina Freeway.

Cheryl Miller—A four-time All American, she starred at center on the NCAA championship basketball team fielded by the University of Southern California (USC) in 1983 and 1984 and led the victorious U.S. women's Olympic team in scoring, rebounding, steals, and assists at the 1984 games in Los Angeles. She was named to coach the USC women's basketball team in 1993.

Julie Krone—By riding Colonial Affair to victory in the 1993 Belmont Stakes, she became the first woman to win a Triple Crown race. She has won more money than any other female jockey, and in 1993 was among the top ten jockeys, regardless of gender.

Why did the name Angel Island not summon up heavenly memories for many Chinese women?

Chinese people hoping to enter the United States between 1910 and 1940 were interrogated and given physical examinations at the Angel Island Immigration Station in San Francisco Bay. After enduring seasickness on the ship crossing, they had to sit in uncomfortable barracks for weeks or months, waiting for clearance to enter the country. Modest women had to stand naked before a male doctor; they were also asked tricky questions about their family history to see whether they qualified for legal immigration.

Once they were released from Angel Island, they faced harsh lives either in West Coast cities or in rural areas. Women worked on family chores in cramped quarters and often tried to bolster family income by sewing at home. Later they worked in garment factories and canneries. Whole families worked together to run restaurants or laundries. Some created successful grocery stores in the South by serving black people not allowed to shop in white-owned businesses. Work was so hard and so time-consuming that women of this generation had little chance to learn English.

Like many other immigrant groups, the Chinese believed in the value of education. Until about 1930, however, girls often did not receive as much schooling as boys because they stayed home to do chores and care for smaller children. Despite their increasing education, many Chinese-American women could find work only as domestics or "Oriental" hostesses well into the 1940s. Banks would hire Chinese-American women only for their branches in Chinatown. A few women did break the barriers into the professions, with **Sau Ung Loo Chan** graduating from Yale Law School in 1928 and **Bessie Jeong** graduating from medical school in 1930. In this era, even a successful actress like **Anna May Wong** usually had to play stereotyped roles.

Chinese-American women, who by tradition had stayed within the home or worked in their family business, became increasingly active in the 1920s and 1930s. They formed women's social and civic clubs. In San Francisco in 1938, they went on strike for better working conditions in the garment industry, staying on the picket line for thirteen weeks. Before World War II, Chinese-American women helped raise money for war relief in China, which had been invaded by the Japanese. During the war, Chinese-American women served as nurses, WACs, and WAVEs. **Emily Lee Shek** of New York City became the first Chinese-American officer in the WACs, and **Helen Pon Onyett** rose to colonel in a thirty-five-year career in the Army nursing corps. **Maggie Gee** of Berkeley ferried military planes within the United States as part of the Women's Airforce Service Pilots. Chinese-American women also were able to get more secretarial, professional, and industrial jobs during the war.

After the war, many Chinese women entered the United States, either as refugees or as war brides. Speaking little English, these women faced problems as they sought employment and often had to work for low wages as domestics or in the garment districts. Their children wrestled with how they could fit in as Americans while retaining their language and customs. Girls did not face marriages arranged by their parents, but they were under pressure to wed Chinese-Americans. By 1970, however, more than one-fourth of young Chinese-American women were marrying non-Chinese. Stereotypes still kept Chinese-American women from many jobs in which they would face the public; "more were accountants, nurses, and health technicians than were lawyers, business executives, and physicians," wrote Judy Yung in *Chinese Women of America*.

Who was the First Lady of the Air?

From the moment she made her celebrated first flight—although not as a pilot—across the Atlantic in 1928, **Amelia Earhart** (1897–1937) drew headlines. To be sure, her promoter/publisher and later husband **George Putnam** generated much of the hype, including dubbing her "First Lady of the Air." But much of her celebrity came genuinely from a public looking for heroes and fascinated with the new wonder, aviation. Earhart made her first flight, with **Bill Stultz** as pilot and **Lou Gordon** as mechanic, only one year after **Charles Lindbergh** had made his daring solo flight from New York to Le Bourget Field outside Paris. She was the one who caught the public's fancy—not the men who flew her. With her resemblance to Lindbergh, she was soon nicknamed "Lady Lindy."

Earhart worked as a nurse in Canada at the end of World War I and later as a social worker. She had no clear course in life until she took her first flight in an open-cockpit biplane from an airstrip along Wilshire Boulevard in Los Angeles. That did it. "As soon as we left the ground I knew I myself had to fly," she wrote later. She took lessons, bought a small plane, and by 1922 she had set the unofficial women's altitude record, fourteen thousand feet.

The fact that she was not the pilot but rather a passenger for the 1928 flight bothered her, although she was well aware that she lacked the training in instrument flying to make the crossing at night and in the fog. She knew, too, that if she did undertake a solo crossing, she would have to answer questions about what advancement that achievement might bring for aviation; she decided she would just tell people she did it because she wanted to do it. She loved adventure, and she wanted to prove that her career didn't depend just on going along for the ride. She practiced instrument flying and, by 1932, she was ready for her own Atlantic solo flight, the first by a woman.

On the fifth anniversary of Lindbergh's crossing, May 20, she took off from Newfoundland. A few hours into the flight, according to Mary S. Lovell's biography *The Sound of Wings,* Earhart's altimeter stopped working, so she had no idea how far above the water she was. Another instrument, however, did tell her how much altitude she gained or lost. Farther on, she picked up ice on the windshield, then went into a spin. She came out of that, flew on through the clouds, and later turned on her reserve fuel tank only to discover fuel leaking onto her shoulder in the cramped cockpit. When she spotted land, she decided that she should not take a chance on flying on, tried to find an airport where there was none, and finally landed in a pasture near Londonderry in Northern Ireland. She had traveled 2,026 miles in fourteen hours and fifty-four minutes. That set a nonstop distance record for women and also represented the shortest flying time across the Atlantic. Earhart also became the first person, male or female, to cross the Atlantic twice by plane.

Hailed as a hero, Earhart later had other famous firsts—the first person to fly solo from Honolulu to Oakland, California, across the Pacific and the first to fly solo from Los Angeles to Mexico, both in 1935. She also took **Eleanor Roosevelt** on a flight, and the First Lady returned to the White House announcing that she wanted to take lessons. Since she was notorious for driving too fast, the president said, thank you, but he didn't want to have to worry about her flying as well. Throughout the 1930s, Amelia Earhart's celebrity status called attention to a new area and era of achievement for women. "Never just out for her own personal and professional advancement," wrote another biographer, Susan Ware, "Earhart consistently identified her individual accomplishments as victories for women as a whole."

On June 1, 1937, Earhart started from Miami on a round-the-world flight, with only navigator **Fred Noonan** as her companion. The pair crossed the Atlantic and Africa, flew on to Karachi, then to Rangoon, Singapore, Port Darwin in Australia, and finally Lae in New Guinea, twenty-two thousand miles in all. On July 2, her plane disappeared after taking off from New Guinea for Howland Island in the South Pacific. Neither the crew nor the plane was ever found. Many theories circulated about what might have happened—that they had been on a secret mission for the U.S. government, that they were captured by the Japanese, or, most likely, that they died in a crash at sea or drowned soon after. While there were other female pilots who set records and established celebrated careers, her death at sea and the surrounding mystery cemented Amelia Earhart's place in American history and folklore.

Why was First Lady Eleanor Roosevelt ridiculed—or revered?

Eleanor Roosevelt (1884–1962) entered marriage with her cousin **Franklin Delano Roosevelt** schooled in turn-of-the-century propriety and notions of a wife's appropriate role. Her ideas of public service changed as she encountered other women working as educators, social workers, or political organizers. Her marriage changed as well after her husband had an affair with her social secretary, then battled back from polio. By the time FDR became president in 1933, his wife had made herself into a politically powerful woman. Her influence deepened—not without cries of outrage from conservatives in the press and public—as she worked with her husband to haul the country out of the Great Depression.

Born into an upper-class family in New York City, young Eleanor was at her happiest at school at Allenswood in England after her mother and then her father died. She married FDR, the not-too-serious but adored only son of **Sara Delano Roosevelt,** in 1905, and was upstaged at her own wedding by the man who gave her away, her uncle, President **Theodore Roosevelt.** Although she had enjoyed working with the National Consumers' League and teaching calisthenics at a settlement house before her marriage, she was a dutiful political wife and concentrated on raising the couple's five children.

With the outbreak of World War I, ER, as friends, staff, and writers often called her, was able to move more into the public sphere. She served coffee and sandwiches to soldiers as they moved through Washington's Union Station bound for training camps, then visited wounded or shell-shocked young men. During this period she helped improve conditions for the mentally ill at St. Elizabeth's Hospital in Washington. She also learned to drive; she liked to drive fast, a trait that years later almost killed her when she totaled her car turning into the gates of the Roosevelt home at Hyde Park, New York. She had to have dentures made after that experience, explaining why pictures of a young

Eleanor show toothy smiles and those of an elderly Eleanor don't.

FDR ran for vice president on the ticket with **James Cox** in 1920. The Democratic candidates were swamped by **Warren G. Harding** and **Calvin Coolidge.** The Roosevelts returned to New York, where Eleanor happily plunged into teaching at the Todhunter School, which she and her friend **Marion Dickerman** had purchased. ER assumed more of an identity of her own, thus attracting controversy in an era when few women were politically influential. She became involved in the League of Women Voters and the Women's Trade Union League and then in Democratic Party, organizing at the state and national levels.

During this period the Roosevelts built Val Kill, Eleanor's cottage on the grounds of the family estate at Hyde Park. It was her home of choice from then on until FDR died in 1945 and her principal residence thereafter. The small cottage, now a national historical site, tells much about the unpretentious way that ER liked to live amid overstuffed chairs, cozy wood paneling, casual dinnerware, and photographs of family, friends, and admirers. She and her friends also established a furniture factory there.

The Roosevelts underwent two major crises: first, FDR's liaison with **Lucy Mercer,** then his lasting paralysis from polio. In 1918, when Eleanor discovered her husband's affair, she offered him a divorce. His mother, ever an enforcer of propriety, negotiated an agreement through which their marriage survived in public form if not in private substance. Three years later, FDR was stricken with polio after a swim at the family's vacation home at Campobello on the Maine/New Brunswick border. Eleanor learned from his aide **Louis Howe** how to best represent her husband's interests and how to speak better in public. She organized Democratic women in New York in 1924 and lobbied at the national convention for legislation in their interest. In 1928, she traveled the state for her husband when he ran for governor.

In 1932, Franklin D. Roosevelt was elected president of the United States. Eleanor was at first uncomfortable with the role of First Lady because it would take her away from the projects she had launched in New York. Soon, however, she saw the broader national horizon, especially with the enormous task her husband's administration faced in restoring the economy in the midst of the Great Depression. Millions of people were out of work, drought and foreclosure were ravaging the farm states, and banks were failing. The business class that had run (and some would say ruined) the economy felt that the Roosevelts were taking the country down the road to socialism, or worse. They scorned Franklin as a betrayer of his class as he announced New Deal measures to combat unemployment and try to save the banks; they ridiculed Eleanor for her appearance, her voice, her unconventional friendships, and her independence.

Franklin Roosevelt often used his wife as a lightning rod to deflect criticism of his programs from himself, and Eleanor herself plunged willingly into controversy by visiting coal miners, poor farmers in Appalachia, and black and white labor union activists. A teetotaler herself, she no sooner became First Lady than she had to tackle the question of whether alcohol would be served at the White House as Prohibition ended. She announced the decision (wine only, with preference to domestic labels) at a news conference open only to the female reporters who regularly covered her and the supposedly "distaff side" of the White House. She frequently featured the work of women, in government and out, at her news conferences.

Franklin Roosevelt, who aged visibly as World War II progressed, died on April 12, 1945. Eleanor Roosevelt was soon named a delegate to the new United Nations by his successor, **Harry S. Truman.** Underestimated by some of the international politicians much as she initially had been at home, she helped the United Nations produce a Universal Declaration of Human Rights in 1948. She remained active in the American Association for the United Nations after resigning her delegate's post when Republican **Dwight D. Eisenhower** was elected president in 1952.

In 1952 and 1956, Eleanor actively supported the presidential candidacy of Illinois Governor **Adlai Stevenson.** In 1960, she still supported Stevenson and was wary of the young Massachusetts senator who received the party nomination, **John F. Kennedy.** She remembered too well how Kennedy's father Joseph had made his money bootlegging during Prohibition and had urged accommodation with Hitler while he was Ambassador to Britain. ER was also not sure how sensitive the younger Kennedy had been to the threats to individual freedom brought on by the government anticommunist witch-hunts of the 1950s.

Kennedy asked to meet with her at Val Kill. Shortly before that meeting, one of Mrs. Roosevelt's grandchildren was killed in an accident. Kennedy called to offer condolences, suggesting they postpone their appointment. She insisted that he come, and Kennedy convinced her that he was his own man. Eleanor Roosevelt, turning seventy-six that fall, campaigned extensively for him in the general election. Kennedy named her to chair his Commission on the Status of Women, her last political task. She died in 1962.

Who organized the Black Cabinet?

In August 1936, **Mary McLeod Bethune** (1875–1955) organized the Federal Council on Negro Affairs, consisting of blacks working in the Roosevelt administration. Popularly known as the Black Cabinet, the group met most Friday evenings at Bethune's home in Washington and attempted to see that blacks were hired for more federal jobs as well as head off government decisions that might harm blacks. The move to coordinate these activities was typical of Bethune, who had founded a college in Florida, served as president of the leading national black women's group, and established a new superorganization to try to increase the effectiveness and unity of black women.

The child of slaves freed by the Civil War, Bethune wanted to be a missionary in Africa but found that the Presbyterian Mission Board did not hire African-Americans as missionaries. She turned to teaching, settling after a failed marriage in Daytona Beach, Florida, where she established a school for girls. Bethune had only $1.50 with which to start her school in a rented house in 1904. From five students (and her son), Bethune's school grew to three hundred students on a twenty-acre campus with eight buildings and a farm in 1923. Eventually, the school was merged with another and became Bethune-Cookman College.

From 1924 to 1928, Bethune was president of what was then the leading group for black women, the National Association of Colored Women (NACW). She saw the need for a powerful coalition of all black women's groups, especially one that would focus its efforts not solely on the home, as the NACW was increasingly doing. To develop programs with national and even international impact, Bethune organized the National Council of Negro Women in 1935. She headed the group with its network of professional societies, sororities, and metropolitan councils until 1949. Bethune, a staunch advocate of African-Americans doing for themselves whenever possible, also worked in integrated groups like the Council of Interracial Cooperation. She felt whites should do more to combat lynchings, so in 1930 she challenged Southern white women to take a stand. Within a month, **Jessie Daniel Ames** called a meeting in Atlanta that resulted in the founding of the Association of Southern Women for the Prevention of Lynching.

In the course of her work, Bethune met **Eleanor Roosevelt** and helped acquaint the president's wife with the problems African-Americans faced. Through their friendship, Bethune had access to the White House, which she used with savvy to defuse problems that she would learn about from contacts around the country. In 1935, Bethune was named to the advisory council for the National Youth Administration (NYA) and then made director of its Office of Minority Affairs. She became the highest-ranking black woman in federal government service to that time. The NYA was set up to help find jobs for sixteen- to twenty-four-year-olds, and Bethune did her best to see that black youths got some of those jobs, although she was not always successful.

Despite its ties to Southern Democrats, the Roosevelt administration was one of the first in which African-Americans got jobs in any numbers and of any significance. At first this "black braintrust," which included Bethune, **Robert Weaver, Frank Horne,** and **William Hastie,** was pulling in different directions. In 1936, Bethune called together the Federal Council on Negro Affairs and helped it develop a unified approach to employment and civil rights questions. Leaders from the civil rights movement such as **A. Philip Randolph** and **Walter White** conferred with the Black Cabinet and helped develop strategy. As author Harvard Sitkoff put it in his study of blacks and the New Deal: "Never before had civil rights organizations had so inside a view of a national administration. Never before had black government employees had such outside leverage at their disposal." The Black Cabinet also helped develop two National Negro Conferences, in 1937 and 1939, sponsored by the NYA and presided over by Bethune.

Bethune retired to Florida in 1949 and died there in 1955. Although there are few statues of women in the nation's capital, one of them is of Mary McLeod Bethune, fittingly located where children can play near it in Lincoln Park on Capitol Hill.

What was a "picture bride"?

Japanese women who entered the United States in the early part of the twentieth century often came in response to proposals by mail from Japanese men already working in the country—proposals that involved exchanging photographs. It was an era of arranged marriages in Japan. For many of the brides the practice itself was not out of the ordinary, but the process of exchanging photographs could be disconcerting when they learned that the men's pictures had been taken many years earlier.

Japanese men had immigrated to the United States with the plan of earning money and returning home. Many found only low-paying jobs in the fields, in mines, or on railroads and so could not realize their dream. As they decided to remain in the country, they sought wives. However, few Japanese women had entered the country, and marriage with whites was often illegal and certainly unlikely, given racial prejudice at the time. White workers were concerned that Asians were taking jobs away from them and so immigration restrictions, imposed on men entering the country, meant the Japanese could leave the country but might not get back in. So they exchanged photographs with women at home and were married by proxy. The Japanese women could then come into the country because of a loophole in the so-called Gentleman's Agreement between the Japanese and U.S. governments in 1907–1908 that allowed entry of wives and relatives of men already here. The Japanese government cut off passports for the "picture brides" in the early 1920s after antagonism to the practice developed in the United States. In the intervening years, almost forty-five thousand Japanese brides traveled to America.

The voyage, often in steerage, to an unknown country was hard enough. But the man that a woman was to meet was unknown as well. As Evelyn Nakano Glenn, author of *Issei, Nisei, War Bride*, described it, "The man meeting her frequently bore little resemblance to the person shown in the photograph." Some had had the pictures retouched to remove baldness or blemishes. "Suave, handsome appearing gentlemen proved to be pock-marked country bumpkins." On seeing their husbands, some of the women threatened to return to Japan on the same boat; some of the men who had worked as farmers had aged badly and the young brides were disappointed, having expected more. But one woman that Glenn interviewed said that even though her husband looked older than a neighbor the same age at home, she stayed because she wanted to see the United States. She didn't care what the man looked like. Her husband ran a laundry in Alameda, California, and she worked with him there. They helped others in the community find jobs.

This first generation of Japanese women—called *issei*—often worked in the fields with their husbands or entered domestic work to help support their families. Far more of the *issei* generation of married women worked than was common among the general population of married women. Because of lack of education and later because of discrimination, succeeding generations of Japanese-American women also became domestic workers. Although doing laundry, cleaning floors, ironing, and cooking for other families often proved a bridge to higher-skilled and higher-paying jobs for immigrants from Europe, that was not the case for Asian-American women (or black women). Even in the years immediately before World War II, over half of the Japanese women in the San Francisco Bay area worked as domestics. Japanese women who entered the United States as "war brides" of U.S. servicemen after World War II often did domestic work or waitressing because few other jobs were open to them.

Although excluded from many public functions, these women formed their own organizations to help them save money, to learn embroidery or other handicrafts, or to serve their churches. They also worked within their families to preserve Japanese culture. Because in many cases their husbands earned little money, they also made clothing and food at home that was needed to supplement the family budget.

These women often were caught between two cultures. In *Stubborn Twig: Three Generations in the Life of a Japanese American Family,* Lauren Kessler described the teaching career that a young **Shizuyo Miyake** had carved out for herself in Japan. Yet once she arrived in Hood River, Oregon, in 1912, she maintained total devotion to her husband and family—with no career and little knowledge of English. A "picture bride" herself, she had at least known her husband, **Masuo Yasui,** as a child growing up, although she had not seen him for several years when his marriage proposal arrived from America. Often isolated from mainstream American life in the small town where her husband owned a store and land, she raised a generation that straddled the old and the new. With her, that generation faced World War II internment, despite having tried to be 200 percent American.

Is "Annie, Get Your Gun" and go to war a prospect for today's military women?

Increasingly. But equality for women in the U.S. military has yet to be achieved.

The only women around military encampments in early America were not soldiers but camp followers—wives, mothers, girlfriends, prostitutes. General **George Washington** loathed the nuisance of having women around the camps, but since the revolutionary forces usually could not afford to feed or clothe soldiers decently, women's contributions were vital. A few women—such as **Deborah Sampson** during the American Revolution—disguised themselves as men and fought in battles. **Lucy Brewer** served three years in the Marines as "George Baker" during the War of 1812, and **Sarah Borginis** achieved the rank of brevet colonel in the war against Mexico in 1846. Perhaps four hundred women served during the Civil War and others worked as spies.

In 1916, Navy Secretary **Josephus Daniels** felt that women would be needed as clerical personnel as the war in Europe proceeded. He authorized enrolling women in the reserves so they could be enlisted once the United States entered the war. These "yeomanettes" served in clerical jobs and did translating and other tasks that freed men for combat. In all, thirty-four thousand women served in the American military during World War I. Nonetheless, the Army remained reluctant to use women in any role but nursing.

America's isolationist impulses yielded little support for the military in general between the two world wars—and even less for increasing women's opportunities to serve. During the 1920s two military-preparedness plans called for using women in wartime in clerical, cleaning, and cooking jobs. One set of proposals, submitted in 1928, even anticipated the mistakes that the War Department eventually made in setting up the Women's Army Auxiliary Corps (WAAC). It urged training women in advance to understand military thinking and training men to understand the problems involved in militarizing the women. That didn't occur.

As war spread in Europe in 1941, Representative **Edith Nourse Rogers,** a Republican from Massachusetts, introduced a bill to establish the WAACs. Rogers had already tried to secure health care for those women adversely affected by their World War I service. She did not want women to serve in the military again "without the protection the men got." After making jokes and fretting about who would do "the cooking, the washing, the mending, the humble, homey tasks to which every woman has devoted herself," Congress passed the bill to set up the WAACs in May 1942. The women who served would not receive the same pay, benefits, or rank as men in the Army. **Oveta Culp Hobby,** who became secretary of health, education, and welfare in the Eisenhower administration, was the first WAAC director. The Army took its own sweet time uniforming women properly, and WAACs found that often their skirts and jackets didn't match, that the jackets had been made flat-chested, that the skirts were too narrow, and that the low-heeled oxfords and men's ties were unattractive. In contrast, the women's arm of the Navy—the WAVES—went to Mainbocher, a New York fashion designer, and uniformed enlistees more successfully.

More than one thousand women ferried planes to air bases across the country, towed gunnery targets, and taught flying as pilots for the Women's Airforce Service Pilots during World War II; thirty-eight of them died while in service. These women, headed by **Jacqueline Cochran,** flew every variety of plane, often piloting them on their first flights, but they were abruptly dismissed in 1944. They had logged some three hundred thousand hours of flying. Not until 1976 would the Air Force allow women to become pilots.

Black women served in segregated units commanded by black female officers. Those women were often the only black officers at a base, meaning that they led extremely isolated lives. Four thousand black women were recruited for the WAACs, or 4 percent of its strength.

Army and Navy nurses distinguished themselves during World War II. Army nurses, for example, followed the troops ashore at the Anzio beachhead; six died when the Germans bombed the hospital. In all, two hundred Army nurses died during the war and seventeen of those are buried in cemeteries overseas.

In all, 350,000 women served during World War II, or 2.3 percent of the total U.S. military strength. "If, indeed, the enlisted women were a lot of trouble, as many men perceived them to be," wrote retired Major General Jeanne Holm in her history of women in the military, "it was due in part to the tendency to segregate and overprotect them."

Congress passed the Army-Navy Nurse Act in 1947, finally establishing nurses as a permanent staff corps of the Army and Navy. These women were limited in the rank they could achieve—lieutenant colonel for those in the Army and commander for those in the Navy. Their chiefs could be colonels or captains. In 1948, Congress passed the Women's Armed Services Integration Act, with Representatives Rogers and **Margaret Chase Smith** pushing for the legislation. The law limited women enlistees to 2 percent of the total military service and contained many other restrictions. For example, women could not aspire to being generals or admirals, the top ranks in each service. Navy women could only serve on hospital ships and transports. Air Force women could not serve aboard aircraft in combat, and the Army made no pretense of absorbing women. As Holm wrote in *Women in the Military: An Unfinished Revolution,* the law was not intended to open new doors for women but rather to consolidate the ground gained in World War II and prepare for mobilization in case of another war.

Had military policy toward women changed by the mid-twentieth century?

Not much. Women made up less than 1 percent of the country's military strength when the Korean War broke out. There were twenty-two thousand women on active duty, one-third of them in health-related jobs. But fifty-seven U.S. nurses arrived in Pusan four days after American troops landed in Korea; one hundred were in Korea within a month. Despite prodding of the Defense Department by **Margaret Chase Smith,** by then a U.S. Senator, women were not widely utilized during the Korean War. Recruitment suffered because the conflict in Korea did not stir American patriotism as had World War II and because women were starting to find better opportunities elsewhere.

In 1967, Congress took off the 2 percent cap on enlisted women and allowed women to hold ranks of general or admiral. The law also eased bottlenecks in promotions for women at other levels. The first female general was the head of the Army Nurse Corps, **Anna Mae Hayes,** a twenty-eight-year-veteran, who got her stars in 1970. The Women's Army Corps director **Elizabeth Hoisington** also became a general as did **Jeanne Holm** of the Air Force. The Navy's first female rear admiral was its nursing chief, **Alene B. Duerk,** promoted in 1972.

How did the Vietnam War affect U.S. military women?

Many of the 11,500 U.S. military women who served in Vietnam were nurses. They saw and treated the particularly vicious mutilating injuries of jungle warfare, often serving under fire. As a tribute to their skill—and to advances in treating combat wounds and speed in evacuating those wounded—fewer than 2 percent of the casualties treated died as a result of their wounds. Television may have brought the Vietnam War into our living rooms, as Laura Palmer wrote in *The New York Times Magazine,* "but it was the war the soldiers fought. It was the bang-bang footage that made the evening news, and that was awful enough. The war the women fought was different. It imploded. There was no film footage of the relentless horror that was hidden in hospitals."

Four Navy nurses injured in a terrorist attack in 1965 were the first women to get the Purple Heart award in Vietnam. Eight Army nurses died, mostly in crashes, although one was killed in a rocket attack on an evacuation hospital. One Air

Force nurse was killed when a transport plane evacuating Vietnamese orphans crashed. Yet President **Ronald Reagan** never mentioned women during a 1981 Medal of Honor ceremony at the Pentagon. In contrast, Palmer reported the candor of General **Colin L. Powell,** chairman of the Joint Chiefs of Staff and a Vietnam veteran who had himself been wounded, when he spoke at the ground-breaking ceremony in July 1993 for the memorial to the women who served in Vietnam. "I didn't realize," he said to the nurses, "how much your sacrifice equaled and even exceeded that of the men. I realized for the first time that for male soldiers, the war came in intermittent flashes of terror, occasional death, moments of pain; but for the women who were there, for the women who helped before the battle and for the nurses in particular, the terror, the death and the pain were unrelenting, a constant terrible weight that had to be stoically carried."

American troops had more limbs amputated in Vietnam than in World War II and Korea combined. Nurses saw such constant carnage that they, too, suffered the emotional trauma of war. **Joan Furey,** then a twenty-three-year-old Army nurse in the intensive care unit at Pleiku, South Vietnam, remembered being determined that one young soldier would live even though he was marked as hopeless for survival. She had been working in intensive care seven days a week for nine months since her arrival in the country. She gave the young man a transfusion and started to unbandage his head. "All the blood she has been pumping into the soldier suddenly pours out over her. Blood and brains, the whole back of his head, are lying in her hands," Laura Palmer wrote. "Calmly, she puts his head together and secures it neatly with a clean dressing. She's in a fugue state. Someone comes and gets her, takes her out for a cigarette. After a couple of Parliaments, she goes back to work. The other nurses and medics don't talk about what has just taken place. Too risky."

Why did the military shift from resisting women's entry into the service academies to sending women to the Persian Gulf War?

The women's movement and creation of the all-volunteer force combined to advance women in the military, with assists from Congress and the courts.

Early in his presidency, **Richard M. Nixon** named a commission to study changing personnel needs should the increasingly unpopular military draft be replaced with an entirely volunteer force. That commission never addressed the question of women as a possible military resource, but it helped destroy the notion that most service jobs involved combat. "Twenty to 30 per cent of active duty billets are directly related to combat missions," the commission said. "The remaining positions are required for logistical support, administration, maintenance and training."

Military women's roles were hotly debated during congressional consideration of the Equal Rights Amendment (ERA) and its ratification drive. Questions about whether women should be drafted or serve in combat touched many nerves. Congress had rejected amendments to the ERA excluding women from the draft or combat, but the nation as a whole evidently wasn't as far along in its thinking about women's changing roles. The ERA never became law, in part because of these concerns.

Much uncertainty surrounded the switch to all-volunteer military service. Would there be enough qualified men to fill the military's needs? A Defense Department task force started studying the use of women in the military and drew up recruiting plans should there be a shortfall of men in the early years of the volunteer service. Key members of Congress were criticizing the services for tokenism regarding use of women. And change occurred. In *Women in the Military: An Unfinished Revolution,* Jeanne Holm reported that in 1972 one out of every thirty recruits enlisting was a woman; by 1976, that ratio was one in thirteen. In 1977, the end of the first phase of the transition to an all-volunteer force, 110,000 women were on active duty.

After the military had slowly opened its Reserve Officer Training Corps (ROTC) programs on college campuses to women, Congress in 1975 required that service academies admit women as well. The first Army and Air Force female cadets and Navy midshipwomen began study in the fall of 1976.

Many military jobs remained closed to women, and the services resisted policy changes that would help women with families. Lawsuits in the late 1960s and early 1970s pressed the military on the question of whether women who became pregnant could remain in the service or, if they had children when they joined, whether they could keep the children with them. Women were being discharged on either grounds or, when they challenged the rules, the services would grant individual waivers to finesse the point. Finally, the Defense Department told the services to issue policies making separation from the military for pregnancy voluntary by May 1975. In 1973, the U.S. Supreme Court ruled that services had to give the same family benefits to women as to men.

Barriers to desirable duty—and thus better chances for promotion—still existed for women. Not only were they barred from any assignment that might involve them in combat, those in the Navy couldn't even go to sea. The Coast Guard, however, assigned women to sea duty as permanent parts of its crews starting in 1977. In 1972, the Navy experimented with a mixed male and female crew aboard the recommissioned USS *Sanctuary*, which functioned mainly as a dispensary ship. The vessel's commander reported that "women can perform every shipboard task with equal ease, expertise and dedication as men do." That ship was decommissioned in 1975, however.

A Navy electrician named **Yona Owens** decided to challenge her denial of a shipboard assignment that had come open in 1974. She and three other women filed a class-action suit, known as *Owens v. Brown*. In 1978, Federal Judge **John J. Sirica** ruled that the Navy's policy of excluding women from sea duty was unconstitutional. "What problems might arise from integrating shipboard crews are matters that can be dealt with through appropriate training and planning," Sirica wrote. The Navy started assigning women to noncombat vessels that fall. The Navy secretary told members of Congress that his service was trying to avoid having women as part of the combat team, although he acknowledged that "there is no hand-to-hand combat in the Navy. There just is none. You don't board enemy ships with a cutlass in your teeth any more. This is all done by electronics and long-range missiles and that sort of thing."

In 1983, some 170 women were among the U.S. troops landing in Grenada, many of them military police. In 1989, Captain **Linda Bray** led 30 MPs to take control of kennels for attack dogs used by Panamanian forces during U.S. military operations in that country. The kennels weren't as lightly guarded as anticipated, and a three-hour shootout occurred. That incident focused new attention on the supposed noncombat role of women.

In the 1980s, there were steps forward and backward. The Army opened 10,000 more support positions to service by women while the Navy was increasing the number of its ships closed to women's service. When **Ronald Reagan** took over as president from **Jimmy Carter,** 173,450 women were on active duty. Plans called for increasing the proportion of women in the military from 8.5 percent to 12 percent by 1986. However, the military services tried to slow the pace of recruitment of women, despite the general military buildup during the Reagan administration. The Army contended that women hampered military readiness because of lost time due to pregnancy and family situations. Senator **William Proxmire** retorted that a General Accounting Office study showed that men lost more time because of problems with alcohol and drug abuse than women did for pregnancy and substance abuse combined, yet the military would still recruit men. By 1982, Defense Secretary **Caspar Weinberger** made clear to the Pentagon that women's role in the military should increase. By 1990, women made up 12 percent of the nation's active military—with 83,200 in the Army, 57,100 in the Navy, 73,580 in the Air Force, and 9,320 in the Marines.

What did the Persian Gulf War reveal about women's status?

Women were so integrated into the military that action was clearly not possible without them as the United States sent troops and mobilized reserves after Iraq invaded Kuwait in August 1990. The media focused intently on the women who had been deployed—even though it was just as wrenching for many of the men to say good-bye to their children. But women were the news. Operation Desert Shield, which preceded the air and ground war, was the largest U.S. military action since Vietnam and the first in which so many women had played a role. In all, there were 537,000 U.S. troops in the Persian Gulf War; 33,300 were women in key combat-support positions.

In desert warfare, the military front is hard to pinpoint. Who, then, could say what was a combat job and what wasn't? In Operation Desert Storm, women directed artillery, fired Patriot missiles to intercept incoming Scuds, constructed buildings, flew airplanes, and refueled tanks. Services interpreted the rules on excluding women from combat on an ad hoc basis: Air Force women serviced and armed combat aircraft at bases in Saudi Arabia, subject to Iraqi Scud attacks, while Navy women could not get assignments on offshore carriers from which combat aircraft were launched. Women proved more than capable of taking care of themselves. Said Captain **Carol Barkalow,** one of the first female graduates from West Point, who served as a transportation officer in the Gulf War: "In the desert, I witnessed the same type of relationships forming between men and women as traditionally occur among men— mutual respect and caring borne of enduring similar dangers and hardships. My division ended up 50 kilometers west of Basra, Iraq. At one point, I lived in a tent with six men and another woman. There were no problems."

Eleven Army women died during the operation. Among them was Specialist **Adrienne Mitchell,** twenty, the daughter of a career master sergeant in the Air Force. He had done thirty years' service without a scratch, he said. "My daughter's been in for five months, and she's dead." Another of the dead was one of the first Army helicopter pilots to go into Iraq with troops and supplies, Major **Marie T. Rossi.** She was killed with three crewmen when their chopper hit a tower in bad weather the day after the cease-fire began. Her husband was flying in a different unit in Saudi Arabia. Two women were also among those held prisoner by the Iraqis; both received the Purple Heart. Major **Rhonda Cornum,** a flight surgeon whose plane was shot down, breaking both her arms, was assaulted while a prisoner when one of her captors stuck his fingers in her vagina and rectum and fondled her breasts.

Semantically, the Gulf War brought a major change. Government officials and the press started referring to men and women, not just men, in the armed forces and to service personnel, not servicemen. Said President **George Bush** in announcing the start of the air war in January 1991: "No president can easily commit our sons and daughters to war."

In the euphoria after the Gulf War, a measure rescinding the ban on women flying combat planes, introduced by Representatives **Patricia Schroeder** and **Beverly Byron,** swept through the House of Representatives in May 1991. Said Schroeder: "The Persian Gulf helped collapse the whole chivalrous notion that women could be kept out of danger in a war." By the time the Senate took up the measure, the opposition had mobilized. The Senate Armed Services Committee tried to finesse the issue by calling for a study commission rather than for repeal of the combat-flying exclusion. Then women organized as well, forming a new group called Women Military Aviators that included veterans of the Persian Gulf. The Senate not only specifically allowed women to fly combat planes for the Air Force and Navy, it also gave the defense secretary the option to waive other combat exclusions.

In April 1993, **Les Aspin,** President **Bill Clinton**'s first defense secretary, announced that women could serve as combat pilots and aboard combat ships, although they were still barred from ground combat. The carrier USS *Eisenhower* became the first Navy warship with women in its crew. One of them, Lieutenant **Shannon Workman,** became the first woman to qualify as a combat-ready Navy pilot. The Navy also made slacks the standard attire for female sailors on all ships. Skirts would be worn only for formal events. In 1994, despite military cutbacks, women still made up twelve percent of U.S. armed forces.

From Tailhook to Tomcat Follies, what was the Navy doing about attitudes toward women in the military ranks and leadership?

Events of the early 1990s showed the gap that still existed between official policy making about women in the military and informal behavior toward them. Nineteen ninety-one was the year of the notorious Las Vegas meeting of Navy pilots—a gathering called "The Tailhook Association"—at which drunken, groping men made women run a gauntlet in a hotel hallway and harassed them in other crude ways. Superior officers present did nothing to stop the incident nor to discipline those involved, and admirals later alerted to the problem also failed to act decisively. A report from the Defense Department's inspector general in 1993 found that as many as 83 women had been assaulted or harassed and that 140 service members engaged in improper behavior.

In October 1993, the Pentagon censured three admirals and reprimanded thirty other top-ranking officers for failing to stop or report the incidents. The report said that the men attending the three-day party "viewed the annual conference as a type of 'free fire zone' wherein they could act indiscriminately and without fear of censure or retribution in matters of sexual conduct or drunkenness." However, the U.S. Senate allowed the Navy's top admiral, **Frank B. Kelso II,** who attended Tailhook, to retire at his four-star rank and full pension. Republican and Democratic women in the Senate united on the issue, led a heated debate on the Senate floor, and forced a close 54–43 vote on that decision in April 1994.

The year after Tailhook, Navy officers put on a show called

"Tomcat Follies" at the Miramar officers club in San Diego. A banner in the show contained an obscene sexual remark about Congresswoman **Patricia Schroeder,** who had been critical of the Navy's investigation into the Tailhook incident. A female officer complained and the Navy relieved five officers of their command and disciplined sixteen others.

President **Bill Clinton** said that the conduct described in the Defense Department's report on Tailhook "has no place in the armed services." But one female Navy pilot doubted that change would be rapid, saying, "I don't think the Navy will ever end sexual harassment until it has ended sex discrimination."

How did a black singer from East St. Louis end up working for the French Resistance in World War II?

The flamboyant **Josephine Baker** (1906–1975), an entertainer who traveled throughout Europe in the 1930s, had access to the crème de la crème of society. For her work gathering information, she earned the Croix de Guerre and the Rosette de la Resistance.

Indeed, Baker, who had appeared in American vaudeville and in New York clubs, became more identified with France than with the United States. She debuted at the Folies Bergere and became a jazz sensation in the 1920s and 1930s, living life to the hilt, walking leopards and swans up the Champs-Élysées. After World War II, she set up an interracial orphanage at the property she and her husband, a bandleader, owned in the Dordogne.

In the 1950s and 1960s, she appeared often in the United States—but only in clubs and theaters where blacks could be served—and she became a crusader against racism. Down and out in 1969, she saw her estate sold for her debts. But she appeared again at Carnegie Hall in 1973 and triumphed back in France in a 1975 show celebrating her fifty years in Paris. She died in 1975.

How did a woman become an official in the 1940s with a union that represented brawny autoworkers?

Mildred M. Jeffrey (b. 1911) became the first director of the women's division of the United Auto Workers (UAW) as women started joining that union in substantial numbers during World War II. She was no stranger to activism, having signed up with the Socialist Party and the Minnesota Farm Labor Party as an undergraduate at the University of Minnesota and picketed with striking building tradesmen. On campus the YWCA was "just about the most radical organization," Jeffrey said, and it became her principal activity. Through the Y, she heard such speakers as Reinhold Niebuhr and various pacifists, labor, and civil rights leaders. She worked for six weeks in the summer of 1930 at a Baby Ruth candy factory in Chicago as part of her "industrial education" through a Y program. While in graduate school at Bryn Mawr, she helped organize garment workers and later worked at shirt shops in Allentown while signing up members for the Amalgamated Clothing Workers of America.

Jeffrey served on the Pennsylvania Joint Board of Shirt Workers and organized at a cotton mill and clothing plants in Tennessee, Georgia, and Louisiana for the Congress of Industrial Organizations, which later merged with the American Federation of Labor. Union organizing could be a dangerous business for both the worker and the organizer. Jeffrey went to jail briefly three times for her union activity but was never convicted on any charge. Once when she was in West Point, Mississippi, trying to organize workers at a clothing plant that had left Pennsylvania and hired many people from rural areas, she realized that she was constantly being shadowed. She decided not to visit any of the workers at their homes because they would surely be fired for meeting with her. Whip in hand, the sheriff in Meridian, Mississippi, ordered her out of town.

During the war, her husband took a job at the Ford Rouge airplane division plant in Michigan. **Victor Reuther,** then head of the UAW, hired Millie Jeffrey to work with the women who were joining his union. Some women had jobs on the production line, but most still worked sewing seat covers or occasionally doing wiring. Today Jeffrey's work would be called "empowerment"—teaching women to get the most out of their union by learning parliamentary procedure, union history, and their rights within the union. She wanted to ensure that they would bring up their grievances and receive the benefits intended from the contract. Jeffrey also had to make sure that the male regional representatives lived up to the union's principles for women. To help women see the results of their work for the war effort, Jeffrey took 150 women from three midwestern states to Fort Knox to watch troops training with the tanks they had helped manufacture.

Political activity and union activity often merged as Jeffrey was a coordinator of Michigan efforts for **John F. Kennedy** in 1960. In the middle 1960s, she was active on the Democrats' committee rewriting party rules established as a result of the black-led challenge to the all-white Mississippi delegation at the 1964 convention. She helped shepherd the successful challenge by an integrated Mississippi delegation against that state's party regulars through the 1968 convention.

The daughter of Iowa's first registered female pharmacist, Jeffrey was a founder of the National Women's Political Caucus and was elected its chair in 1975. She was one of a handful of women who not only discussed the general possibility of a female vice presidential candidate in 1984 but also focused specifically on one of the many qualified women for the job. This group helped convince then Congresswoman **Geraldine Ferraro** of New York to let her name be floated as a leading contender. One night, the women, who included one of Ferraro's staff members and other Washington political activists, gathered to eat Chinese food. All the fortune cookies were rigged with predictions pointing in the political direction the women hoped Ferraro would go. She got the point—and the nomination.

How did the internment of Japanese-Americans during World War II affect the women?

The American government's decision to relocate 110,000 Japanese-Americans, including children born in the United States, after the Japanese attack on Pearl Harbor was a massive denial of civil rights. President **Franklin D. Roosevelt** signed the order on February 19, 1942, as a war security measure. Families living on the Pacific Coast and in parts of Arizona had a week to shut down their businesses and decide what to do with their homes. They were allowed to take only what they could carry, and were sent to camps in California, Utah, Colorado, Idaho, Wyoming, Arizona, and Arkansas.

The camps were places of little privacy and lots of people—more Japanese-Americans in one place than many of the youngsters had ever seen before. Modesty was one of the first standards to change in barracks rooms with partitions that did not reach to the ceiling, toilets with no doors, and group showers. The camps were in swampy locations in Arkansas and windy, dusty places elsewhere, so many people found themselves getting used to harsh new climates. Food was often poor.

Feelings of shame and anger surrounded the entire internment. But some of the older women, who had labored in the fields or in other people's homes from dawn to dusk, had unaccustomed leisure time in the camps. Some took courses on flower arranging and other elements of Japanese culture. **Michiko Tanaka,** interned in Arkansas with her husband and children from California, where they had done farmwork and other labor, said that her biggest worry until that point had been money for food and shelter. "In camp that burden was wiped out. The government fed us and gave us a monthly allowance of $10.50." Her husband proved a popular actor and singer in the camp talent shows. As a result, she remarked, "He was never home to fight with."

The younger women of the *Nisei*, or second generation, had the opportunity to mix with more Japanese-American young people than they might have met at home. The young women, often limited to domestic work before internment, sometimes were able to find jobs as accountants or secretaries. Since some college-bound students were able to leave their camps, young women whose families might otherwise have insisted that they stay at home were able to go away to school. Historian Valerie Matsumoto wrote that a study of one thousand relocated students showed that 40 percent were women.

Because of the cramped quarters and lack of privacy, everyone spent more time away from their families. That further strained ties already weakened by the increasing Americanization of the second generation. Internment had a lasting effect on the Japanese-Americans forced to endure it.

Whose work helped launch the modern environmental movement?

Biologist **Rachel Carson**'s book *Silent Spring* about the devastation caused by DDT and other pesticides appeared in 1962. The controversy surrounding its publication focused Americans' attention on the degradation of the environment being brought in the name of progress.

Carson's work showed the truth of the adage "write what you know." The daughter of a woman who loved nature, Carson (1907–1964) spent time as a child out-of-doors learning about woods and bugs and plants even as she prepared to be a writer. She had a story published when she was ten and seemed destined for a literary career until she switched her college major from English to biology. There were few women in that field in 1929 when she graduated from college. Nonetheless, she enrolled for graduate study at Johns Hopkins University in Baltimore, earned a master's degree in zoology, spent summers learning about the sea at the Marine Biological Laboratory in Woods Hole, Massachusetts, and landed a job as a biologist with the federal government in Washington.

She had little time to write for many years. She was not only managing the publications of the U.S. Fish and Wildlife Service and editing booklets about wildlife preserves, but also bringing up the two children of a sister who had died. But after writing in her spare time and on vacations, in 1951 she published *The Sea Around Us,* which became a bestseller and won a National Book Award. Its success, and award of a Guggenheim Foundation Fellowship that year, allowed her to leave government work and write *The Edge of the Sea* in 1955. But it was *Silent Spring* in 1962 that shocked Americans who had come to think of DDT as a positive force in controlling mosquitoes. Government studies on pesticides followed, DDT was ultimately banned, and Americans became far more aware of what was happening to the natural world around them and what they could do to preserve that environment.

Why did the expression "Ride, Sally, Ride" describe history in the making?

All around the Kennedy Space Center in Florida, on June 18, 1983, banners proclaimed "Ride, Sally, Ride," as Dr. **Sally Ride** (b. 1951) became America's first female astronaut. The U.S. space program had been launched two decades earlier during the administration of President **John F. Kennedy,** and finally an American woman would be launched into space as well.

To Ride, science and the scientific method offered clear ways to examine and solve problems. Ride had been an honor student at Westlake School in Los Angeles but was bored with many of her subjects and school activities until a science teacher helped hook her on that field. America's space program was in its heyday as she was growing up; she was eighteen years old when U.S. astronauts landed on the moon. Starting college at Swarthmore in Pennsylvania, Ride took only science and mathematics classes. When she transferred to Stanford, she continued her emphasis on science, especially astronomy, as well as studying Shakespeare. An outstanding tennis player, she wrestled with a decision about turning professional but decided to remain in school to become a space scientist. She stayed on at Stanford for graduate school, majoring in astrophysics.

The National Aeronautics and Space Administration, which ran the space program and had had no women among its first seven teams of astronauts, advertised for scientists as well as pilots for its shuttle program, women as well as men. She was one of 1,000 women who applied. She made the cut to 208 men and women—and later was named one of 35 new astronauts. Six of those selected to be mission specialists were women. Ride's principal assignment during the year of training that followed was working with fellow astronaut **John Fabian** to learn how to operate a robot arm that would release and retrieve satellites while the shuttle was in orbit.

When Ride was chosen in 1982 to become the first American woman in space, the press clamored to talk to her. Mission Commander **Robert Crippen** told the press why he wanted Ride on his crew: "I wanted a competent engineer who was cool under stress. Sally Ride demonstrated that talent. She also has a pleasing personality that will fit in with the group." Finally Crippen put an end to further questions by asserting flatly: "She is flying with us because she is the very best person for the job. There is no man I would rather have in her place."

On June 18, 1983, Ride rode the *Challenger* into space with Crippen, pilot **Rick Hauck,** John Fabian, and **Norman Thagard.** The trip into space was like having a ticket on Disneyland's best ride, the nation's first female astronaut to go into space said at the time. During the mission Ride helped launch Canadian and Indonesian communications satellites. She and Fabian also launched and picked up a West German satellite that took the first live photographs of the entire spaceship while it was orbiting Earth. The *Challenger* landed successfully in California after a ninety-eight-orbit mission that took slightly more than six days.

The attention focused on Ride at the end of the mission was reminiscent of the hoopla surrounding **Amelia Earhart**'s first transatlantic crossing when she had not even been the pilot. Ride soon stopped accepting invitations unless all the mission crew was included.

After another *Challenger* spacecraft exploded on liftoff in early 1986, killing all seven astronauts, including teacher **Christa McAuliffe** and space scientist **Judith Resnik,** Ride served on the special panel named to determine the cause of the disaster. In May 1987, Ride left the space program to teach at Stanford University's Center for International Security and Arms Control. Later she joined the faculty at the University of California at San Diego.

Where is "mankiller" a term of respect?

Among Native Americans such as the Cherokees, "mankiller" is a term of respect for the warriors who guarded the villages. It is a surname given wider exposure when **Wilma Mankiller** (b. 1945) was elected chief of the 150,000-member Cherokee Nation. As such, she was also chief executive of Cherokee Nation Industries, a major corporation that runs factories, gift shops, a ranch, and a lumber company. She has a ready sense of humor, one she needs at times when someone dwells too much on her name. "Some people do earn their names in native culture," she told one reporter. "I didn't, but I don't always tell people that. Sometimes I just say that Mankiller is my name, I earned it, and I let 'em wonder."

She grew up in Oklahoma in Mankiller Flats, then moved in 1956 to California under a federal relocation program. She had a miserable adolescence, she said, in a land far from the one in which she was born. In San Francisco, she found that she often dressed and acted differently than other children. The one place she felt at home was at the American Indian Center in the Mission District. In 1969, the Indian takeover of Alcatraz Island in San Francisco Bay stirred her consciousness more deeply about the injustices and broken treaties involving Native Americans, and she started studying sociology, treaty rights, and education issues. The emerging women's movement affected her as well.

Her marriage to an Ecuadoran businessman was becoming too confining, so Mankiller became active with the Native

American Youth Center in East Oakland and volunteered with the Pit River people in that tribe's fight against Pacific Gas and Electric Company over millions of acres of land in northern California. Divorced in 1974, Mankiller was attending college and raising two daughters. Before she could move back to Oklahoma, her ex-husband kept their nine-year-old daughter away from her for almost a year. Reunited with her daughter, Mankiller moved back to her home state by the late 1970s and was hired in October 1977 as an economic stimulus coordinator for the Cherokee Nation of Oklahoma.

In 1983, **Ross Swimmer** asked her to run for deputy chief of the Cherokees and in 1985 she succeeded him when he became assistant interior secretary for Indian affairs. She won full four-year terms as principal chief in elections in 1987 and 1991. The first woman to head a major North American tribe, Mankiller worked to improve community development, health care, and early childhood education for the Cherokees. In 1986, she married Charlie Soap, a fellow Cherokee organizer.

Ms. magazine named Mankiller as one of its women of the year in 1985. In 1993, she was honored by the National Women's Hall of Fame in Seneca Falls, New York. In 1994, she announced her resignation as chief, citing the biblical passage, "To every thing there is a season," and adding, "My season here is coming to an end."

In 1979, Mankiller had been on her way to her graduate school classes at the University of Arkansas at Fayetteville, just over the state line from Oklahoma. She survived a head-on crash with another car driven by one of her best friends, who was killed. Mankiller's face and right leg were crushed and her left leg and her ankles were broken as were many of her ribs. "That accident changed my life," she has written. "I had experienced death, felt its presence, touched it, and then let it go. It was a very spiritual thing, a rare natural gift. From that point on, I have always thought of myself as the woman who lived before and the woman who lives afterward."

CHAPTER 9

~

Time Out for Culture

Why were so many of Emily Dickinson's poems so morbid?

Why were only 11 of Emily Dickinson's 1,775 poems published while she was still alive?

How did Mary Cassatt and Georgia O'Keeffe become prominent artists?

Who might be called the queen of American theater's "royal family"?

Who were the first female winners of the Pulitzer Prize for their novels?

Who is the only movie star to have a life preserver named after her?

Milestones: Women as the Movies Saw Them

Who ran the Depression-era Federal Theatre Project?

Who was the woman who sat at the Round Table and did her jousting with words?

Why did Marian Anderson give a concert at the Lincoln Memorial?

What impact did Agnes de Mille have on American dance (and was she related to movie spectacle director Cecil B. DeMille)?

Milestones: Women in the Arts

Which American women have won the Nobel Prize for literature?

Whose name and artistry are linked with the famous New Mexico black clay pots?

What culture did Katherine Siva Saubel help preserve?

How did the play *A Raisin in the Sun* mirror the life of its playwright?

How did Maxine Hong Kingston find that being an outsider helped her writing?

Milestones: Women Writing

Why were so many of Emily Dickinson's poems so morbid?

Poet **Emily Dickinson** (1830–1886) lived in an era in which people were surrounded by deaths that regularly occurred at an early age. In addition, she grew up in a religious revival atmosphere; while she withstood attempts to bring her to a conversion as a young woman, she sought regularly to find meaning in life—and death—through her writing.

Dickinson lived her entire life in Amherst, Massachusetts, the granddaughter of **Samuel Dickinson,** who was financially ruined by his devotion to the establishment of Amherst College, and the daughter of **Edward Dickinson,** whose firm handling of the college finances ultimately steered the school onto a stable course. Her mother's family seemed plagued by tuberculosis, and her mother, a shy and emotional woman, was frequently depressed. At two, when her younger sister was born and both mother and infant were sick for several months, Emily was sent to visit relatives. There, her aunt was caring for yet another relative who would eventually die of tuberculosis. When Emily returned to Amherst, her grandfather and grandmother, near whom she had lived all her short life, had left for Cincinnati to try to repair their fortunes; she never saw them again. Emily was gone from Amherst only a few months, but her whole world may have changed in that period. Biographer Cynthia Griffin Wolff speculated that the experiences at that time—fear of the death of her mother after a childbirth so severe that she had no more children, the concern over the approaching death within her aunt's home, the unexplained separation from her grandparents—formed questions with which she would later grapple in her poetry.

Wolff, who had worked as a guide at the Emily Dickinson House, testified to the number of people who visited the home seeking explanation there—and in Dickinson's life—for her poetry. Was there a thwarted romance that created the love poetry? How could she write in the mature voice of the wife when she had never been one? Why was she so preoccupied with God and death? Did an eye disease that she suffered in the 1860s spur her production of poetry, and how did it affect the poetry's content? Why did she remain increasingly secluded after about 1860?

One can never conclusively know the answers. Twentieth-century poet **Adrienne Rich** said of Dickinson: "Genius knows itself; . . . Dickinson chose her seclusion, knowing she was exceptional and knowing what she needed." Given the restraints on women in the nineteenth century, she might have gone mad without such practical self-discipline, Rich indicated, adding: "Given her vocation, she was neither eccentric nor quaint; she was determined to survive, to use her power, to practice necessary economies."

Emily Dickinson lived her solitary life, writing in a remote, small town even as the country was facing great spiritual and cultural tests as industry developed, cities boomed, immigrants poured in from other countries, and slavery and war divided the country. Had she been a direct participant in the affairs of her day, she would not have had the time nor the energy to pursue the sweeping themes of nature, love, and death that occupied her. As Wolff summarized, it may be that she had always suspected, "even before she was well under way, that such would be the case: wrestling the Lord is an intimate undertaking, not a public entertainment."

Dickinson did not totally lack experience in life. She knew well that women were the ones who faced death in childbirth, cared for the ill, buried the dead. She had the imagination and command of language to tell, in a few lines, much about the heartbreak of death and the knowledge that life goes on:

> The Bustle in a House
> The Morning after Death
> Is solemnest of industries
> Enacted upon Earth—
>
> The Sweeping up the Heart
> And putting Love away
> We shall not want to use again
> Until Eternity.

#1078

Why were only 11 of Emily Dickinson's 1,775 poems published while she was still alive?

Emily Dickinson's most productive period centered around 1862. She lived another twenty-four years and yet only a minute amount of her work was published in her lifetime.

Dickinson may have had few intimates beyond her immediate family but, as a person educated at Amherst Academy and Mount Holyoke, then a female seminary, she maintained a wide correspondence with the intellectuals of her day. There were not the strictures against women publishing their work that there had been in early centuries; many American novelists were women. But there were strictures, biographer Cynthia Wolff wrote, against women who were serious intellectuals, who *thought*.

She could have easily had her poems privately published, and she had contact with other poets and newspaper editors who could have helped. Indeed, six of those poems that did appear while she was alive were published in the Springfield, Massachusetts, *Republican,* edited by her friend **Samuel Bowles.** Early on, she had written to essayist and reformer **Thomas Higginson** seeking his opinion on her poetry. He did not consider it publishable—her rhyming and meter were unorthodox to a traditionalist's eye—but she wrote on, privately, doubling her output in the year after starting her correspondence with Higginson.

Dickinson may have realized that her poetry spoke in a different voice than that readers were willing to hear from a woman at mid-nineteenth century. Thus she tucked the verse away in packets that her younger sister Lavinia discovered, "tied together with twine," in a small box after her death of Bright's disease in 1886. Higginson helped with publication of that first volume in 1890 and even then, he was so put off by Dickinson's style and what he perceived might be public reaction that he altered meter, rhyme, and metaphor as he prepared the copy.

Despite **Adrienne Rich**'s warning not to read too much autobiography into poetry, one could easily see Dickinson speaking for herself with these lines:

> How many Flowers fail in Wood—
> Or perish from the Hill—
> Without the privilege to know
> That they are Beautiful—
>
> How many cast a nameless Pod
> Upon the nearest Breeze—
> Unconscious of the Scarlet Freight—
> It bears to Other Eyes.

#404

How did Mary Cassatt and Georgia O'Keeffe become prominent artists?

Women learned painting and embroidery in the nineteenth century to display ladylike refinement, not to become creative artists—and never to earn a living. **Mary Cassatt** (1844–1926) stepped into uncharted territory for a young American woman when she not only studied painting seriously but also went to Paris where she emerged as one of the few prominent women among the Impressionists. Furthermore, she supported herself and later her parents with her painting commissions.

Mary Cassatt was born in Pittsburgh, Pennsylvania. From the time she was seven until she was eleven, her family lived in France and briefly in Germany. Returning to the United States, she applied to study at the Pennsylvania Academy of the Fine Arts in Philadelphia in 1860 and worked there for two years, then studied privately until she returned to Paris in 1866. The Ecole des Beaux-Arts, *the* place to study, did not admit women; Cassatt took private classes but learned the most by copying the works of the great masters displayed at the Louvre. The first painting that she had accepted for the giant exhibition called the Salon, which specialized in landscapes or dark, gloomy portraits, was of a young woman playing a mandolin; this work showed some of the techniques she had learned while working at the Louvre. Cassatt left Paris during the Franco–Prussian War, returning in 1873.

She wrestled with the artist's dilemma: should she inhibit her style and paint in a manner acceptable to the Salon and the public taste of that time, or should she let her style expand the way the Impressionists were doing? She did first the one, then the other, becoming a successful portraitist but later using brighter colors and experimental painting techniques in scenes of everyday life. Her long friendship with Impressionist **Edgar Degas** helped motivate her. It was he who urged her to move beyond the Salon's shows and prizes and join the Impressionist exhibitions, which she did in 1879.

Cassatt's work increasingly focused on women and children. In 1880, she painted her mother reading to her grandchildren as well as a scene of two women having tea; in 1886, a girl arranging her hair; in 1897, a mother and child having breakfast in bed. She was also trying new techniques, moving from oils to watercolors to pastels, and was strongly influenced by Japanese art, as shown in *The Letter,* done in 1890–1891. One of her best-known paintings, *The Boating Party,* showing a man rowing a woman and child across the water, was completed by 1894.

While the European public warmed slowly to the Impressionists, Americans still knew little about them. Cassatt's long-time friend **Louisine Havemeyer,** wife of a sugar refiner, came often to Europe after 1895 to add to her art collection. Cassatt helped her find the best paintings at the best prices, and also encouraged her brother, by then a Pennsylvania Railroad official, to buy Impressionists. Louisine Havemeyer left much of her collection to the Metropolitan Museum in New York when she died; Mary Cassatt had done her part to promote and preserve the art of her era.

As much as anyone since Mary Cassatt, **Georgia O'Keeffe** (1887–1986) "raised the awareness of the American public to the fact that a woman could be the equal of any man in her chosen field," wrote Edith Evans Asbury in O'Keeffe's obituary in *The New York Times.*

Fiercely independent, O'Keeffe studied, painted, and taught for twelve years before winning attention on the art scene. She was born in Sun Prairie, Wisconsin, and moved with her family at fourteen to Williamsburg, Virginia. She had decided early on that she wanted to become an artist and after high school enrolled at the Art Institute in Chicago. She took classes in New York City and at the University of Virginia and taught art in the Amarillo, Texas, public schools from 1912 to 1916, when she became head of the West Texas Normal College's art department. Frustrated, as she recalled later, she said to herself, " 'I can't live where I want to. I can't even say what I want to.' I decided I was a very stupid fool not at least to paint as I wanted to."

In 1916, a friend, **Anita Pollitzer,** showed her work to photographer **Alfred Stieglitz,** a key figure in the New York art world. He exclaimed: "At last, a woman on paper!" and staged a show of her work, much to O'Keeffe's dismay. Stieglitz soon became her manager and her husband, as well as taking some five hundred photographs of her body in various stages of dress and undress. Despite a tempestuous relationship and many long separations when O'Keeffe chose to live in New Mexico, the pair was married until Stieglitz died in 1946. O'Keeffe lived and worked for many years at Abiquiu in the sere countryside north of Santa Fe. She died at ninety-eight in 1986.

Voluptuous, brilliantly colored flowers. Stark, sun-bleached skulls and pelvic bones. Adobe buildings against New Mexico blue skies—O'Keeffe's choice of subjects was always ahead of her time, sometimes erotic, often ambiguous, rarely humdrum. She would never explain, choosing to let her art speak for itself. At times she sat on the roof of her home in New Mexico, waiting for the right impression for a scene taking shape in her mind. "That there should be light of such clarity, architectural forms of such simple nobility and such a largesse of lion-colored space was a continual astonishment to her," wrote art critic John Russell, "and one that irradiated painting after painting."

Who might be called the queen of American theater's "royal family"?

With brothers Lionel and John, actress **Ethel Barrymore** (1879–1959) reigned over theater and movies for more than fifty years. The daughter of an actor and a comedienne, she made her debut in Sheridan's *The Rivals* in Montreal in 1894. She was still at it and won an Academy Award as best actress in 1944 for her role as a charwoman in *None But the Lonely Heart.*

In between, she had become a star as early as 1901 while appearing in *Captain Jinks of the Horse Marines.* She married and had three children, was a leader in the Actors Equity union, played on Broadway and toured with a hit in *The Constant Wife,* had a Broadway theater named after her, and then became a character actress as she grew older. She played the schoolmistress in *The Corn Is Green* for several years starting in 1940 in both New York and on the road. Moving to California, she turned to appearing in movies.

Who were the first female winners of the Pulitzer Prize for their novels?

Edith Wharton (1862–1937) won for *The Age of Innocence* in 1921, and **Willa Cather** (1873–1947) for *One of Ours* in 1923.

A list of Wharton's ancestors reads like a New York gazetteer—Rhinelander, Schermerhorn, Gallatin, and so on. Born into old New York society, she wrote about its clash with new money and new ideas. "Clash" may actually be too harsh a word, because New York society preferred a look of disdain or quiet words behind drawing room doors to direct, distasteful confrontation with anyone they felt lacked their breeding.

In *The Age of Innocence,* for example, the elite of society finds its views fluctuating about one of their own who is not really their own—Madame Ellen Olenska, member of an old family, who had been raised largely in Europe and wed to a count there. Escaping from a bad marriage, she is at first welcomed back into her family until her relatives think a potential divorce case might bring an accompanying scandal. Wharton's story centers on Newland Archer, his growing captivation with Ellen and his eventual capitulation to his wife, May. Wharton described life as it was in her childhood—the conversation among young men at the opera, the lethargy of life in an uppercrust New York law firm, the relations of hypochondriac husbands and humorless wives, summer life in Newport—and especially the intolerance directed at anyone, family member or not, who overstepped the bounds of supposed good taste.

As Wharton's biographer R. W. B. Lewis indicated, the characters of Newland Archer and Ellen Olenska in some ways represented the pulls and tugs on the author herself. Archer, more interested in writers and painters than most of his relatives, grew fascinated with Olenska but pulled back because of a sense of duty, almost as Wharton, who traveled extensively in Europe as a child, finally succumbed to New York rituals herself. After a broken engagement, she married a banker thirteen years older than she. For her part, Olenska tried to fit in with New York society but ultimately returned to Paris and theaters, art, people who liked good conversation, and, as Wharton described it, "the incessant stir of ideas, curiosities, images and associations thrown out by an intensely social race in a setting of immemorial manners." Wharton herself lived in France—with one house in Paris, another in the Riviera—after 1910. After her husband had a nervous collapse and was hospitalized, she divorced him in 1913. Having independent means, she was able to travel and move in literary circles until she died at seventy-five.

Wharton did not overdo her aphorisms, but she did have Ellen Olenska, tired of New York society despite its off-and-on kindnesses, talk to Newland Archer about "the blind conformity to tradition—somebody else's tradition" that she saw among their friends. "It seems stupid to have discovered America only to make it into a copy of another country," she told him with a smile. "Do you suppose Christopher Columbus would have taken all that trouble just to go to the Opera with the Selfridge Merrys?"

Willa Cather's fictional world was far from the mannered society folk of Edith Wharton's novels, although both were influenced by the writing of **Henry James**. Cather, born in Virginia, was a product of the Nebraska prairies where she moved as a child, and it was the life of the pioneers and their descendants around which much of her best fiction was centered. She crafted many of her characters after the Bohemians, Germans, and Swedes from that area.

Cather attended the University of Nebraska in Lincoln and worked on the local newspaper to help pay her way through school. She reviewed plays and traveled to Chicago to see her first opera, which then became a lifelong interest. Moving to Pittsburgh in 1897, she continued her journalistic career and began to write poetry and fiction. She taught high school English in Pittsburgh after leaving the newspaper job, and then **S. S. McClure** hired her to help edit his muckraking magazine. She was *McClure's* managing editor from 1908 to 1912.

Sarah Orne Jewett, author of *The Country of the Pointed Firs,* strongly influenced Cather. Writing to Cather in 1908, four years before she took the plunge into full-time fiction, Jewett said that she thought the younger woman's writing was being hindered by her responsibility as a magazine editor. "If you don't keep and guard and mature your force, and above all, have time and quiet to perfect your work," Jewett said, "you will be writing things not much better than you did five years ago."

It was an admonition that must have stuck in Cather's mind: After 1912 and publication of *Alexander's Bridge,* she turned to writing fiction full-time. *O Pioneers!* appeared in 1913, *The Song of the Lark* in 1915, and *My Ántonia* in 1918. In *My Ántonia,* for example, Cather described both the hardships that beset a Bohemian family that moved to the Nebraska plains and the stalwart spirit that kept the daughter, Ántonia, working hard and living with contentment. The book was especially evocative of the colors and silences of the land and of life in Nebraska's small towns. Later, Cather won the Pulitzer Prize in 1923 for

One of Ours, which, despite mixed reviews, sold well and made her financially independent. She was also famous for two works of historical fiction: *Death Comes for the Archbishop,* published in 1927 and set in the Southwest, which she had explored fifteen years earlier while on leave from her magazine job, and *Shadows on the Rock,* published in 1931. She died at her home in New York City in 1947.

Who is the only movie star to have a life preserver named after her?

The Mae West life vest can, when inflated, endow anyone with some of the charms of the very buxom actress (pneumatic, one writer called her), who had a long and provocative career.

Forty years old when she made her first movie in 1932 after a song-and-dance career that had started when she was seven, **Mae West** (1893–1980) postured before, slunk around, sang to, upstaged, teased, or seduced some of Hollywood's leading men during her long film career. But she never gave away her soul. **Cary Grant** had his first leading-man roles with West, and she appeared with **George Raft, Gilbert Roland, Randolph Scott,** and later **W. C. Fields**. She was bold and brassy when few other women would never have dared invite anyone, on screen or off, to "come up and see me some time." As Richard Griffith and Arthur Mayer wrote in *The Movies,* each picture's end "found her wealthy, wicked and well loved."

Her one-liners, considered risqué or even racy for their time, have lasted better than her portrayals of saloon girls or outrageous Gay Nineties belles. For example:

"When I'm good, I'm very good, but when I'm bad, I'm better."

"It's better to be looked over than to be overlooked."

"Between two evils I always pick the one I haven't tried before."

"It's not the men in my life that count—it's the life in my men."

"Goodness, what lovely diamonds," the hatcheck girl says to West, who replies, "Goodness had nothing to do with it, dearie."

Milestones: Women as the Movies Saw Them

Mary Pickford (1893–1979)—"America's Sweetheart," she was innocence personified in her roles. She starred in *Daddy Long Legs* in 1919 after playing both an ugly housekeeper and her beautiful employer in *Stella Maris* the year before. A gifted comedienne, she was also a shrewd businesswoman and, along with **Charlie Chaplin, D. W. Griffith,** and **Douglas Fairbanks** she founded United Artists. She and Fairbanks were married in 1920; after divorcing him, she married actor **Charles "Buddy" Rogers** in 1937.

Lillian Gish (1896–1993)—Director D. W. Griffith's heroine in many movies, Gish appeared in his most famous and controversial film, *The Birth of a Nation,* which opened in 1915. She also played the sacrificing innocent in *True Heart Susie,* in which she almost loses the boy next door to a woman with city ways. Ultimately, however, virtue is rewarded when her rival proves an unfaithful wife and dies of pneumonia. In 1987, at ninety, she made *The Whales of August* with **Bette Davis.**

Gloria Swanson (1897–1983)—Best known today for her portrayal of an aging and forgotten star in *Sunset Boulevard,* released in 1950, Swanson started her Hollywood career in the **Mack Sennett** silent comedies. Ever adaptable, she became known as a clotheshorse flapper for her roles in the 1920s and starred in *Why Change Your*

Wife? in 1920, which featured one of Hollywood's staple portrayals of female rivals in a kicking and scratching "catfight." With help from her lover **Joseph P. Kennedy,** father of the future president, she produced her own films, including *Sadie Thompson* in 1928 and *The Trespasser* in 1929.

Joan Crawford (1904–1977)—One of Hollywood's most enduring stars, Crawford showed the freedom of the "new woman" as she danced a celebrated Charleston in the 1928 picture *Our Dancing Daughters* and starred with **Douglas Fairbanks, Jr.,** in *Our Modern Maidens* in 1929. Her career lasted from 1925 until 1970 and featured films ranging from *Grand Hotel* and *Mildred Pierce* to *Whatever Happened to Baby Jane?*

Greta Garbo (1905–1990)—She made the transition from seductive silent-screen success in *Flesh and the Devil* to enduring fame after her debut in "talkies" in *Anna Christie* in 1930. Always mysterious and leaning more toward tragic roles in the Thirties, she appeared in *Grand Hotel, Queen Christina, Anna Karenina,* and *Camille,* then played a Russian spy in *Ninotchka,* retiring at the top of her fame in 1941.

Katharine Hepburn (b. 1907)—Hepburn. The name itself conjures up the smart but slightly brittle roles that she played in the 1930s, the on- and off-screen relationship she had with **Spencer Tracy,** and the caustic but usually loving roles she later played, such as her Academy Award–winning portrayal of an elderly woman mediating between her aging husband and prickly daughter in *On Golden Pond* in 1981. That was merely the latest of her four Oscars, the others awarded for *Morning Glory* in 1933, *Guess Who's Coming to Dinner?* in 1967, and *The Lion in Winter* in 1968. Her acting range runs from comedy, such as *Bringing Up Baby,* to character studies, such as her memorable role as a missionary in *The African Queen* with **Humphrey Bogart** in 1951.

Rosalind Russell (1908–1976)—Gifted with extraordinary timing, Russell specialized in wisecracking career women with roles in *Take a Letter, Darling,* and *His Girl Friday,* director **Howard Hawks**'s version of the classic newspaper story *The Front Page.* In this case, Russell played the star reporter. Her best star turns in later years came in *Picnic* in 1956 and in the title role in *Auntie Mame* in 1958.

Jean Harlow (1911–1937)—Sexy and comic, Harlow appeared in *Platinum Blonde* and was one herself. She appeared with **Clark Gable** in *Red Dust* and *Hold Your Man* in the early 1930s. She also starred in *The Girls from Missouri,* which had been originally titled *Born to Be Kissed* until MGM decided that might offend the revised and puritanical Production Code.

Ginger Rogers (b. 1911)—Ginger Rogers is best known for whirling around the screen with **Fred Astaire** in such elegant musical films as *Top Hat, Swing Time,* and *Carefree* in the 1930s. She did what he did, only backwards. But she also won an Academy Award for her dramatic role in *Kitty Foyle* in 1940.

Myrna Loy (1905–1993)—After playing a series of exotic vamps early in her career, she became a star as the acerbic Nora Charles with **William Powell** as Nick in *The Thin Man* movies starting in 1934. She later appeared with **Fredric March** in *The Best Years of Our Lives.* Never nominated for an Oscar, she received an honorary Academy Award in 1991 for her career that had stretched from silent films and *Ben Hur* in 1925 to *Just Tell Me What You Want* in 1980.

Ingrid Bergman (1915–1982)—Coming to America from Sweden, she starred with **Leslie Howard** in *Intermezzo,* Humphrey Bogart in *Casablanca,* **Gary Cooper** in *For Whom the Bell Tolls,* and **Charles Boyer** in *Gaslight.* Her affair with director **Roberto Rossellini** while still married to **Peter Lindstrom** caused great scandal in post–World War II America. After her marriage to Rossellini she was barred from U.S. films for seven years. Later she won an Oscar for *Anastasia*.

Doris Day (b. 1924)—The epitome of the wholesome heroine, Day was a major box-office draw in such 1950s and 1960s romances and comedies as *On Moonlight Bay, April in Paris, Calamity Jane, Love Me or Leave Me, The Pajama Game, Pillow Talk,* and *Please Don't Eat the Daisies*.

Audrey Hepburn (1929–1993)—An elegant former model, Hepburn made a string of successful films in the 1950s and into the 1960s, including *Roman Holiday, Sabrina, Funny Face, Breakfast at Tiffany's,* and *My Fair Lady* (even though the musical parts of her role were dubbed by a singer). In later years she became active in humanitarian relief activities.

Elizabeth Taylor (b. 1932)—British born, this stunningly beautiful actress became a star in adolescence in *Lassie Come Home* and *National Velvet,* moving later to key roles in *Little Women, A Place in the Sun, Giant, Cat on a Hot Tin Roof, Suddenly, Last Summer, Butterfield 8, Cleopatra,* and *Who's Afraid of Virginia Woolf?* The marrying kind, her husbands have included producer **Mike Todd,** singer **Eddie Fisher,** actors **Richard Burton** (twice) and **Michael Wilding,** and U.S. Senator **John Warner**.

Judy Garland (1922–1969)—As Dorothy, she was swept away from Kansas and into Americans' hearts in *The Wizard of Oz* in 1939. She was already starring in the Andy Hardy movies with **Mickey Rooney** and sang in such popular films as *Meet Me in St. Louis, The Pirate,* and *Easter Parade*. She had meaty dramatic roles in *A Star Is Born* in 1954 and *A Child Is Waiting* in 1962, making her last film the following year. In her last years, her life was not as sunny as her early movie roles had been; she died less than two weeks after her forty-seventh birthday.

Dorothy Dandridge (1923–1965)—The first black woman ever nominated for an Academy Award as best actress for her sizzling performance in *Carmen Jones,* Dandridge lost the Oscar to **Grace Kelly**. Bigger stardom always seemed to beckon, but Hollywood was not ready to do much more than cast her in "tragic mulatto roles." Still, she won a Golden Globe for *Porgy and Bess* and also appeared with **Harry Belafonte** in *Bright Road,* **Curt Jurgens** in *Tamango,* and **John Justin** in *Island in the Sun.* She died at forty-one of a drug overdose in 1965.

Marilyn Monroe (1925–1962)—Monroe seemed first to be "simply" a busty, lusty blonde but emerged as a first-class comedienne. Her roles included *Asphalt Jungle, Gentlemen Prefer Blondes, The Seven-Year Itch, Bus Stop,* and *Some Like It Hot,* and her husbands included baseball star **Joe DiMaggio** and playwright **Arthur Miller**. She died of an overdose of sleeping pills in 1962.

Anne Bancroft (b. 1931)—She re-created her Broadway success in the film version of *The Miracle Worker* in 1962 but may be best remembered as Mrs. Robinson, who seduces a young **Dustin Hoffman** in *The Graduate*. A superb dramatic actress, her other key roles include *The Pumpkin Eater, The Turning Point, Agnes of God,* and *'night, Mother.*

Julie Andrews (b. 1935)—Andrews appeared in the stage versions of *My Fair Lady* and *Camelot* but saw those roles go to other actresses when movies were made of them. But she won an Academy Award in 1964 in her first film, *Mary Poppins,* and also helped make a hit of *The Sound of Music* the following year. Later she showed a talent for comedy in *Victor, Victoria.*

Jane Fonda (b. 1937)—The sex object of *Barbarella* became Nazi-fighting Lillian Hellman in *Julia,* a television reporter in *The China Syndrome,* and a daughter often at odds with her aging father in *On Golden Pond.* She often seemed as well known for her radical politics during the 1960s and 1970s, and later for her fitness enterprises, as for her film roles.

Jane Alexander (b. 1939)—From *The Great White Hope* to *Testament,* Alexander, also noted for stage roles and her television appearance as Eleanor Roosevelt, became head of the National Endowment for the Arts in 1993.

Barbra Streisand (b. 1942)—A singer who brought new tempos to her songs, such as the dirgelike "Happy Days Are Here Again," Streisand starred in the musical *Funny Girl* and in *What's Up, Doc?* and *The Way We Were,* then directed herself in *Yentl.* That film was nominated for an Academy Award for best picture but she was not among the finalists for best director, causing immense controversy in Hollywood. Streisand also directed and appeared in *The Prince of Tides.* Although two of the film's stars were nominated for Oscars, Streisand was again ignored.

Meryl Streep (b. 1949)—Seemingly a woman of a thousand accents and certainly of numerous Academy Award nominations, Streep slept with a senator in *The Seduction of Joe Tynan,* left her child for her ex-husband to raise in *Kramer vs. Kramer,* and was forced to make a cruel decision in *Sophie's Choice.* She has also starred in *The French Lieutenant's Woman, Silkwood, Out of Africa,* and *A Cry in the Dark.*

Whoopi Goldberg (b. 1949)—Gaining attention initially through her comedy routines, she made her name nationally in *The Color Purple,* and then became one of Hollywood's most bankable stars in a series of comedies, including *Sister Act.* She won an Academy Award for her performance in *Ghost.*

Susan Sarandon (b. 1946)—At her best playing working-class women, Sarandon appeared in *Atlantic City* as the waitress that **Burt Lancaster** watched from afar as she sensuously applied lemon to her skin to clean away the smell of the fish she had served that day. Her role most symbolic of women's resistance to sexual violence came as she and **Geena Davis** ran away from it all in *Thelma and Louise*. But as so often happens in the movies, even women trying to take charge of their lives end up as criminals, sailing off a cliff to their doom.

Who ran the Depression-era Federal Theatre Project?

The short-lived Federal Theatre Project, set up during the 1930s to support out-of-work actors and other creative people, created the underpinnings for the later flowering of regional theater. But the project bogged down when conservative lawmakers disliked some of its socially conscious messages. **Hallie Flanagan** (1890–1969), who had taught at Grinnell College, her Iowa alma mater, and Vassar College in New York, headed the project.

Flanagan had taught drama privately in Colorado Springs to earn money as her young husband was dying of tuberculosis. When he died in 1919, she took voice and dance lessons and started writing plays, rather than going on the stage, so that she could spend time with her two young children. One son died of meningitis three years later. She went east with her younger son, got a master's degree, and returned to teach at Grinnell.

In 1925, Flanagan was invited to teach at Vassar and to set up an experimental theater. A year later, she received a Guggenheim Foundation fellowship to travel in Europe, one of the first women so honored. On her travels, she saw how much more deeply some European governments were involved in the arts than the U.S. government was. On her return, she staged innovative productions at Vassar Experimental Theatre. One of them, *Can You Hear Their Voices?*, dealt with congressional indifference to starving Arkansas farmers and foreshadowed the techniques used in the Federal Theatre Project's Living Newspapers.

The Federal Theatre Project staged more than 1,200 productions across the country, bringing live theater to millions of people who had never seen it before. The regional theaters that developed took theater outside the domination of Broadway and added new voices to the dramatic mix. As Flanagan put it, it was a switch in audiences from "the 400 to 4 million." There was a bit of everything—Shakespeare, musicals, circuses. Black theater was also supported at a time when there were few opportunities for African-Americans.

She considered theater "not the frosting on the cake but the yeast which makes the bread rise" and also felt that one of the functions of the theater is "giving apoplexy to people who consider it radical for a government-sponsored theater to produce plays on subjects vitally concerning the governed." The project inevitably drew intense scrutiny from Congress. During hearings about the project, one congressman asked Flanagan about the play *Doctor Faustus.* "You are quoting from this Marlow," he said. "Is he a Communist?" No, just the greatest dramatist before Shakespeare, she replied, but to no avail as Congress cut off the project's funds during the summer of 1939. Flanagan continued writing and teaching, first at Vassar and later at Smith College. She retired in 1955 and died in 1969.

Who was the woman who sat at the Round Table and did her jousting with words?

At the celebrated literary Round Table at the Algonquin Hotel in New York—as opposed to the Arthurian gatherings of early England—**Dorothy Parker** (1893–1967) was the wittiest of the wits that included humorist **Robert Benchley**, playwright **Robert Sherwood**, journalists **Franklin P. Adams** and **Alexander Woollcott** and editor **Harold Ross**. She was a writer with the right stuff at the right time as the smart-set magazines like Ross's *The New Yorker* and *Vanity Fair* were created.

Dorothy Parker wrote for *Vanity Fair* from 1917 to 1920 and later was the chief book critic for *The New Yorker* from 1927 to

1931. Her wit was acerbic, as when she panned one play by saying, "If you don't knit, bring a book." In the late 1920s and
early 1930s, even as she was pursued as a celebrity, she also published short stories and poetry. In 1929, she was awarded the
O. Henry Prize for her story "Big Blonde" about an alcoholic
woman who tries to commit suicide. Parker, whose drinking was
legendary, had tried suicide once or twice herself. In 1934, she
went to Hollywood and worked on screenplays for about twenty
films, including the original *A Star Is Born*.

Many of her best stories concerned the frustrations and pain
of relations between men and women. As one critic has written,
that was a prominent theme among women in the nineteenth
century, and Parker examined the question from the changing
vantage points of the twentieth century. She did not feel sorry
for the women who waited by the phone and wept and begged,
wrote Joan Acocella in a *New Yorker* piece on the one-hundredth
anniversary of Parker's birth. These women "made her wince,
and we wince as we read the stories—for, burning with resent-
ment though they are, they are even more emphatically a record of shame. Female shame is a big subject, and for its sake
Parker should have been bigger, but she is what we have, and
it's not nothing."

Parker was also intensely political, crusading against the
death sentence given anarchists Sacco and Vanzetti, working
with the Screenwriters Guild in Hollywood to help organize the
film industry writers, and, in the end, leaving much of her
money to support the civil rights work of Dr. Martin Luther
King Jr.

Still, Parker is best remembered for her Parkerisms. A few
more:

"Men seldom make passes
At girls who wear glasses."

From a review of *House at Pooh Corner:*
"Tonstant Weader Fwowed Up."

"Brevity is the soul of lingerie."

"You know, that woman speaks 18 languages. And she can't say 'no' in any of them."

On learning that former President Calvin Coolidge had died: "How could they tell?"

Reviewing a play starring Katharine Hepburn: "Miss Hepburn runs the gamut of emotions from A to B."

To a young man who said he could not bear fools:
"That's odd. Your mother could."

Why did Marian Anderson give a concert at the Lincoln Memorial?

Maestro **Arturo Toscanini** remarked of contralto **Marian Anderson** that a voice like hers was heard once in a hundred years. But it was not to be heard at Constitution Hall in Washington in 1939 because Anderson was black. The Daughters of the American Revolution (DAR) owned Constitution Hall and refused to let her sing there, despite her fame. First Lady **Eleanor Roosevelt** resigned from the DAR in protest and Anderson gave a free concert sponsored by Secretary of the Interior **Harold Ickes**, and highlighted with her singing "My Country, 'Tis of Thee," from the Lincoln Memorial steps.

Anderson (1902–1993) grew up singing in the Baptist church in her hometown of Philadelphia and made what she considered a disastrous concert debut at New York's Town Hall in 1924—disastrous because of severe criticism of her command of German for the lieder she sang. She studied in Europe and gave concerts throughout the continent, returning to far more successful appearances in New York in 1935 and 1936 under the management of impersario **Sol Hurok**. In her contracts, she insisted that blacks be given equal seating with whites.

During World War II, Anderson gave concerts for servicemen and bond drives. In 1955, she debuted at the Metropolitan Opera in *Un Ballo in Maschera*. She retired in 1965 and died in 1993.

What impact did Agnes de Mille have on American dance (and was she related to movie spectacle director Cecil B. DeMille)?

Agnes de Mille (1905–1993) showed that American material and everyday movement could be incorporated into ballet, first when she danced her own choreography for *Rodeo* in 1942 and then when she staged the dances for the musical *Oklahoma!* in 1943. And, yes, the movie producer-director was her uncle. (He just wrote the name a little differently.)

De Mille's father was a Broadway playwright and so she grew up around theater people. She studied ballet and decided after seeing **Anna Pavlova** and **Ruth St. Denis** perform that she, too, wanted to be a dancer. Her father was less than keen on that idea, so she majored in English at UCLA. Later, in New York, she made her debut as a choreographer in 1928. She traveled to Europe, performing there and doing the choreography for a **Cole Porter** show in London, *Nymph Errant*, starring **Gertrude Lawrence**.

After her success with *Rodeo*, staged for the Ballet Russe de Monte Carlo, which was performing in America during the war, de Mille was asked to work on Broadway with a musical being developed from a play called *Green Grow the Lilacs*. It became the highly acclaimed *Oklahoma!* and ran for five years. As her obituary in *The New York Times* said, "What made Miss de Mille's contributions to 'Oklahoma!' seem distinctive to audiences of the 40s was the way that dancing, far from being a mere diversion or spectacle, was integrated into the show's dramatic action. This was especially true of the principal choreographic sequence, 'Laurey Makes Up Her Mind,' in which the work's heroine was shown torn between two suitors."

De Mille also choreographed *Carousel, Allegro, Brigadoon, Gentlemen Prefer Blondes,* and *Paint Your Wagon,* among others, during the heyday of the musical. She also created dances for the American Ballet Theater, including *Fall River Legend,* about Lizzie Borden, a nineteenth-century woman accused of murdering her parents. Disabled by a cerebral hemorrhage in 1975, de

Mille fought back to resume her career. A keen supporter of federal and state financial aid for the arts, de Mille wrote several volumes of memoirs and a biography of modern dancer and choreographer **Martha Graham** in 1991. She died in 1993.

Milestones: Women in the Arts

Art and architecture

Romaine Brooks
Mary Cassatt
Judy Chicago
Elaine Fried de Kooning
Marisol Escobar
Helen Frankenthaler
Meta Fuller
Harriet Hosmer
Clementine Hunter
Edmonia Lewis
Julia Morgan
Anna Mary Robertson "Grandma" Moses
Louise Nevelson
Georgia O'Keeffe
Anna, Margaretta, and Sarah Peale
Beverly Pepper
Irene Pereira
Augusta Savage
Laura Wheeler Waring

Dance

Irene Castle
Evelyn Cisneros
Agnes de Mille
Isadora Duncan
Katherine Dunham
Suzanne Farrell
Martha Graham

Judith Jamison
Gelsey Kirkland
Rita Moreno
Ruth St. Denis
Maria Tallchief
Twyla Tharp
Gwen Verdon

Photography

Berenice Abbott
Diane Arbus
Alice Austen
Margaret Bourke-White
Imogen Cunningham
Dorothea Lange
Annie Leibovitz

Music

June Anderson
Marian Anderson
Joan Baez
Kathleen Battle
Antonia Brisco
Grace Bumbry
Sarah Caldwell
Rosemary Clooney
Judy Collins
Doris Day
Geraldine Farrar
Ella Fitzgerald
Aretha Franklin
Judy Garland
Mary Garden
Billie Holiday
Lena Horne
Marilyn Horne

Whitney Houston
Mahalia Jackson
Janis Joplin
June Kuramoto
Peggy Lee
Jeanette MacDonald
Madonna
Bette Midler
Liza Minelli
Jessye Norman
Odetta
Rosa Ponselle
Leontyne Price
Linda Ronstadt
Diana Ross
Dinah Shore
Beverly Sills
Bessie Smith
Kate Smith
Risë Stevens
Barbra Streisand
Gladys Swarthout
Helen Traubel
Mary Travers
Sarah Vaughan
Shirley Verrett
Ellen Taaffe Zwilich

Which American women have won the Nobel Prize for literature?

Pearl Buck (1892–1973) and **Toni Morrison** (b. 1931).

Buck grew up in China, where her parents were Presbyterian missionaries. After winning prizes for her writing as a child, she published articles and short stories in American magazines in the early 1920s. Her first published novel, *East Wind: West Wind,* about clashing values in China, appeared in 1930. Her next novel, *The Good Earth*, published in 1931, was also her most famous. She won the Pulitzer Prize in 1932 for this portrayal of a Chinese peasant family. A prolific writer, she published more than one hundred books and won the Nobel Prize in 1938, the first American woman ever so honored. She was also active in promoting Asian-American understanding and in finding homes for Asian-American children.

It was fifty-five years before another American woman would receive the Nobel Prize for literature. Again it was awarded to a writer who reached into her own heritage, this time African-American, to capture not only its central themes but also the tone and poetry of its language. Toni Morrison, born Chloe Anthony Wofford in Lorain, Ohio, in 1931, had studied literature and the classics at Howard University and Cornell, writing her dissertation on Virginia Woolf and William Faulkner. She was a professor at Princeton University when her Nobel award was announced in October 1993. She had gone to Princeton after an eighteen-year career as a Random House editor and other teaching assignments.

Morrison's first novel, *The Bluest Eye*, was published in 1970, followed by *Sula* in 1974, *Song of Solomon* (1977), *Tar Baby* (1981), *Beloved* (1987), and *Jazz* (1992). Her writing, at times almost mystical, at other times brutally realistic, has combined folklore and history. For example, *Beloved*, for which she won a Pulitzer Prize, was based on an 1851 incident. The novel told about a fugitive slave woman who killed her daughter to prevent her return to slavery. The child, Beloved, haunts her mother and helps her restore herself through her community. As Carolyn Denard wrote in *Black Women in America: An Historical Encyclopedia*, this novel, "full of intertwining plots and layered time sequences ... keeps readers challenged and attentive." Morrison's award was celebrated by many women for her refusal to gloss over the rough truths of women's lives.

Whose name and artistry are linked with the famous New Mexico black clay pots?

Maria Martinez (1886?–1980) and her husband, **Julian**, per-fected the black-on-black pottery that put their San Ildefonso pueblo and others nearby on the arts-and-crafts map. Maria, whose principal language was always her native Tewa, had learned to make red clay pottery from her aunt when she was seven or eight years old. Later, in 1908 and 1909, she became interested in another form of pottery when an archeologist named Dr. **Edgar Lee Hewitt** was excavating in Tyuonyi and Fri-joles Canyons near San Ildefonso, which itself is about twenty-five miles northwest of Santa Fe, New Mexico. Hewitt found some shards of black pottery unlike others he was recovering. He asked Maria, by then a young married woman, if she could make any that was similar. She and her husband Julian experi-mented and, by smothering the fire around the pottery with dried horse manure, they could change the iron-red color of their clay pots into black. The heavy black smoke produced car-bon that did the trick. Their first efforts were undecorated; by 1918, they had the first firings of black pots that Julian had decorated.

The Martinezes demonstrated their technique at the Mu-seum of New Mexico in Santa Fe as early as 1911 and started selling their pots to the public. They started making larger ves-sels a few years later, and then pottery sales fell off during World War I. By the 1920s, the pots started to have real com-mercial value and Maria was encouraged to sign them. She did not use a potter's wheel in pursuing her craft, but instead coiled the clay into whatever shape she needed and meticu-lously smoothed it before it was decorated and fired. Sales in-creased after the first Santa Fe Indian Market was held in 1922 and after a bridge was built across the Rio Grande near San Ildefonso. That allowed more tourists to travel to the pueblo to buy directly from the artists. Maria taught her technique to oth-ers at San Ildefonso and the pueblo's pottery making became an important factor in its economy. By 1924, she was earning about three dollars for a small bowl and twelve dollars for a vase or larger, special bowl. Half a century later, when the Smithsonian held an exhibit of her pottery in 1979, it was selling for from $1,500 to $15,000 a piece.

Julian Martinez died in 1943. Maria Martinez continued making pottery into the 1970s and was the matriarch of five generations of potters when she died in 1980.

Other Indian women also contributed to the economy of the Southwest. Among the Acoma of New Mexico, for example, women controlled pottery production and experimented with abstract designs. **Lucy M. Lewis** and her family were among the leading Acoma potters.

What culture did Katherine Siva Saubel help preserve?

The Native American ancestors of **Katherine Siva Saubel** (b. 1920) once lived throughout what is today Riverside County in Southern California, and Saubel has worked to preserve her heritage and make it better known to others. She believes that her fear of leaving home when she was little to go to an Indian school run by the government is the reason that today she knows her own language, Cahuilla, fluently. "I know all the things that were handed down to me. We lived the way our people lived many years ago."

Saubel, born on the Los Coyotes Reservation on the border between modern Riverside and San Diego Counties, struggled in her early days in school. She knew no English and had had no contact with non-Indians, but she became the first Indian girl to graduate from Palm Springs High School. She loved history, although she later discovered that her early hero, **Andrew Jackson,** had forced the Cherokees off their land. She received Ds and Fs in history, even though she loved the subject, because she dared to argue with her teachers about how Native Americans were portrayed. "I said, 'That is not right. This is the way it was told to me by the old people.' "

She realized that most of her classmates did not speak Cahuilla (pronounced Cah-wee-uh) or know their history. "So I used to sit in class and when it didn't interest me, I would write down in a notebook I kept the names of plants, where they grew, how you prepared them and for what." Years later, she published that folklore in a book that she prepared with a California State University anthropologist. It is called *Temalpakh*, which means "From the Earth," and it is about the two-way relationship between plants and people.

Saubel was named by California's governor to the state's Native American Heritage Commission and ran the small Malki Indian Museum on the Morongo Indian Reservation where she lives outside Banning, California. In 1993, she was selected for the National Women's Hall of Fame at Seneca Falls, New York. Saubel has tried to widen people's acquaintance with the Cahuilla and other Indians, pointing out, for example, that the model for writer **Helen Hunt Jackson**'s famous character Ramona was Cahuilla.

How did the play *A Raisin in the Sun* mirror the life of its playwright?

Lorraine Hansberry (1930–1965), the first African-American woman to have a play produced on Broadway, had been about eight years old when her family moved into a white neighborhood. Her father, a graduate of Alcorn State in Mississippi and a successful real estate broker in Chicago, was defying the practice of racially segregating neighborhoods. At one point, a mob gathered outside the Hansberry home and someone threw a brick through the window, just missing Lorraine. When the child would walk to school, whites would make fun of her and call her names, an experience she never forgot. Hansberry's father, Carl, and the National Association for the Advancement of Colored People took their charges of discrimination to the Supreme Court, which ruled in 1940 that whites had no right to keep blacks from their neighborhoods, although many continued to do so.

People often write what they know, and Hansberry knew both discrimination and real estate because, in addition to her father's involvement, her mother managed many buildings. She discovered her affinity for the theater during two years at the University of Wisconsin. After a stint as a reporter for the black newspaper *Freedom* in New York City, Hansberry used the conflict in her childhood neighborhood as the basis for her play, which opened on Broadway in 1959. The cast included **Sidney Poitier, Ruby Dee, Ivan Dixon,** and **Glynn Turman.** Hansberry later became the first African-American playwright to win the New York Drama Critics Circle Award for best play. *A Raisin in the Sun,* one of the first productions ever to present a realistic portrayal of a black family on the New York stage, later became a film. It focuses on the Youngers, their debate over what constitutes success—the mother's dream of a better home or the son's of more materialistic gains—and the love that holds them together despite their disagreements.

Hansberry died of cancer at thirty-four, shortly after her second play, *The Sign in Sidney Brustein's Window,* had opened on Broadway.

How did Maxine Hong Kingston find that being an outsider helped her writing?

When she was a child, **Maxine Hong Kingston** (b. 1940) read all of **Louisa May Alcott**'s books, "identifying with all those girls," then being pulled up short when someone described marrying a "little Chinaman" who was "so odd." There were no Chinese-Americans in any of the stories she found in her local public library in Stockton, California. "In a way, it's not so horrible to be left out," she said years later, "because then you could see at a very early age that there's an entire mother lode of stories that belong to you and nobody else. You think, my goodness, I know a lot of girl stories. You could make up half of literature because of all the women that have been left out. And Chinese Americans."

Kingston read voraciously as a youngster and wanted to put the people around her, whose lives and stories she considered dramatic, into literature, but she didn't know how. Then she read books by **Howard Pease,** who lived in Stockton, too. When she saw how exciting it was to read about places she knew, she decided that she, too, could write about familiar places, people, and stories. Her first book, *Woman Warrior,* a fact-and-fantasy memoir based on stories that her mother had told her, won the National Book Critics Circle Award in 1976; her second was *China Men,* which told about the men who came to the United States from China to build the nation's railroads and work in its mines. With both books, she helped direct attention to people who until that point had been largely ignored in American history books. Her third book, and first novel, was *Tripmaster Monkey,* published in 1989.

In her first two books, Kingston wrote the Chinese scenes mainly from the memories told her by her parents, who had been born in China and had not returned. She deliberately did not go to China herself until she had written those books so that she could re-create "the myth of China." Later, she traveled throughout China, visiting, among other places, her family's village in Guangdong province. Although she saw little things that made her wish she had visited the village before writing *Woman Warrior,* basically "everything was very much as I had imagined. The people were just as dramatic as I thought they'd be."

Milestones: Women Writing

Fiction writers

Alice Adams	*Superior Women*
Louisa May Alcott	*Little Women*
Julia Alvarez	*How the García Girls Lost Their Accents*
Djuna Barnes	*Nightwood*
Ann Beattie	*Chilly Scenes of Winter*
Kay Boyle	*Thirty Stories*
Rosellen Brown	*Civil Wars*
Pearl Buck	*The Good Earth*
Willa Cather	*My Ántonia*
Kate Chopin	*The Awakening*
Sandra Cisneros	*The House on Mango Street*
Joan Didion	*Play It As It Lays*
Ellen Douglas	*Can't Quit You Baby*
Louise Erdrich	*Love Medicine*
Edna Ferber	*Giant*
Marilyn French	*The Women's Room*
Ellen Gilchrist	*Victory Over Japan*
Gail Godwin	*A Mother and Two Daughters*
Shirley Ann Grau	*The Keepers of the House*
Elizabeth Hailey	*A Woman of Independent Means*
Frances Ellen Watkins Harper	*Iola Leroy*
Pauline Elizabeth Hopkins	*Contending Forces*
Zora Neale Hurston	*Their Eyes Were Watching God*
Helen Hunt Jackson	*Ramona*
Shirley Jackson	*Bird's Nest*
Sarah Orne Jewett	*The Country of the Pointed Firs*
Nella Larsen	*Quicksand*
Harper Lee	*To Kill a Mockingbird*
Ursula Le Guin	*The Left Hand of Darkness*
Katherine Mansfield	*The Stories of Katherine Mansfield*
Paule Marshall	*Brown Girl, Brownstones*
Bobbie Ann Mason	*In Country*

Mary McCarthy	*The Group*
Carson McCullers	*The Member of the Wedding*
Margaret Mitchell	*Gone with the Wind*
Lucy Maud Montgomery	*Anne of Green Gables*
Toni Morrison	*Beloved*
Bharati Mukherjee	*The Middleman and Other Stories*
Gloria Naylor	*The Women of Brewster Place*
Joyce Carol Oates	*Because It Is Bitter, and Because It Is My Heart*
Flannery O'Connor	*Everything That Rises Must Converge*
Cynthia Ozick	*The Shawl*
Dorothy Parker	*A Treasury of Dorothy Parker*
Anne Petry	*The Street*
Katherine Anne Porter	*Ship of Fools*
Anne Rice	*The Queen of the Damned*
Carolyn See	*Rhine Maidens*
Leslie Marmon Silko	*Almanac of the Dead*
Mona Simpson	*Anywhere But Here*
Jane Smiley	*A Thousand Acres*
Harriet Beecher Stowe	*Uncle Tom's Cabin*
Amy Tan	*The Joy Luck Club*
Anne Tyler	*Dinner at the Homesick Restaurant*
Alice Walker	*The Color Purple*
Margaret Walker	*Jubilee*
Eudora Welty	*Delta Wedding*
Jessamyn West	*Friendly Persuasion*
Edith Wharton	*The Age of Innocence*
Laura Ingalls Wilder	*The Little House on the Prairie*
Anzia Yezierska	*Bread Givers*

Mystery writers

Amanda Cross	*Death in a Tenured Position*
Marcia Muller	*Eye of the Storm*
Sara Paretsky	*Bitter Medicine*

Essayists, letter writers, and memoirists

Abigail Adams	*The Book of Abigail and John: Selected Letters of the Adams Family, 1762–1784*
Jane Addams	*Twenty Years at Hull House*
Mary Catherine Bateson	*Composing a Life*
Annie Dillard	*Teaching a Stone to Talk: Expeditions and Encounters*
M. F. K. Fisher	*The Art of Eating*
Jeanne Wakatsuki Houston	*Farewell to Manzanar*
Harriet Ann Jacobs	*Incidents in the Life of a Slave Girl*
Maxine Hong Kingston	*The Woman Warrior: Memoirs of a Girlhood Among Ghosts*
Sarah Kemble Knight	*The Private Journal of a Journey from Boston to New York in the Year 1704, Kept by Madam Knight*
Anne Moody	*Coming of Age in Mississippi*
Mary White Rowlandson	*The Sovereignty and Goodness of God, Together with the Faithfulness of His Promises Displayed; Being a Narrative of the Captivity and Restoration of Mrs. Mary Rowlandson*
Susan Sontag	*A Susan Sontag Reader*
Elizabeth Cady Stanton	*Eighty Years and More*
Gertrude Stein	*The Autobiography of Alice B. Toklas*
Ida Wells-Barnett	*Crusade for Justice: The Autobiography of Ida B. Wells*

The voices of feminism

Susan Brownmiller	*Against Our Will*
Kim Chernin	*In My Mother's House*
Andrea Dworkin	*Pornography: Men Possessing Women*
Susan Faludi	*Backlash*
Betty Friedan	*The Feminine Mystique*
Margaret Fuller	*Woman in the Nineteenth Century*
Charlotte Perkins Gilman	*Women and Economics: A Study of the Economic Relations Between Men and Women as a Factor of Social Evolution*
Sarah Grimké	*Letters on the Equality of the Sexes and the Condition of Women*
Emma Goldman	*Anarchism and Other Essays*
bell hooks	*Talking Back: Thinking Feminist, Thinking Black*
Catharine MacKinnon	*Sexual Harassment of Working Women*
Kate Millett	*Sexual Politics*
Judith Sargent Murray	*On the Equality of Sexes*
Tillie Olsen	*Silences*

The scholars

Sandra Gilbert and Susan Gubar	*The Madwoman in the Attic: The Woman Writer and the Nineteenth Century Literary Imagination*
Carol Gilligan	*In a Different Voice*
Carolyn Heilbrun	*Writing a Woman's Life*
Gerda Lerner	*The Creation of Patriarchy*
Margaret Mead	*Coming of Age in Samoa*
Laurel Thatcher Ulrich	*A Midwife's Tale: The Life of Martha Bullard, Based on Her Diary, 1785–1812*

The poets

Maya Angelou	*Poems*
Anne Bradstreet	*The Tenth Muse, Lately Sprung Up in America*
Gwendolyn Brooks	*Annie Allen*
Ana Castillo	*My Father Was a Toltec*
Emily Dickinson	*The Complete Poems of Emily Dickinson*
Rita Dove	*Thomas and Beulah*
Nikki Giovanni	*The Women and the Men*
Maxine Kumin	*Up Country*
Audre Lourde	*Our Dead Behind Us: Poems*
Phyllis McGinley	*Times Three: Selected Verse from Three Decades*
Edna St. Vincent Millay	*A Few Figs from Thistles: Poems and Sonnets*
Marianne Moore	*Observations*
Sylvia Plath	*Ariel*
Adrienne Rich	*Diving into the Wreck*
May Sarton	*Letters from Maine: New Poems*
Anne Sexton	*Awful Rowing Toward God*
Sara Teasdale	*Love Songs*
Mona Van Duyn	*Near Changes*
Phillis Wheatley	*Poems on Various Subjects, Religious and Moral*

And the playwrights

Caryl Churchill	*Top Girls*
Betty Comden (with Adolph Green)	*Applause*
Gretchen Cryer	*I'm Getting My Act Together and Taking It on the Road*
Frances Goodrich (with Albert Hackett)	*The Diary of Anne Frank*
Angelina Weld Grimké	*Rachel*
Lorraine Hansberry	*A Raisin in the Sun*
Lillian Hellman	*Toys in the Attic*
Beth Henley	*Crimes of the Heart*
Jean Kerr	*Please Don't Eat the Daisies*
Anita Loos (with John Emerson)	*Gentlemen Prefer Blondes*
Clare Boothe Luce	*The Women*
Eve Merriam	*The Club*
Marsha Norman	*'night, Mother*
Ntozake Shange	*For Colored Girls Who Have Considered Suicide/When the Rainbow is Enuf*
Mercy Otis Warren	*The Adulateur*
Wendy Wasserstein	*Uncommon Women and Others*

CHAPTER 10

〜

From Civil Rights
to Women's Rights

Why were white Southern politicians afraid of a black sharecropper with a sixth-grade education named Fannie Lou Hamer?

Why did women play such a prominent role in the civil rights movement?

If Rosa Parks was too tired to move to the back of the bus in Montgomery, Alabama, why didn't she just take a cab home?

Milestones: From the Pews to the Pulpit

Since women landed on Plymouth Rock when men did, why did it take them three centuries to get the vote?

Why were black suffragists often at odds with their white counterparts?

Why were women who sought the right to vote

thrown into the workhouse in Occoquan, Virginia, and force-fed?

Who were the "bra burners" and "women's libbers"?

After "consciousness raising," what did women do about changing their lives?

Why did the coat hanger become a powerful symbol for American women?

What was the backlash against the women's movement?

Why the hoopla when tennis star Billie Jean King met tennis hustler Bobby Riggs on the courts in 1973?

Who coined the phrase "displaced homemaker," and what did she mean?

How did women land jobs in newsrooms, supposedly "no place for a lady"?

What were the stages of major advancement for women in the newsroom?

Why did Helen Thomas of United Press International call the National Press Club balcony "purdah"?

Milestones: Fighting Sex Discrimination at *The New York Times*

Why would any self-respecting female sports reporter want to go into a steamy locker room full of sweaty, half-clothed or naked men?

Milestones: Pulitzer Prize-Winning Women

Who was considered the dean of women broadcast journalists?

Where have all the female network anchors been?

Why didn't the Equal Rights Amendment win ratification?

Milestones: Women and the Law

What paths did Sandra Day O'Connor and Ruth Bader Ginsburg travel to become Supreme Court justices?

Why did Anita Hill's charge of sexual harassment reverberate so loudly?

Why have women in the White House always been First Ladies, not Commanders in Chief?

Who was the first female member of Congress?

Who were the nation's first female governors?

Why was 1992 "The Year of the Woman" in politics?

Did Hillary Rodham Clinton bring First Ladydom a new look?

~

Why were white Southern politicians afraid of a black sharecropper with a sixth-grade education named Fannie Lou Hamer?

Fannie Lou Hamer (1917–1977), a forty-six-year-old former sharecropper, sat in the national spotlight as she testified at the 1964 Democratic National Convention about the dangers black Mississippians faced. At a dramatic televised hearing—in the days when political conventions were not so tightly scripted as to be total bores—she told how she had lost her job and been jailed and brutally beaten for her attempts to register to vote and to help others register. Mississippi had long kept its black citizens from voting and thus from using any political strength toward seeking better schools or public services, and Hamer wondered aloud whether America truly believed in justice.

"Is this America," she asked, "the land of the free and the home of the brave where we have to sleep with our telephones off the hooks because our lives be threatened daily because we want to live as decent human beings, in America?"

Hamer attended the convention with the predominantly black Mississippi Freedom Democratic Party that was challenging the seating of the state party's all-white delegation. She came up against an even more immovable object than herself: President **Lyndon Johnson.** Johnson had succeeded the assassinated **John F. Kennedy** and wanted nothing to mar his nomination for a full term in the White House. He tightly controlled the convention to try to avoid walkouts by angry Southern whites.

The convention did not seat the Freedom Democrats, who had argued that the regular Democrats' delegation had been selected illegally because blacks had been systematically denied their constitutional right to vote. The convention did, however, vote that henceforth delegates would not be seated from any state that had discriminated in their selection. That decision started the process of rewriting party rules, eventually providing greater political participation by minorities, then women and other underrepresented groups. Growing political participation by blacks and women threatened the jobs and power of Southern white males. This growing activism also threatened what tranquillity some black Southerners had managed to establish, and some wished a Fannie Lou Hamer would go away so that the danger might pass.

The following year, Hamer and two other Mississippi women, **Victoria Gray** and **Annie Devine,** challenged the seating of the state's five-member congressional delegation in Washington. They lost, but again took the issue to the politicians and dramatized for the nation the lack of black participation at the polls across the South. While they were challenging the five white congressmen, legislators were also debating and ultimately passing the Voting Rights Act that helped increase the political influence of African-Americans and other minorities.

Fannie Lou Hamer remained active in efforts for social change in Mississippi. She helped organize a 1967 conference between poor women and county officials in Sunflower County in the days before such meetings were common. In 1968, she was seated as a member of the racially integrated delegation that successfully challenged the regular Democratic Party's right to represent Mississippi at the Democratic National Convention in Chicago. She sued her county voting supervisor to open the registration process to more applicants and to win new elections in 1967 in two small towns near her home. She sued the Sunflower County school system in 1970 to seek more school desegregation and to prevent demotion of black principals and firing of black teachers. She ran Freedom Farm, a cooperative aimed at bringing some independence to farm laborers who had lost their jobs through mechanization of agriculture. She spoke vigorously at the 1971 founding meeting of the National Women's Political Caucus, urging the mainly middle-class women not to forget that black women had twin struggles against not only sexism but also racism. And she ran for the state senate in 1971 and lost, although once again she was able to bring economic and educational issues to the forefront that might not otherwise have gotten attention. At the

1972 Democratic National Convention, Hamer seconded the vice presidential nomination of **Frances Farenthold** of Texas. She died in 1977 and is buried beneath a headstone that proclaims her motto: "I am sick and tired of being sick and tired."

Why did women play such a prominent role in the civil rights movement?

In virtually every town or rural hamlet across Mississippi, there was an organizer like **Fannie Lou Hamer,** outraged by the injustice with which she had lived and enabled by the grassroots nature of the civil rights movement in Mississippi to help plan strategy and carry it out. African-American women in the South were strangers to neither hard work nor physical danger, and their efforts in the movement entailed both. Active in their churches, they were "the ones that supports the deacon board," as **Unita Blackwell** said. "They holler the amen. The women is the ones that support the preacher. . . . So in the black community the movement, quite naturally I suppose, emerged out of all the women that carried out these roles."

Hamer worked in Ruleville, Blackwell in the even smaller town of Mayersville hard by the Mississippi River. In Palmers Crossing near Hattiesburg, there was **Victoria Gray;** in Canton, **Annie Devine;** in Drew, **Mae Bertha Carter;** in Leake County, **Winson** and **Dovie Hudson.** And others elsewhere across the state. The young people working in Mississippi in the early 1960s sought out these local people who both understood the benefits of voting and possessed the confidence of their neighbors so that some might join them in risking trying to register. With this bottom-up organizational approach, these young people of the Student Non-Violent Coordinating Committee (SNCC) differed from the top-down, minister-led Southern Christian Leadership Conference (SCLC) headed by Dr. **Martin Luther King Jr.** Women may not have directed programs, but they were often the people who brought their neighbors to voter-registration meetings, who distributed food and clothing to those who lost their jobs because of movement activity, and who housed and sustained the young civil rights volunteers.

The focus on seeking out grassroots leadership stemmed in part from the ideas of **Ella Baker,** who grew up in a community that she described as having "no sense of hierarchy" and a "Christian concept of sharing." Born in Virginia and educated in North Carolina, Baker became an organizer in New York during the Depression of the 1930s, then set up youth branches of the National Association for the Advancement of Colored People (NAACP) across the South. Later, she became the first female president of the NAACP's New York chapter. She returned to the South as an aide for King at the SCLC. Increasingly frustrated by the leadership styles she found within SCLC, which relied on charismatic leaders who sometimes risked thinking *they* were the movement, Baker welcomed the emergence of the students and their sit-ins. She helped the young people organize SNCC at a conference over the Easter weekend of 1960 at her alma mater, Shaw University, in North Carolina. She encouraged the SNCC workers who fanned out across the South to find and help local leaders so that when individual SNCC members moved on, they would leave behind people better able not only to understand the cause of their problems but also how to try to solve them. It was in this role that she helped organize the Mississippi Freedom Democratic Party.

The civil rights movement in which Hamer and Baker and other women figured so prominently did not ignite itself by spontaneous combustion. Even as the injustices festered for many years, blacks and their white allies started to organize and educate for change. The Highlander Folk School in the mountains of Tennessee welcomed people of all races who went there to learn teaching techniques to help others learn to read and pass the voter literacy tests in use across much of the South. One of the people who devised Highlander's teaching techniques was **Septima Clark,** an educator from Charleston, South Carolina. Long active in South Carolina in the drive for equal pay and fair treatment for black teachers, Clark was fired for refusing to give up her NAACP membership. Although she had taught for forty years, she was denied her retirement pay and had to wage a twenty-year struggle to regain her pension. Despite her contribution to the SCLC training program, Clark also found her participation in the leadership questioned by men like the Reverend **Ralph Abernathy.** "They just didn't feel as if a woman, you know, had any sense," she said.

Across the South, local women acted, sometimes singly, often in concert with other women. There was **Modjeska Simkins** in South Carolina, **Gloria Richardson** in Cambridge, Maryland, **Amelia Boynton** in Selma, Alabama, and there were the younger women who stood beside them—**Bernice Johnson Reagon, Dorie** and **Joyce Ladner, Colia Liddell, June Johnson, Diane Nash, Eleanor Holmes Norton, Marian Wright Edelman,** and many others. Sometimes these women achieved leadership where it was too dangerous for African-American men to assert themselves, but they were no strangers to violence or economic intimidation themselves. Fannie Lou Hamer never fully recovered from the beating she received while jailed in Winona, Mississippi. June Johnson and **Annell Ponder** were beaten there as well. The Reverend **Fred Shuttleworth**'s wife was stabbed in the hip during one protest during the fight to desegregate Birmingham schools. And the firehoses in Birmingham were turned on women as well as men, girls as well as boys. As a chain of bondage was being broken, new links were forming in the bonds of freedom.

If Rosa Parks was too tired to move to the back of the bus in Montgomery, Alabama, why didn't she just take a cab home?

In Montgomery, Alabama, in 1955, jobs for African-Americans were limited, the pay was low, and the transportation system was segregated. Cabs were essentially out of the question, at least for routine trips, for seamstress **Rosa Parks** (b. 1913), who made twenty-three dollars a week.

White and black rode the same buses, but blacks were expected to take their seats from the back forward (the less desirable seats over the hot engine, the rear wheels, and the exhaust pipes) while whites were seated from the front. If all seats were taken when a white person boarded the bus, black riders were expected to stand. This, after being also required to pay their fares at the front of the bus, get off, and board from the back door. Rosa Parks did not move on that day in December 1955 when the driver ordered her and several other black passengers to move to give a white person a seat. She had a bag of groceries, was on her way home, and later told someone that she simply was tired. But it wasn't that simple. For twelve years, Parks had run the local office of the National Association for the Advancement of Colored People as the chapter's elected secretary to its leader, activist and railroad porter **E. D. Nixon.**

She had also attended workshops that **Septima Clark** taught at Highlander Folk School. Parks recalled her first meeting there with Clark in 1955: "When I saw how well she could organize and hold things together in this very informal setting of interracial living, I had to admire this great woman. She just moved through the different workshops and groups as though it was just what she was made to do, in spite of the fact that she had to face so much opposition in her home state and lost her job and all of that." Describing herself as tense and nervous, Parks said she was nonetheless "willing to face whatever came, not because I felt that I was going to be benefited or helped personally, because I felt that I had been destroyed too long ago." But she hoped that young people would benefit.

Two months after her Highlander workshop, Parks refused to move from her seat on a Montgomery, Alabama, bus. She had been thrown off buses several times earlier for refusing to move; sometimes buses passed her by for that reason. Her action that day, and the driver's reaction in having her arrested, inspired a year-long boycott as blacks in Montgomery walked to work or carpooled rather than ride the buses. The Women's Political Council in Montgomery, headed by **Jo Ann Robinson,** was instrumental in organizing that boycott. These black women had endured the injustices of the segregated buses for years. They had flyers on the street proclaiming the bus boycott within two hours of learning of Parks's arrest. It was during these protests that Dr. **Martin Luther King Jr.** emerged as a national leader.

Milestones: From the Pews to the Pulpit

1808—**Elizabeth Seton** founded the Sisters of Charity, the first Catholic order native to America.

1853—**Antoinette Brown,** later Blackwell, was howled down as she attempted to speak before the World's Temperance Convention in New York. Later that year, however, she was ordained as the first female minister in a major U.S. religious denomination, in her case, the First Congregational Church in Wayne County, New York.

1855—Female "assistant missionaries" outnumbered ordained male missionaries from Protestant groups. As interest in missionary work, both at home and especially overseas, increased, an interdenominational Woman's Union Missionary Society of America was established in 1861. Women in the principal Protestant denominations set up missionary societies between 1868 and 1884. They, and their Southern counterparts established soon afterward, ran hospitals, schools, and orphanages.

1860—Even though their clergy was virtually all male, American Protestant churches became increasingly feminized during the nineteenth century. Women not only filled the pews but increasingly taught Sunday school classes and directed many other church social activities. The churches' theology also became less harsh; for example, infants were no longer doomed to damnation because they died before being baptized.

1869—The Hebrew Ladies' Sewing Circle was organized in Boston to support a project for poor women.

1871—The Hebrew Ladies' Relief Society was established in Kansas City.

1880—**Anna Howard Shaw** was ordained as the first female minister in the Methodist Protestant Church, having been refused ordination earlier by the larger Methodist Episcopal Church.

1886—The National Christian Scientist Association was founded to link followers of **Mary Baker Eddy,** whose theology argued basically that through positive thinking and stress on spirituality one could achieve well-being and good health.

1889—**Lina Hecht** started a Sunday school for girls at a Boston synagogue.

1895—**Elizabeth Cady Stanton,** long critical of organized religion's patriarchal stance toward women, published the first of two volumes of *The Woman's Bible.* It analyzed and reinterpreted the Bible's references to women that ministers often used to keep women in their place and out of leadership.

1898—**Marion F. Curney** established the first Catholic settlement house, St. Rose's, on New York's West Side.

1900—The first Catholic institution of higher education for women—Trinity College—opened in Washington, D.C. (Nearby Catholic University did not admit women.)

1912—The Jesuits were given permission for coeducation at Marquette University.

—Hadassah, the women's arm of Zionism in America, was established.

1913—Five thousand women belonged to the newly founded National Federation of Temple Sisterhoods to unite fifty-two groups doing community work through their Reform Jewish temples.

1915—Black Baptist women issued a report grading the performance of their clergymen, calling the lowest-ranking among them "intellectually inept" and accusing some of them of exploiting their congregations.

1918—The women's missionary society of the Colored Methodist Episcopal Church met for the first time.

1919—Two Methodist women started the American Association of Women Preachers. Prospects for women's ordination in Protestant denominations brightened because of the successful culmination in 1920 of the suffrage movement and because of women's contributions to the war effort during World War I.

1923—Evangelist **Aimee Semple McPherson** dedicated the Angelus Temple—"the Church of the Foursquare Gospel"—in Los Angeles, where she often preached to five thousand or more people.

1927—The Catholic bishop of Providence, Rhode Island, urged clergymen to follow the earlier dictum of Pope **Pius X** that women be eliminated from church choirs.

1929—Pope **Pius XI**'s encyclical on education proclaimed that coeducation "mistakes a leveling promiscuity and equality for the legitimate association of the sexes."

1930—The Presbyterian Church in the USA denied ordination to women but did allow them to become church elders.

—Pope Pius XI said that women who sought social equality were acting unnaturally and debased themselves.

1948—The African Methodist Episcopal Church approved the ordination of women.

1951—**Paula Ackerman** of Meridian, Mississippi, became the first woman to serve as spiritual leader of a Jewish congregation, succeeding her husband, a rabbi, on his death. She insisted on serving only until a suitable rabbi was found.

1955—**Mrs. Sheldon Robbins** became Judaism's first female cantor.

1956—Presbyterians and Methodists voted to ordain women.

1968—**Mary Daly**'s *The Church and the Second Sex* was published. It made the feminist case against the Catholic Church and yet expressed hope and "modest proposals" toward partnership.

1969—The National Coalition of American Nuns was founded, in part to work for women's equality within the Catholic Church.

1970—The Lutheran Church of America and the American Lutheran Church voted to ordain women.

—Catholic bishops and the heads of seven nuns' groups met in Washington, D.C., to discuss women's role in church policy making.

—The Episcopal Church voted to allow women to become deacons, usually the final step before the priesthood.

1972—**Sally Priesand** became the first female Reform Jewish rabbi in America.

—Pope **Paul VI** reaffirmed that women could have no formal role in the Catholic ministry.

1973—Conservative Judaism ruled that women could be counted with men to determine the number of people present to allow congregational worship.

—The Episcopal Church voted to keep the priesthood open to men only.

1974—Three retired Episcopal bishops ordained eleven women as their church's first female priests in a ceremony conducted in Philadelphia, without the official sanction of the church.

—The National Leadership Conference of Women Religious called for the ordination of women as Catholic priests.

1975—More than 1,200 people launched the Women's

Ordination Conference at a meeting in Detroit at which they discussed scriptural and theological material that supported ordaining women as Catholic priests.

1976—The Episcopal Church voted that women could become priests and said it would recognize those women ordained in Philadelphia if they would have the ordination "regularized" in ceremonies within their own diocese.

1977—The Vatican issued its "Declaration on the Question of the Admission of Women to the Ministerial Priesthood," repeating the church's opposition to ordaining women "in fidelity to the example of the Lord."

1979—Sister **Mary Theresa Kane,** speaking at a prayer service being conducted by the visiting Pope **John Paul II** at the National Shrine of the Immaculate Conception in Washington, D.C., challenged the pontiff to reconsider his opposition to ordination of women and asked him to "be mindful of the intense pain and suffering which is part of the life of many women." Sixty nuns, wearing blue armbands, rose in support of her protest.

—**Sonia Johnson** was tried by the Mormon Church for supporting the Equal Rights Amendment (ERA), which her church leadership opposed. She was excommunicated in 1980, as much for challenging her church as for supporting ERA.

1980—**Marjorie Matthews** became the first female Methodist bishop in the United States.

1984—After New York's Archbishop **John J. O'Connor** urged parishioners not to vote for the Mondale-Ferraro ticket in the presidential election because of its stand on abortion, twenty-four Catholic nuns signed a *New York Times* ad saying that Catholics held "a diversity of opinions" on abortion. Church leadership did not acknowledge such diversity and sought retractions from the nuns. Two of them, **Barbara Ferraro** and **Patricia Hussey,** ultimately left their order, the Sisters of Notre Dame de Namur, over the controversy.

1988—Reverend **Barbara Harris** became the first female Bishop of the Worldwide Anglican Communion.

1989—Radical feminist theologian Mary Daly, author of *Beyond God the Father,* was denied a full professorship at Boston College, run by Jesuits.

1992—The National Conference of Catholic Bishops could not muster the two-thirds vote needed to pass a pastoral letter on the role of women in the church and society. Debated for nine years, the draft of the letter was heavily weighted toward conservative views but still did not pass.

1994—**Laura Geller** became the first woman named senior rabbi of a major metropolitan Jewish congregation when she was selected as the spiritual leader for Temple Emanuel in Beverly Hills, California.

—Pope John Paul II, in a letter to Catholic bishops, warned that the idea of women being ordained as priests was not "open to debate."

Since women landed on Plymouth Rock when men did, why did it take them three centuries to get the vote?

For most women in the early American colonies, politics was hardly uppermost in their lives; survival was. Even so, one of the earliest colonial landowners, **Margaret Brent,** who arrived in St. Mary's City, Maryland, in 1642, demanded a vote in the legislature. She had been named executor of the estate of the colony's governor, **Leonard Calvert,** and as such had raised enough money to pay off rebellious soldiers. Not long thereafter, she asked the colonial assembly for the vote that would have been hers as a landowner had she been male. Her request was denied.

The Maryland assembly's decision reflected the prevailing view that women should be subsidiaries to their husbands; an unmarried woman of property like Margaret Brent was a relative rarity. Thus, it was not surprising when the Founding Fathers not only excluded any Founding Mothers from the discussions leading to independence but also declared that only all men were created equal. The Constitution gave only men the right to vote. With women's sphere perceived to lie exclusively in the home, no one argued with that provision. Only as women started to perceive their unequal standing under the law and in their daily lives did they start considering how best to redress their grievances. Men assured them that their fathers, husbands, and brothers voted in their interests, but some quickly saw through that argument when they tried to change divorce, property, or liquor laws.

Inertia slowed the suffragists in their campaign because the women who attended the Seneca Falls, New York, convention in 1848 were uncertain how to proceed. Many other women, especially those economically more privileged who felt well protected at home, either opposed women's suffrage outright or considered the political arena degrading and shuddered at women's participation.

Suffragists faced opposition from some abolitionists who felt nothing should dilute the fight against slavery. The women who favored suffrage suspended their campaigns during the Civil War, but then their former allies insisted that protecting the Negro by giving him—not her—the vote was more important than giving women the vote. When one of **Frederick Douglass**'s listeners pointed out in 1869 that there were black women as well as black men deserving of protection, Douglass, who had attended the first meeting at Seneca Falls, replied that the lynchings from lampposts, the insults, and the discrimination that befell a black woman occurred "not because she is a woman but because she is black." Republicans running the government after the Civil War may have favored giving blacks the vote because they figured that blacks would vote for the party whose leader, **Abraham Lincoln,** had emancipated the slaves. These Republicans considered female voters unpredictable— women might simply follow their husbands' leads. Some clergymen opposed the vote for women because they said the Bible dictated an inferior position for women; they may also have been offended by the fact that many suffragists also favored a greater role for women in their churches.

One must not discount the basic conservatism of people as a factor in opposing votes for women. With the frontier closing and industry consolidating its gains, many people, especially business leaders, did not want change. Some business leaders felt, rightly, that adding women to the voting rolls would lead to legislation to change labor laws, especially those affecting women and children. Where traditional business interests were less entrenched in western states, women won the vote first.

The liquor lobby financed many campaigns against giving women the vote because women were the most fiery temperance campaigners. In California, for example, during the referendum campaign to try to win statewide women's suffrage in 1896, the wholesale liquor dealers in San Francisco urged saloon-keepers, hotel operators, and grocers to work against the amendment. They received just enough votes in the Bay Area to turn back the majority favoring women's right to vote in the rest of the state. Women's suffrage didn't pass in California until 1911.

With all these forces at play and with lawmakers standing, as they usually do, with their fingers testing the wind, is it any surprise that it took until 1920 for women to win the vote?

Why were black suffragists often at odds with their white counterparts?

The division began after the Civil War when the leaders of the movement for the women's vote split over seeking universal suffrage or universal manhood suffrage, the latter meaning that black men would get the vote but not women, black or white.

One faction felt that the need for blacks to try to protect their rights through the vote was so overwhelming that the Fifteenth Amendment, giving suffrage only to black males, was acceptable. **Susan B. Anthony** and **Elizabeth Cady Stanton** disagreed.

In the latter part of the nineteenth century and early twentieth, white suffragist leaders, especially younger ones no longer bringing with them a background of abolitionism, often compromised with white Southerners by downplaying or disavowing the vote for black women. Nativism, or the distrust of foreigners, combined with racism to lead some suffrage leaders to advocate the vote for white women to overcome what they considered the negative impact of voting by impoverished, illeducated immigrants and black men. For example, a resolution passed by the National American Woman's Suffrage Association (NAWSA) in 1893 pointed out that there were "more women who can read and write than all negro voters; more American women who can read and write than all foreign voters; so that the enfranchisement of such women would settle the vexed question of rule by illiteracy of home-grown or foreign born production."

The following year, Susan B. Anthony found it expedient to ask **Frederick Douglass,** the black leader who had been present at the first women's rights meeting at Seneca Falls, New York, not to attend the suffrage association's first Southern convention, held in Atlanta. She also declined to help black women who sought her aid to organize a NAWSA branch. Anthony and her allies thought that suffrage needed all the support it could get—and that meant keeping Southern white women in the fold at the expense of black women. **Carrie Chapman Catt,** Anthony's successor as NAWSA president, suggested to the Southern whites that they not attend her organization's convention in Chicago in 1916 because the Chicago delegation would consist largely of black women. When the Northeastern Federation of Colored Women's Clubs sought affiliation with NAWSA in 1919, suffragist leader **Ida Husted Harper** urged that the women wait to apply for membership until after the Nineteenth Amendment passed, again to avoid stirring up fears among Southern white women.

Nonetheless, black women continued to believe that obtaining the vote would help curb problems they faced on grounds of both race and gender. Reactionary Southern leaders' fears of the impact of the black women's vote "were not illusionary," as author Rosalyn Terborg-Penn has pointed out, because those votes had already been significant in a Chicago aldermanic election and in a New York state assembly race in the years just before the suffrage amendment came up for a vote. Furthermore, black women were organizing in Alabama, Georgia, Tennessee, and Texas as well as in northern states and cities. After the Nineteenth Amendment was passed, however, black women encountered obstacles when they tried to vote, just as black men had faced in the South since at least 1890. Poll taxes and elaborate qualifying tests kept black women from registering. But because their problems were deemed the result of race issues, not women's issues, the National Woman's Party leadership declined to help as it kept its focus solely on securing an Equal Rights Amendment.

Why were women who sought the right to vote thrown into the workhouse in Occoquan, Virginia, and force-fed?

In 1917, the National Woman's Party, more militant than the traditional leaders in the fight for votes for women, sought to bring the suffrage question to greater public attention. Its members were led by **Alice Paul** (1885–1977), who had been influenced by her work with the British women's movement. When women who had been picketing the White House during their campaign to force congressional action were arrested, they were jailed in Occoquan because, on principle, they refused to pay their fines. Like their British counterparts, they started hunger strikes and were force-fed.

The single-minded Paul, a Quaker, was a 1905 graduate of Swarthmore College in Pennsylvania. In the years between earning master's and doctoral degrees from the University of

Pennsylvania, she did settlement house work in New York and in England, where she became active in the drive for women's rights headed by **Emmeline** and **Christabel Pankhurst.** The Pankhursts and their followers staged marches, interrupted men's political meetings, and unfurled banners in Parliament demanding women's rights. Paul and her soon-to-be colleague, **Lucy Burns,** were arrested during some of these demonstrations.

Back home, Paul and Burns started lobbying for votes for women as the Congressional Committee of the National American Woman's Suffrage Association (NAWSA) in 1912. NAWSA sought to achieve its goal through education, not intimidation, and Paul and Burns soon parted company with the association and formed the Congressional Union and later the National Woman's Party. To the more cautious, their tactics seemed likely to anger rather than persuade their targets, but the old-line suffragists may have benefited. The National Woman's Party made NAWSA look moderate.

Paul and Burns believed that women had to hold the party in power responsible for not passing the suffrage amendment, and so they led campaigns against Democratic officeholders in 1916. NAWSA disagreed, and invited President **Woodrow Wilson** to a meeting at which he declared his support for suffrage.

On January 10, 1917, the National Woman's Party picketed the White House carrying banners saying, "Mr. President, How Long Must Women Wait for Liberty?" In March a thousand women walked around the White House in the rain during President Wilson's second inauguration. None of the pickets was arrested until June, when they were charged with obstructing traffic and received as much as sixty days in the workhouse at Occoquan, Virginia. There, bedding was not changed between prisoners' use, the same piece of soap was used for all the prisoners, the food contained worms, and the women had to undress in front of their fellow prisoners (in an age, remember, of great modesty). In November, a group of suffragists, taken to Occoquan after their arrest, started a hunger strike to protest that they were not being treated as the political prisoners they considered themselves. That night the workhouse superintendent had them hauled roughly into cells. When Lucy Burns persisted in calling the roll to determine whether all the women were present, one of the guards handcuffed her wrists and fastened them above her head on the cell door.

After several days of the hunger strike, several of the women were forcibly fed because jail authorities, already confronted with bad publicity, feared worse if any of the inmates died from lack of food. One woman described being held down by five people while a tube was pushed down her throat and fluid began pouring in. In a note smuggled out of jail, Lucy Burns wrote of having a tube forced into her nose. "It hurts nose and throat very much and makes nose bleed freely. Tube drawn out covered with blood. Operation leaves one very sick. Food dumped directly into stomach feels like a ball of lead."

After the United States entered World War I that year, the woman's party had started referring to the president as Kaiser Wilson, angering many as patriotism swept the country. When Alice Paul was taken into custody during the ongoing protest, she said that she was being arrested "not because I obstructed traffic, but because I pointed out to President Wilson the fact that he is obstructing the progress of justice and democracy at home while Americans fight for it abroad." She, too, began a hunger strike that lasted three weeks and a day; she was force-fed for the last two weeks of that time. The authorities sent a psychiatrist to question Paul. Asked if she would talk to him, Paul laughed and said, "That's our business to talk," and proceeded to give an hour-long history of the suffrage movement. Although she received a favorable report, she was nonetheless sent to the psychopathic ward where mentally unbalanced patients were allowed to peer into her room through a grated door.

Released by early December, the women stepped up the drive for the amendment. The following January 10—one year after the first White House picketing—the House passed the suffrage amendment. The Senate, however, did not. NAWSA targeted four senators who had voted against the amendment and beat two of them in the 1918 elections. In 1919, the House passed the amendment for the second time, and on June 4 the Senate finally passed it. It was ratified and took effect in 1920.

Who were the "bra burners" and "women's libbers"?

"Bra burning" and "women's lib" came to be media short-hand for the modern wave of feminist thought and action that emerged in the 1960s. There was no bra burning. That image stemmed from one of the earliest attention-getting stunts for the women's liberation movement, a demonstration against the Miss America pageant at Atlantic City in September 1968. Some two hundred activists crowned a sheep as Miss America to illustrate their point that women were judged like livestock; they also threw girdles, curlers, high heels, and—yes, some bras—into a trash can. Nothing was burned, however.

In the 1960s, women in the civil rights movement and the student and antiwar movements found themselves making coffee and making love, not making policy. More women began examining their own lives, relationships, and jobs and discovering that they did not always like what they found. They formed "consciousness-raising" groups to talk among themselves about everything from sexual satisfaction to household chores. They wanted "women's liberation" from the stereotypes and male dominance that they felt restricted their lives. Headline writers quickly shortened (and trivialized) their demand into "women's lib."

This modern incarnation of the women's movement did not rise out of nowhere. During the 1940s women had pressed for larger roles in wartime, and not all female workers left their jobs cheerfully when servicemen came home from overseas. The steady movement of women into the workforce and their realization that they were not paid, promoted, or treated equally planted the seeds for the modern movement. More women were graduating from college who felt as well prepared for work as men—although they still might be told, "We don't hire (m)any women." Development of the birth control pill also contributed greatly to women's new freedom.

While feminist activity seemed largely dormant after World War II, women were making a few political gains. With **India Edwards,** a former journalist, as executive director of the women's division of the Democratic National Committee constantly pushing him, President **Harry S. Truman** named the first female ambassador. She was **Eugenia Anderson,** who was sent to Denmark. He also named **Georgia Neese Clark** to the largely symbolic position of U.S. treasurer (one of two people who sign our paper money). She was a banker where no treasurer had been before. Truman, however, selected no women for his cabinet and was talked out of naming Federal Judge **Florence Allen** to the U.S. Supreme Court because the justices felt that her presence would prevent their sitting around with their shoes off to talk over cases. Women's national political standing advanced only a little during **Dwight D. Eisenhower**'s administration, but he did name **Oveta Culp Hobby,** head of the Women's Army Auxiliary Corps during World War II, as secretary of the new Department of Health, Education, and Welfare.

When **John F. Kennedy** was elected president, he named longtime activist **Esther Peterson** as assistant secretary of labor and director of the Women's Bureau. Kennedy had no female cabinet secretaries, so Peterson, a dynamo as a lobbyist, was the ranking woman in his administration. In 1961, Kennedy created a Presidential Commission on the Status of Women at Peterson's urging. **Eleanor Roosevelt** was named to chair the commission, with Peterson as executive vice chairman. Roosevelt died the next year, but because she had devoted so much of her life to advancing women, the appointment had great symbolic value.

The major debate before the commission concerned whether there needed to be an equal rights amendment, a point of division between Esther Peterson and labor advocates on one side and feminists from the National Woman's Party on the other. The commission report, issued in 1963, finessed the question by stating that equality under the law between men and women was essential but not calling for an equal rights amendment at that point. The commission did urge an end to sex discrimination in the federal civil service, equal pay for comparable work, paid maternity leave, and improved child care. The property of married couples should belong to both members of the couple, not just the husband, the commission said, a concept that may seem natural today but wasn't at that time. The report of this prestigious commission not only focused the public's attention anew on issues of concern to women, it also gave invaluable experience to many women who continued to work to implement these recommendations.

In 1963, Congress also passed the Equal Pay Act. Despite weaknesses in the bill, the legislation placed the federal government behind women's rights to hold jobs under the same conditions as men. Within ten years, the law led to 171,000 people receiving $84 million in back pay.

Laws and commissions are not all that influence social movements. Books can, too. Published in 1963, **Betty Friedan**'s *The Feminine Mystique* outlined the frustrations of women who found themselves increasingly isolated in the suburbs and unable to use their educations fully. They suffered from an ennui that she called "the problem that has no name." While the book did not necessarily reach across race and class lines, it nonetheless captured the attention of the women who did have the education and time to analyze their own situations and helped create the climate that would galvanize the women's movement.

Although lawmakers viewed the Civil Rights Act of 1964 as dealing mainly with the employment grievances of black Americans, they were persuaded to ban sex discrimination as well in Title VII of the legislation. Some thought that provision was a joke, but it would prove an important basis for later court cases.

After "consciousness raising," what did women do about changing their lives?

What women always do—they formed associations to air their grievances and lobby for change. By 1966, the women and some men who were following up the recommendations of the Presidential Commission on the Status of Women were growing frustrated with the laggardly pace of the federal Equal Employment Opportunity Commission (EEOC) in responding to sex discrimination cases. At a 1966 meeting of state status-of-women commissions in Washington, they tried to introduce a resolution expressing their impatience, but **Esther Peterson** told them the meeting's purpose was to exchange information, not take action. That did it. They took action. They decided to form the National Organization for Women (NOW) to pressure agencies like the EEOC and to work on roadblocks to women's full participation in American society. **Betty Friedan** was NOW's first president. Within a year, the group had convinced President **Lyndon Johnson** to issue an executive order forbidding firms holding federal contracts from discriminating against women.

One of the other major, enduring organizations guiding the women's movement—the National Women's Political Caucus—was formed in 1971 at a meeting in Washington that included Congresswomen **Bella Abzug** and **Shirley Chisholm,** Betty Friedan, **Fannie Lou Hamer,** and **Gloria Steinem.** The caucus was established to elect more women to public office and to lobby for their appointment to federal and state jobs. The following year many of the women were at the Democratic National Convention working (unsuccessfully, as it turned out) to win stronger support for reproductive rights and to try to nominate a female candidate, **Frances "Sissy" Farenthold** of Texas, for vice president, also unsuccessfully.

A leading activist at that 1972 convention was Gloria Steinem, who that same year had helped found *Ms.* magazine, the first overtly feminist national women's magazine. With her aviator glasses, stylish appearance, and soft-spoken wit, Steinem became a "media star" of the movement, admired by many who didn't want feminists to seem to be man-haters but did want to be woman-identified. Being a star meant, however, that she was also "trashed"—with her motivation and commitment questioned—by those who felt she received too much attention. Trashing occurred as a by-product of the desire among some of the more radical feminist groups not to conduct their organizations in the same hierarchical way that men did. They favored not only collective action but also collective leadership, which was not an oxymoron in their thinking; for example, **Ti-Grace Atkinson** of New York NOW—and later The Feminists—advocated having women rotate in leadership positions. In this context, many women's groups refused to put leaders forward, but the press felt it needed leaders to quote and so anointed them itself. That led some in the rank and file to criticize those anointed for supposedly seeking celebrity rather than blending in with a movement seeking autonomy and equality.

The attempt to ratify the Equal Rights Amendment (ERA), passed by Congress in 1972, drew much of the energy of the women's movement during the 1970s and early 1980s. Within about a year after ERA's passage, thirty states had ratified it and it seemed headed for victory. But reaction set in and ERA backers could win only five of the remaining eight states needed for final ratification. It was during this era that **Eleanor Smeal** emerged as the leader of NOW and architect of the successful drive to convince Congress to extend the ratification period. But even an extra thirty-nine months didn't help. The opposition by then was firmly dug in.

As a follow-up to a 1975 international women's conference in Mexico City, President **Jimmy Carter** appointed an International Women's Year commission to plan a national meeting in the fall of 1977. Twenty thousand women converged on Houston to debate a series of resolutions on abortion, day care, gay rights, support for ERA, and various economic issues, while across town conservatives led by **Phyllis Schlafly** and **Nellie Gray** held what they called a "pro-life, pro-family" meeting. The battle lines were being drawn for the approaching retrenchment of the 1980s.

Why did the coat hanger become a powerful symbol for American women?

Coat hangers represented the crudest instrument that women might use to abort their own pregnancies, and so became a symbol of the deaths or injury to women unable to obtain safe, legal abortions before the 1973 Supreme Court *Roe v. Wade* decision.

In that controversial landmark decision written by Justice **Harry A. Blackmun,** the court based its opinion on the right of privacy. It said that during the second trimester of pregnancy, states could regulate abortion but only to protect a woman's health and that states could forbid abortion in the third trimester except when the procedure was necessary to save the woman's life. This decision would pit the Catholic Church and some conservative Protestant denominations against the women's organizations that backed reproductive rights and thus divert much of their attention from other causes. The groups squared off semantically as well, with one side wanting to be called "right to life" supporters, not antiabortion, and the other preferring "pro-choice," not proabortion.

Roe v. Wade altered American politics as well as political language. Groups on both sides of the issue used it—and it alone—as a litmus test to determine their support. Presidents **Ronald Reagan** and **George Bush** addressed right-to-life conventions and antiabortion marchers, while President **Bill Clinton** moved to ease those abortion restrictions that he could affect within days of taking office in 1993. He lifted the "gag rule" imposed during the Reagan and Bush administrations that had forbade clinics receiving federal aid from providing any information to women about abortion. He also dropped the restriction on U.S. foreign aid to countries that financed abortions and eliminated the ban on bringing the abortifacient RU-486 into the country.

Lawmakers at the federal and state levels debated limitations on government financial aid and access to abortions, and each time a new law was passed, it faced court challenges. Supreme

Court nominations drew especially intense scrutiny and lobby-ing, although court observers were aware of the unpredictabil-ity of justices once they were confronted with specific cases and convincing arguments from their colleagues.

What was the backlash against the women's movement?

For some Americans, women evidently went too far, too fast, in changing their lives. When **Ronald Reagan** was elected pres-ident in 1980, these forces moved into the ascendancy. The women's movement found itself channeling many of its re-sources toward preserving the gains of the last decade and a half. Paradoxically, Reagan's policies and those of his successor, **George Bush,** helped feminist organizations recruit more mem-bers during the 1980s and early 1990s. While Reagan appointed the first female member of the U.S. Supreme Court, **Sandra Day O'Connor,** he appointed fewer women to jobs that re-quired Senate confirmation than his immediate predecessors, encouraged opposition to abortion rights, resisted attempts to pass federal legislation to improve day care for the children of working parents, and cut funds for programs that would help battered women. His first budget director, **David Stockman,** even tried to cut money for the popular Women, Infants and Children (WIC) feeding program, but Congress headed off that move. If corporate America felt any pressure to improve work-ing conditions for women in the 1980s, it came from the courts and the women themselves, not from the White House.

Meantime, as Susan Faludi outlined in her best-selling book, *Backlash: The Undeclared War Against American Women,* moviemak-ers, authors, and the religious Right capitalized on the anxieties of a changing society to portray independent women as mon-sters. Magazines played up the odds against college-educated women getting married, the older they got. Women were get-ting mixed messages, Faludi wrote, including one that said,

"You may be free and equal now . . . but you have never been more miserable."

Women turned their energies to many fields—improving programs for children, electing women to office, preserving reproductive rights, combatting gun violence, helping battered women, heading universities, conducting symphony orchestras—and mainly living their lives, doing their jobs, feeding their families. After ERA failed, the only unifying issue for the movement was the threat to *Roe v. Wade* as Reagan and then Bush appointed justices who they thought would share their views on abortion. Otherwise, feminists went their own way—always, however, forming associations where none existed to work on their own issues. Many young women declined to call themselves feminists but took for granted the opportunities those feminists had opened for them.

Why the hoopla when tennis star Billie Jean King met tennis hustler Bobby Riggs on the courts in 1973?

When 40 million Americans gathered around their television sets on September 20, 1973, they were watching a tennis match promoted in a style suiting the Super Bowl, the World Series, and the NBA finals all rolled into one. What was at stake? The pride of the emerging women's movement versus male ego, at least among the armchair athletes watching at home.

Women were arguing for equal tournament prize money, with **Billie Jean King** as a leader. She had discovered, for example, that she won $600 for capturing the Italian Open while the male winner got $3,500. The U.S. Lawn Tennis Association capitulated in 1973 and started paying male and female winners of the U.S. Open each $25,000. But there was still the argument over whether women played the game as well as men. **Bobby Riggs,** fifty-five, who had been a world-class tournament player years earlier (but no longer), first challenged and beat the reserved Australian champion **Margaret Court** on Mother's Day 1973. Women's tennis honor thus at stake, King rose to the challenge and proved as flamboyant at hype as was Riggs. She beat him easily in three sets (6–4, 6–3, 6–3), which proved nothing except that Riggs had hit more nerves off the court than he was able to hit winners on it.

The contest in sports had moved from the gym floors to the floor of Congress in 1972 as women and male allies fought for passage of Title IX to the Education Act. That legislative section banned any institution receiving federal money from discriminating in any of its programs on the basis of sex. Covering far more than athletics, Title IX nonetheless drew some of its heaviest opposition from men involved with college sports programs. The National Collegiate Athletic Association (NCAA) opposed the measure, saying it would doom intercollegiate sports. Backers of the legislation could point to college after college where women's athletics were shortchanged. At the University of Washington in Seattle, for example, men's sports received $2,582,000, women's, $18,000. The budget for women's programs there the following year alone increased to $200,000.

Once the legislation passed, universities had to start spending more money for better training facilities, equipment, uniforms, travel, and scholarships for women's athletics. Average spending for women's sports in NCAA's Division 1 increased from $27,000 in 1973–1974 to $400,000 by 1981–1982, although men's programs still received far more money. While female athletes prospered, women in the coaching ranks did not. In 1972, 90 percent of women's college coaches were women. By 1987, only 50 percent were. By 1990, 84.1 percent of women's intercollegiate athletic programs were headed by men.

Nonetheless, the combination of money and encouragement for more young women to participate in college athletics drew comment again and again at the 1984 Olympics in Los Angeles as American women emerged as track, swimming, and basketball stars. Of 200 women on the U.S. Olympic team, 170 had participated in college athletic programs, many of which would not have been as strong without Title IX. They were drawn from a pool of female college athletes that grew from 16,000 in 1972 to 150,000 by 1984. As the *Los Angeles Times* editorialized at the time, "Olympians like Tracy Caulkins, Evelyn Ashford and Cheryl Miller have shown that being fair rewards the nation as well as its women."

On the twentieth anniversary of the passage of Title IX, the NCAA reported that women still were being shortchanged. More than twice as many men than women received athletic scholarships. Men's athletic programs and recruiting efforts received more money than women's. A survey by the women's Basketball Coaches Association reported in 1994 showed that male head coaches earned an average $76,566 a year while women earned $44,961.

Women did not take such disparities quietly. In 1993, **Sanya Tyler,** the Howard University women's basketball coach, sued for sex discrimination because her salary had been about half that of her men's basketball counterpart. She won $2.4 million in damages, which was later reduced to $1.1 million. **Marianne Stanley,** women's basketball coach at the University of Southern California, also sued that year over the salary disparities.

That same year, some universities moved to correct inequities. The men's and women's basketball coaches at the University of Virginia were earning the same amount—$106,000—in 1993, and Stanford's women's basketball coach negotiated a contract to bring her salary to parity with the men's coach within eighteen months. The California State University also announced that the nineteen schools in its system had until 1998–1999 to bring funding and participation opportunities for women in line with those for men. That meant some of the campuses might have to cut the money they spent on football, always the stumbling block in promoting gender equity. Cal State didn't act on its own, however, but was sued by the National Organization for Women after the Fullerton campus had dropped women's volleyball. A survey taken in 1988–1989 had shown that even though 53 percent of the system's students were female, only 30 percent of its student athletes were women. Men received 74 percent of athletic department funds, women, 25 percent, and coeducational teams, 1 percent.

Who coined the phrase "displaced homemaker," and what did she mean?

Tish Sommers (1914–1985), cofounder with **Laurie Shields** (1922–1989) of the Older Women's League, described her own situation with the phrase "displaced homemaker." She was a woman displaced from her home after a lifetime as a housewife when her husband abandoned her. Divorced at fifty-seven, Sommers had been out of the job market and dependent on her husband. She was ineligible to receive Social Security and, because she had had cancer twenty years before her divorce, she could not get health insurance on her own. She realized that these problems affected far more women than just herself. Refusing to consider herself a victim, Sommers took up the slogan: "Don't Agonize; Organize," and started lobbying in Sacramento, the capital of California, where she lived, and in Washington for legislation to provide counseling centers for older, divorced women. Then she started tackling broader issues and urging women to prepare better to care for themselves communally as they age.

How did women land jobs in newsrooms, supposedly "no place for a lady"?

Well into the twentieth century, journalists could best be described as men who cursed, drank, chased ambulances, smoked cigars, played poker, and generally didn't want women around the newsroom, at least not as colleagues. The few women who were hired wrote for the society pages—and even the leading columnists there were sometimes men. In the 1920s and 1930s and even beyond, the women's pages, with their news of recipes, fashions, and parties, were edited in a room separate from the tough atmosphere of the newsroom. In the days just before World War I, the only female reporters on the news staff of *The New York Herald-Tribune*—**Ishbel Ross** and **Emma Bugbee**—had to work down the hall from the main newsroom.

From colonial times onward, however, women have written for and published American newspapers. The first American journalist was **Elizabeth Timothy,** who arrived in Philadelphia from Rotterdam with her printer husband Lewis in 1731. They moved to Charleston, South Carolina, three years later, where Lewis was to publish **Benjamin Franklin**'s *South Carolina Gazette.* Four years after that, smallpox claimed Lewis's life and Elizabeth took over the paper for seven years until her son was old enough to run it. In 1740, the *Gazette* provided valuable public service when fire destroyed much of Charleston and people needed a central place to run notices to locate missing relatives, find housing, and obtain other help. From that day to this—from Timothy to **Katharine Graham,** who finished the job her husband, Philip, began by making *The Washington Post* a press giant—widows have succeeded their husbands as publishers. That succession is less likely to occur today, given the nature of corporate America.

During the nineteenth century, women relayed political gossip in print, covered foreign wars, investigated conditions in hospitals and mental asylums, reported on violent labor strikes, and crusaded against lynching. Among them:

Margaret Fuller, editor of the Transcendentalist literary set's journal, *The Dial,* in the early 1840s, also worked for Horace Greeley's *New York Tribune.* At thirty-six, she sailed for Europe, becoming America's first female foreign correspondent. She wrote about education in England, about day-care centers in France, and, from Italy, about the wars of 1848 that changed the map of Europe. She survived the shelling of Rome by the French but died the following year in a shipwreck off Fire Island, New York.

Nellie Bly was the most famous of the journalistic "stunt girls." She feigned illness to investigate mental hospital conditions, wore a scanty costume to write about chorus girls, and pretended she was an impoverished worker to study sweatshop conditions. In 1889, while a reporter for *The New York World*, she decided to see if she could travel around the world in eighty days as novelist **Jules Verne** had conjectured. This was, remember, a time in which it took seven days just to sail the Atlantic, and much of the world had barely developed transportation systems. Bly met Verne, creator of Phileas Fogg who had made the fictional trip, at his estate in France, then continued on through the Mediterranean to Ceylon, Hong Kong, and San Francisco, arriving in Jersey City, New Jersey, as a timer called out seventy-two days, six hours, ten minutes, and eleven seconds.

Ida Wells-Barnett, daughter of a freed slave, entered the news business as a freelancer, writing for a church paper about her lawsuit against a train conductor who tried to make her move into a segregated railroad car. As editor of a small paper in Memphis, *The Free Speech and Headlight,* she denounced the lynching in 1892 of three black grocers. Her newspaper was ransacked and her life threatened. She moved to New York and later Chicago but remained a vigorous voice against lynching.

These women remained the exceptions rather than the rule. A few women covered trials and became known as "sob sisters" for their evocative portrayals. Others left the country in order to succeed. **Dorothy Thompson,** who was educated at Syracuse University, sailed for Europe in 1920 and freelanced (literally writing for free) until she did so many articles for the *Philadelphia Public Ledger* that it hired her as its correspondent. She had a knack for being where the story was, and by 1924 was Berlin bureau chief, covering the political and economic life of the Weimar Republic created after Germany's loss in World War I. The harsh conditions that the western allies had imposed on Germany contributed to the downfall of that republic and to the rise of Adolf Hitler, whom Thompson interviewed and considered "inconsequent and voluble." Soon, however, she decided that he would be the next dictator and started warning the West about fascism. Expelled from Germany, Thompson later became a leading columnist for *The New York Herald-Tribune,* so noted and controversial that she even became a subject for *New Yorker* cartoons. She was married for a turbulent period to Nobel Prize–winning author **Sinclair Lewis.**

Katherine Beebe Pinkham Harris was one of the rare reporters who did not have to work on the women's pages. Starting her journalistic career with the *Oakland Tribune* in the 1920s, she later worked for the Associated Press bureau in San Francisco, where she received choice outside assignments, such as covering the general strike, because the men were uncomfortable having her in the messy bureau. "You'll have to get used to seeing me without my coat on," the bureau chief said.

What were the stages of major advancement for women in the newsroom?

Eleanor Roosevelt helped create the first breakthrough. As First Lady, she made news. Through her friendship with Associated Press reporter **Lorena Hickok,** she knew that women were often the first fired as newspapers trimmed their staffs during the Depression in the early 1930s. Roosevelt announced that only women could cover her news conferences and trips—and she went to coal mines and schools and farms as Americans tried to restore their economy. Local newspapers and Washington bureaus therefore had to have at least one woman on their staffs.

World War II spread the opportunity to help cover and edit the news to women all over the country. Just as wartime created Rosie the Riveter, there was Rosie the Reporter as well. As men went into military service, women filled their spots in the newsroom. They became city editors, copy editors, Washington reporters—even sportswriters. Some women even landed overseas assignments. **Ruth Cowan Nash** of the Associated Press rode with French troops to report on the Battle of the Bulge, and **Marguerite Higgins** arrived at Dachau concentration camp before its liberators and later shared the 1951 Pulitzer Prize for coverage of the Korean War. **Flora Lewis** made it to London just after World War II had ended in Europe but stayed on and became a *New York Times* correspondent and columnist. These women were the exceptions. Most were fired or quit voluntarily when the war ended, whether or not men returned to take their jobs. They had no choice; most had signed an agreement to leave in order to get the job in the first place.

Despite having doors closed in their faces, a few newcomers made it at news organizations in the 1940s and 1950s. Often, the only jobs available for them were on the women's pages. Those who were determined to cover politics or courts or to write features managed by sheer persistence to move to the sections of the paper that the male editors took seriously. Others worked on revising the women's sections themselves, covering news that concerned women about education or economics, health or households. Their sections became the early models for the evolution of women's pages into today's lifestyle sections.

The third turning point in the making of the modern female reporter occurred in the 1960s. More women were graduating from college by the early 1960s, and more women turned to law, medicine, business—and journalism—for careers. In addition, young men's draft status worked against them as the United States built up its forces in Vietnam, so some of their female college classmates got newspaper jobs. Few African-American women and fewer Latino, Asian-American, or Native American women moved into the media in this period. **Marvel Cooke,** who had worked for the *Amsterdam News,* a paper based in Harlem, during the 1930s and 1940s, became one of the first black women hired by a white-run newspaper, in the late 1940s, while **Dorothy Gilliam** came from the black press in Louisville to *The Washington Post* in 1961. In the segregated Washington of that era, there were few restaurants where she could eat lunch.

—Those women who had made it into the newsrooms began to see their careers stunted, their ambitions to go overseas thwarted, or their hope denied to earn what men of comparable experience and talent were being paid. So they sued *The New York Times* in 1974 and the Associated Press in 1978. Others filed complaints at the Equal Employment Opportunity Commission against *The Washington Post;* still others sued *Newsday* and the *Detroit News.* License challenges were leveled against a number of network-owned television stations. Women's caucuses sat in at the offices of *Ladies' Home Journal,* and women at *Newsweek* protested that they were always researchers, never reporters. While few of the women who brought the suits benefited appreciably—and some had their careers seriously blighted—they nonetheless opened the doors for many of the young women who cover national politics and foreign affairs or write popular columns today.

Why did Helen Thomas of United Press International call the National Press Club balcony "purdah"?

The National Press Club, established in Washington in 1908, long reigned as the premier gathering spot for reporters to hear dignitaries visiting Washington. It was also the main afterwork watering hole for the journalists whose offices were concentrated in the National Press Building. There were few women in the press corps, and so little need was perceived to admit them to Press Club membership.

As more women became reporters and worked their way to Washington, they, too, wanted to ask their questions at lunch with the bigwigs. At first, they couldn't attend the luncheons at all. In 1955, they were allowed in but confined to a small balcony overlooking the main dining room—farther away from phones to call in their stories. They were also unable to ask any questions. United Press International's **Helen Thomas** had to cover speeches by important men—and they were always *men*— from the balcony, so she called it "purdah," after the Muslim and Hindu practice of secluding women from men's sight.

The women fought back. They asked questions about various private clubs' discriminatory policies at presidential news conferences and were not taken seriously by chief executives like **Dwight D. Eisenhower,** nor at first by **John F. Kennedy.**

They cabled foreign leaders preparing to visit Washington, asking them to decline to speak at the National Press Club. Some, including Soviet Premier **Nikita Khrushchev** on his 1959 trip, complied. Slowly, the club leadership relented—letting the women eat lunch in one dining room by 1963. But they still couldn't use the Men's Bar. By 1969, they could attend the luncheons but had to leave within half an hour. They still couldn't be members.

Finally, by 1970, the club took a vote by mail on admitting women. The proposal lost. The women had allies within the male club membership who thought the old policy hopelessly antiquated and proposed a decision by those present and voting in January 1971. They heard arguments that women wouldn't want to join, that there might be "unpleasant incidents," that the golf tournament would be ruined (remember, these were grown-up journalists and it was 1971). Said one: "We are not discriminating against them. We want our club as it is."

The final vote was 227 to 56 in favor of admitting women. Many of the journalists, male and female, then went off to the Men's Bar for a victory drink.

Milestones: Fighting Sex Discrimination at *The New York Times*

The lawsuit: Boylan v. *The New York Times* charged the newspaper with discriminating against women in hiring, pay, and promotions. The suit also claimed that the newspaper made prestigious assignments on the basis of sex. Newspaper management denied all charges.

The plaintiffs: **Betsy Wade Boylan** (listed first, and thus the case bore her name), then head of the foreign copy desk; accountant **Louise Carini;** reporter **Joan Cook;** advertising telephone solicitor **Nancy Davis;** reporter **Grace Glueck;** Washington reporter **Eileen Shanahan;** and **Andrea Skinner,** news clerk.

Date filed: November 7, 1974, following a complaint to the Equal Employment Opportunity Commission in 1972 and 1973. On April 11, 1977, a U.S. district judge granted the plaintiffs' request to broaden the case into a class-action suit representing an additional 545 women.

Settled: October 6, 1978, on the eve of trial.

Outcome: The *Times* agreed to a stepped-up affirmative action program, applying to top jobs for the first time, and agreed to $233,500 in back pay for 550 women. **Harriet Rabb,** the women's attorney, pointed out at the time of settlement that in 1970 and 1971, the years immediately before the first complaint, only 6 percent (2 out of 29) of the editors and reporters hired by the *Times* were women. A year after formal charges had been filed, 47 percent of the reporters and editors hired—or 9 out of 19—were female.

Nevertheless, by 1986, when **A. M. Rosenthal** retired as executive editor, there were still no women's names among his likely successors and no women named in the first round of promotions that followed **Max Frankel**'s appointment to Rosenthal's job. By 1993, **Soma Golden** had been named assistant managing editor, joining **Carolyn Lee** as the only women on the newsside masthead; **Linda Mathews** succeeded Golden as national editor. **Rebecca Sinkler** was editor of the Book Review, and **Nancy Newhouse** was Sunday travel editor.

Commentary: **Anna Quindlen** of *The New York Times,* speaking at an anniversary celebration of the lawsuit: "Tonight, I just want to say thank you. I want to say thank you not to Abe Rosenthal, not to Max Frankel, but to a small devoted cadre of women—and I'm not sure I would have had the guts to be one of them—who made it possible for me to have eleven very good years at *The New York Times.*"

Why would any self-respecting female sports reporter want to go into a steamy locker room full of sweaty, half-clothed or naked men?

Media management didn't want women in their newsrooms, and once women were there they found that baseball and football teams didn't want them in their locker rooms, either. Women on sports assignments must catch players for interviews immediately after a game in order to meet their deadlines and to learn about strategy or injuries that may not have shown up on television. So, eyes forward, into the locker room they went as men emerged from their showers and dressed to leave the stadium.

At the 1977 World Series, baseball commissioner **Bowie Kuhn** decided that **Melissa Ludtke** of *Sports Illustrated* couldn't go into the Los Angeles Dodgers locker room. A majority of the Dodgers had voted to let Ludtke in, if she needed to be there, but the commissioner's office rescinded that permission. She sued. She won, but too late to do any good for that World Series. Each woman who came new to the sports beat still risked hostility. In 1990, a celebrated incident in which nude football players harassed *Boston Herald* reporter **Lisa Olson** in the New England Patriots locker room led to an investigation by National Football League commissioner **Paul Tagliabue** and fines for the players involved.

Milestones: Pulitzer Prize-Winning Women

Pulitzer Prizes have been awarded each year since 1917 in the name of editor **Joseph Pulitzer,** one of the founders of the Graduate School of Journalism at Columbia University. The first woman receiving a prize—**Minna Lewinson**—won not a journalistic award but one for newspaper history that she shared in 1918 with **Henry**

Beetle Hough for their history of the American press's services to the public.

Other women first to win in each category:

For reporting, at edition time: **Mrs. Caro Brown** of the Alice, Texas, *Daily Echo,* in 1955, for stories on one-man rule in Duval County.

For reporting, no edition time: **Miriam Ottenberg** of the Washington, D.C., *Evening Star,* in 1960, for stories on a used-car racket.

For correspondence: **Anne O'Hare McCormick,** of *The New York Times,* 1937, for reporting from Europe.

For national reporting: **Lucinda Franks,** of United Press International, sharing the 1971 award with **Thomas Powers** for reporting on the life and death of revolutionary Diana Oughton.

For international reporting: **Marguerite Higgins** of the *New York Herald Tribune,* sharing the 1951 award with five other reporters for coverage of the Korean War.

For editorial writing: **Hazel Brannon Smith** of the *Lexington Advertiser,* Lexington, Mississippi, 1964, for courageous editorials despite community pressure and opposition.

For editorial cartooning: **Signe Wilkinson,** *Philadelphia Daily News,* 1992.

For photography: **Mrs. Walter M. Schau,** a California amateur, 1954, for a photo of a thrilling rescue published in *The Akron Beacon Journal* and distributed by the Associated Press.

For commentary: **Mary McGrory,** of the *Washington Star,* 1975.

For criticism: **Ada Louise Huxtable,** of *The New York Times,* 1970.

For feature writing: **Madeleine Blais,** of the *Miami Herald,* 1980.

Who was considered the dean of women broadcast journalists?

Few women broadcast news on the radio when **Pauline Frederick** (1906?–1990) began her career, making her first appearance in 1939. She went on to cover the United Nations for several decades, becoming a pioneer for women again in television newscasting.

Born in Gallitzin, Pennsylvania, Frederick reported for several newspapers while in high school, then majored in political science at American University, where she received a master's degree in international law. Women were not being hired by newspapers or radio stations in the 1930s, but she hit upon the idea of interviewing wives of diplomats and sold the articles to the *Washington Star*. Later she wrote for the North American Newspaper Alliance. Assigned to cover what were considered women's stories, Frederick said later she didn't consider them limited in interest to women because "news is news."

During World War II she did research and wrote scripts for NBC commentator **H. R. Baukhauge.** She covered the Nuremberg war trials in Germany as a freelancer, getting on the air only once because the regular male reporter wasn't present. **Edward R. Murrow** considered her manner and her material "not ... particularly distinguished," so she was turned down for a job at CBS News.

Stringing for ABC News, she rarely got on the air because she was told women's voices were not sufficiently authoritative. Finally she worked her way into a regular assignment covering the United Nations as an ABC staff member in 1948. She studied issues and cultivated sources diligently and was assigned to help cover the first nationally televised political convention in 1948 (although she had to do her own makeup and that of the women guests, such as Margaret Truman). Hired away from ABC by NBC in 1953, Frederick covered U.N. activity in connection with the Korean War, the Middle East, the Cuban missile crisis, and Vietnam for that network for twenty-one years. Again, she was a pioneer because few women did television news until the Federal Communications Commission required local stations to hire and promote women (and minorities) and make regular reports to the government on their progress. Frederick was the first woman elected president of the United Nations Correspondents Association.

She had to retire at sixty-five in 1974, but provided commentary on National Public Radio for the next five years. In 1976, she added another "first" to her string of accomplishments, becoming the first woman to moderate a presidential campaign debate. She died in 1990.

Where have all the female network anchors been?

In 1976, ABC paid **Barbara Walters** $1 million to co-anchor its evening network newscast with **Harry Reasoner** and do four special broadcasts a year. The pairing lasted a year and a half but was always chilly at best because of Reasoner's reputation as a sexist and because of publicity over what seemed a blurring between news and entertainment in paying Walters. **Diane Sawyer** and others anchored weekend news programs or filled in for vacationing male anchors, and women were mainstays on local news broadcasts, but there were no permanent female anchors on the weekday network evening news programs until **Connie Chung** moved onto "CBS Evening News" with **Dan Rather** in June 1993.

Born in the United States, Chung is the youngest daughter of a former Chinese diplomat and intelligence officer for Chiang Kai-shek. She graduated from the University of Maryland and started her television career as a part-time clerk at a local station in Washington, D.C., while she was still in college. Hired as a newsroom secretary after graduation in 1969, she soon became a writer and then a reporter. She moved to CBS in 1971. Chung was the first Asian-American reporter on network television, covering hearings on Capitol Hill, the presidential campaign of Senator George McGovern, and the Watergate affair. Later she anchored the news for the CBS-owned station in Los Angeles, and at one point she and **Marcia Brandwynne** were the first major-market, all-female anchor team in the country. She worked at NBC before returning to CBS in 1989 to do special interview programs before being named co-anchor with Rather.

The question remains whether women can follow the example of **Walter Cronkite,** that is, staying in their prominent jobs as they grow older. **Marlene Sanders,** whose pinch-hitting at ABC in 1964 earned her the distinction of being the first woman ever to anchor the evening news, told the *Los Angeles Times* at the time of Chung's debut, "I'll know women have succeeded in TV news when there's a woman on the air who looks like David Brinkley."

Why didn't the Equal Rights Amendment win ratification?

The campaign to ratify the Equal Rights Amendment (ERA) to the U.S. Constitution, which ended in defeat three states short of approval in 1982, failed on several levels. Philosophically, the ERA failed to win ratification because the debate concentrated too much on differences that people accepted and not enough on women's disadvantages; politically, it failed because it had shrewd opponents who played on the fears of people who did not want the uncertainty of change.

In 1923, **Alice Paul,** founder of the National Woman's Party (NWP), read the text of an equal rights amendment from the steps of the Presbyterian Church at Seneca Falls, New York, the small town that in 1848 had been the site for the first women's rights convention. Through the next several decades the feminist community remained divided over what form women's equality should take—whether women should acknowledge biological differences and seek legislation that would protect them from abuses in the workplace or whether acknowledging differences would leave women with a weaker legal status. This argument stymied concerted moves toward an equal rights amendment.

The resurgence of women's activism in the 1960s and passage of civil rights and equal pay laws breathed new life into the drive for the amendment. More women were entering the workplace and objecting to the unequal treatment they received. Congress, prodded by Representative **Martha Griffiths,** a Michigan Democrat, completed action on the ERA on March 22, 1972, and sent it to the states for ratification. Within half an hour, Hawaii ratified it. Five other states did so within a week. But ten years later—after one thirty-nine-month extension of the original seven years allotted for ratification, the ERA was dead.

If any one person led the defeat of the ERA, it was **Phyllis Schlafly,** a right-wing attorney who formed STOP-ERA and who drove the amendment's backers nuts during debates on the measure. She distorted the issues but stymied ERA proponents because the truth was far more complicated than the version she presented. Often, her listeners were not ready for the changes that she said ERA would bring.

Combat and toilets figured prominently in the debate over ERA. Opponents said that if the amendment passed, women could be drafted and sent into combat. Proponents had difficulty with this argument, even though the Supreme Court ruled in 1981 that drafting men only was constitutional. ERA backers could also argue that under the War Powers Act, judges would defer to military leadership in decisions on sending women into combat and that military leaders did not want to send women into combat. However, many ERA backers considered that argument to be hedging. Even though many had been active in antiwar movements, they felt women who wanted to serve in the military should have equal opportunity to do so. It followed logically, then, that if there were a draft, women who expected equality should be equally willing to be drafted. Some ERA backers said so.

"Potty politics" should have been easier to handle. ERA opponents said passage of the amendment would force men and women to use the same toilets. The legislative history of ERA clearly showed that regulations based on privacy concerns were exempt. Furthermore, as law professor Deborah Rhode wrote, Schlafly herself survived using unisex toilets on airplane flights traveling to testify against the amendment. The fact that such arguments had to be answered at all indicated that those opposing the amendment consistently determined the terms of the debate.

Just as ERA was beginning the ratification process, the Supreme Court handed down its *Roe v. Wade* decision legalizing abortion in 1973. That further complicated the debate, as did the fact that feminists backed fairer treatment for lesbians. To ensure that lawmakers in states that had not already ratified the ERA made the connection, Schlafly mailed them reports on the 1977 International Women's Year convention in Houston, including its endorsements of the ERA, gay rights, and abortion.

Schlafly's biggest distortion may have been her assertion that if the ERA passed, women would lose their "right" to financial support by their husbands and would have to go to work to provide half the family income. In truth, women had no such right because courts rarely intervened in intact marriages, so women were already at risk. But as Rhode wrote, "Many homemakers were more inclined to reject the messenger than to acknowledge their own vulnerability." Fears of changes in family stability and women's roles that were being debated throughout society played into the hands of the ERA opponents.

The move to stop the ERA also was aided by the difficulty in amending the Constitution. Ratification is required by three-fourths of the states. By 1977, the last state to ratify had done so.

Those who have analyzed the failure of ERA have pointed, however, to lessons learned. Many women became politically active through working on both sides of the issue. ERA backers learned by hard example the need to develop broader grass-roots coalitions and to become involved in the nitty-gritty aspects of politics such as voter registration and redistricting. Finally, wrote Deborah Rhode, the ERA campaign "illustrated the difficulty of achieving informed public analysis of legal issues carrying substantial symbolic freight." People undergoing a fundamental reordering of their lives may not be willing to write those changes into law until well after the fact.

Milestones: Women and the Law

Colonial era into the nineteenth century—The doctrine of coverture prevailed, that is, legally a woman ceased to exist as a separate entity once she married. Her property became her husband's property.

1839 to 1869—Twenty-nine jurisdictions passed laws allowing married women to control their own property, to make contracts, and to retain their own earnings.

1848—Women and men meeting at Seneca Falls, New York, wrote the Declaration of Sentiments, which called for allowing married women to own property and for women's suffrage and other rights.

1868—The Fourteenth Amendment to guarantee citizenship rights for ex-slaves was ratified. Its "due process clause" provided the legal basis for later challenges to discrimination on the basis of race and sex.

1873—In *Bradwell v. Illinois,* the U.S. Supreme Court held that a state law barring women from being lawyers was constitutional. **Myra Bradwell** had passed the state bar examination and edited a legal journal, but she was denied admission to the bar. One justice said that not only did the Fourteenth Amendment not apply in this case but also that "man is, or should be, woman's protector and defender. The natural and proper timidity and delicacy which belongs to the female sex evidently unfits it for many of the occupations of civil life."

1875—The Supreme Court upheld a Missouri law denying women the right to vote.

1908—An Oregon law that limited the working hours of

women was ruled constitutional by the Supreme Court. Attorney **Louis Brandeis,** who later became a justice himself, presented detailed studies on the relationship between long hours of labor and women's health and morals.

1920—The Nineteenth Amendment giving women the vote was ratified.

1923—A minimum-wage law for women was held unconstitutional. The Supreme Court reversed itself in 1937 in a Washington State case, in which an employee sued to have her pay brought to the then-minimum wage of $14.50 for forty-eight hours' work.

1948—A law prohibiting women from working as bartenders unless they were related to the male bar owner was ruled constitutional.

1961—Florida's practice of excluding women from state juries was ruled constitutional. The Supreme Court overturned this decision in a Louisiana case in 1975. Justice **Byron White** wrote then that selection of a jury from a representative cross section of the community "is an essential component of the Sixth Amendment right to a jury trial," and that systematic exclusion of women violated that requirement for a fair cross section.

1963—Congress passed the Equal Pay Act outlawing discrimination in wages on the basis of gender.

1964—Title VII of the Civil Rights Act forbade sex discrimination in employment.

1965—A Connecticut law prohibiting married couples from using contraceptives was ruled unconstitutional in *Griswold v. Connecticut*. **Estelle Griswold,** executive director of the Planned Parenthood League of Connecticut, had been arrested and fined one hundred dollars for giving married couples information about contraception. In his opinion on her case, Justice **William O. Douglas** wrote that marriage was a relationship "lying within the zone of privacy created by several fundamental constitutional guarantees."

1967—President **Lyndon Johnson** issued an executive order forbidding any federal contractor from discriminating on the basis of sex.

1971—The Supreme Court ruled constitutional a law allowing segregation by sex in higher education. In 1982, however, in *Mississippi University for Women v. Hogan,* the court ruled unconstitutional the state's practice of admitting only women to nursing school. In the intervening years, Justice **Sandra Day O'Connor** had joined the court and she wrote the majority opinion. "Rather than compensate for discriminatory barriers faced by women" as the university had contended, its policy "of excluding males from admission to the School of Nursing tends to perpetuate the stereotyped view of nursing as an exclusively woman's job" and helps make that assumption a self-fulfilling prophecy.

—In a case argued by future Supreme Court Justice **Ruth Bader Ginsburg,** *Reed v. Reed,* the court ruled unconstitutional a state law discriminating between men and women as administrators of estates.

1972—Congress passed the Equal Rights Amendment and states began the ratification process. By 1982, after a thirty-nine-month extension of the original seven-year period, thirty-five states had ratified; thirty-eight were needed, so the amendment failed.

—A law prohibiting giving contraceptives to unmarried people was ruled unconstitutional in *Eisenstadt v. Baird.*

—In Title IX of the Education Amendments, Congress forbade sex discrimination by any colleges or universities that received federal money.

1973—In *Roe v. Wade* and *Doe v. Bolton*, the Supreme Court overturned laws prohibiting abortion except in the last trimester of pregnancy.

—A government order prohibiting Help Wanted ads from specifying sex was ruled constitutional.

1974—The Cleveland Board of Education's requirement that teachers leave their jobs when they become five months pregnant was ruled unconstitutional.

—Denying pregnancy disability benefits to workers was upheld in *Geduldig v. Aiello*. In 1975, the court ruled unconstitutional a law denying unemployment compensation to women in the last three months of their pregnancies. But the following year it said that private employers could deny disability benefits to workers who were absent for reasons related to motherhood. In 1978, Congress passed a law forbidding employment discrimination on the grounds of pregnancy.

1976—In *Planned Parenthood v. Danforth*, the Supreme Court struck down most of a Missouri law designed to restrict abortions. In 1977, a Connecticut law denying Medicaid payments for abortions was upheld; in *Harris v. McRae* in 1980 the Supreme Court upheld Congress's ban, through amendments sponsored by Representative **Henry Hyde** (R-Ill.), on paying for abortions through Medicaid. The first of the series of Hyde amendments had passed on September 30, 1976.

1979—The Supreme Court held that the Massachusetts veterans' preference law did not constitute sex discrimination.

—The Supreme Court ruled unconstitutional an Alabama law that only husbands had to pay alimony. The case challenged the basic law of marriage that men had to support women and women had the duty to provide domestic and sexual service to their husbands.

1980—The Equal Employment Opportunity Commission issued guidelines describing sexual harassment as sex discrimination illegal under Title VII of the Civil Rights Act.

1981—A Louisiana law giving husbands the right to dispose of jointly owned property without their wives' consent was declared unconstitutional.

—The Supreme Court held that an Oregon county's practice of paying female jail guards less than male guards violated federal law. However, in 1984, the Ninth Circuit Court of Appeals said that the University of Washington was not guilty of sex discrimination for paying the nursing faculty less than male faculty in other parts of the university. In 1985, the same court, in a decision written by Judge **Anthony Kennedy,** later a member of the Supreme Court, ruled that the state of Washington had not discriminated in the manner in which it paid its female employees despite a study that found wage disparities in jobs of comparable worth. After the union involved asked for a rehearing, the state settled with an agreement that substantially increased the pay for jobs that had been undervalued.

—The Supreme Court upheld the federal law that only men had to register for the military draft.

1983—Three cases in which states or local governments sought to restrict abortions produced mixed results, including a ruling upholding a Virginia law that all abortions after the first trimester of pregnancy must be conducted in a hospital or licensed out-patient clinic.

1984—In *Grove City College v. Bell,* the Supreme Court narrowed the applicability of Title IX to forbid sex discrimination only by college programs that actually received federal funds. Programs elsewhere on a college campus that did not use federal money would no longer be covered. In 1988, Congress passed the Civil Rights Restoration Act reasserting the broader interpretation.

1984—Law firms that discriminated on the grounds of sex in naming partners were found to violate federal law in *Hishon v. King Spaulding.*

1986—An Indianapolis ordinance that selling pornography constituted discrimination against women was ruled unconstitutional on First Amendment grounds. The local law, backed by feminists **Catharine MacKinnon** and **Andrea Dworkin,** was based on the argument that pornography creates a climate that keeps women from functioning freely in their communities.

—The Supreme Court ruled that sexual harassment was discrimination and thus violated federal law. The case, *Meritor Savings Bank v. Mechelle Vinson,* involved a woman who charged that her supervisor not only insisted upon her having sexual intercourse with him, he also fondled her in front of other employees and followed her into the women's restroom. The case left unsettled the degree of employers' liability.

—The Supreme Court upheld a Georgia law criminalizing sodomy. The decision undermined homosexuals' contention that private sexual behavior was protected by privacy rights.

1987—In *California Federal Savings and Loan v. Guerra,* the Supreme Court upheld a California law requiring that employers grant as much as four months' unpaid disability leave to new mothers—and hold jobs for them.

—The Supreme Court said that employers could take the sex of a qualified applicant into consideration for promotions in voluntary affirmative action plans. The case had been brought by a California man passed over when a woman was hired for a county dispatcher's job.

—In a New York State case, the Supreme Court ruled that large private clubs that served meals and where members conducted business could not discriminate against potential members on grounds of sex or race.

1988—The New Jersey Supreme Court awarded custody of "Baby M" to **William** and **Elizabeth Stern** instead of **Mary Beth Whitehead,** who had been a surrogate mother, giving birth to the baby for ten thousand dollars.

1989—With four justices calling for repeal of *Roe v. Wade,* the Supreme Court upheld a Missouri law sharply restricting abortion. But Sandra Day O'Connor, who voted with the 5–4 majority, said *Roe v. Wade* remained intact. The case, *Webster v. Reproductive Health Services,* provided momentum for states to try to restrict abortion further.

—Price Waterhouse accounting firm failed to promote **Ann Hopkins** to partner although she had brought more business to the firm than any fellow candidates for promotion. She sued, and the Supreme Court ruled that the burden of proof was on employers charged with discrimination once the employee presented evidence of biased treatment. "It takes no special training to discern sex stereotyping in a description of an aggressive female employee as requiring 'a course at charm school,' " the court said.

1990—The Supreme Court upheld an Ohio law requiring pregnant teenagers to notify one parent before having an abortion or to get a judge to allow them to bypass this step. It struck down part of a Minnesota law requiring notification of both parents, but said that requirement was acceptable if a teenager could get a judicial waiver instead.

—The Supreme Court found that a government request for university records in a tenure case at the Wharton School of Business at the University of Pennsylvania did not violate the First Amendment. The case was important for women and minorities claiming that discrimination led to their denial of tenure.

1991—The Supreme Court ruled that companies could not exclude women of child-bearing age from jobs involving exposure to potentially harmful toxic substances. The case was brought against the nation's largest auto-battery manufacturer, Johnson Controls. Justice **Harry Blackmun** wrote that Title VII "does not prevent the employer from having a conscience. The statute, however, does prevent sex-specific fetal-protection policies."

—The court ruled acceptable a government regulation barring clinics receiving federal family planning money from counseling about abortion or providing abortion referrals. Doctors argued the rule violated their First Amendment rights.

—A U.S. District Court judge ruled that Virginia Military Institute (VMI) did not have to admit women. He wrote that single-gender schooling "adds a measure of diversity to Virginia's overall system of education that would be missing if VMI were coeducational." A federal appeals court later ordered VMI to provide coeducation but said the school could do so by creating a parallel military-training program at a women's school.

—Congress passed a new Civil Rights Act that broadened protections for women, minorities, and the disabled after adverse court decisions had shifted the burden of proof. The new law provided that those who proved sex discrimination could receive financial damages, and it established a Glass Ceiling Commission to try to reduce barriers to advancement by women and minorities.

1992—In *Planned Parenthood of Southeastern Pennsylvania v. Casey,* the Supreme Court upheld *Roe v. Wade* but also said that some restrictions on abortion were constitutional because of the state's "compelling interest" in potential human life. The restrictions allowed in this case were similar to those held unconstitutional in 1986 and the ruling, coming in the midst of a presidential campaign, highlighted the precariousness of *Roe v. Wade.* But it also showed that the court was more middle-of-the-road on this issue than many had predicted.

1993—Sexual harassment in the workplace can be harmful even if its victim hasn't suffered so severely that she had a nervous breakdown, the Supreme Court ruled in *Harris v. Forklift Systems.*

—Congress passed—and President **Bill Clinton** signed—the Family and Medical Leave Act, giving employees in companies with fifty or more workers as much as twelve weeks unpaid leave for the birth of a child or a close family member's illness.

—**Shannon Faulkner** sued The Citadel after her admission was revoked when the South Carolina military college discovered she was female. She was allowed to attend classes but could not wear the cadet uniform pending the case's outcome.

1994—In a case that involved discrimination against a man, the Supreme Court ruled that equal protection laws barred preemptive challenges of jurors on the basis of sex, holding that gender, like race, should not be a determinant of competence.

What paths did Sandra Day O'Connor and Ruth Bader Ginsburg travel to become Supreme Court justices?

Sandra Day O'Connor (b. 1930) and **Ruth Bader Ginsburg** (b. 1933) have more in common than one might think, given their appointment by presidents with distinctly different philosophies, **Ronald Reagan** and **Bill Clinton.** Both graduated high in their classes from law school in an era when few women were encouraged to enter the profession. Neither could get the kind of job she sought after graduation because of being female. One helped make laws through the legislature and the other as a legal advocate. Both became appellate judges before nomination to the high court.

O'Connor was born in El Paso, Texas, and grew up on her parents' ranch in southeastern Arizona. She learned early to drive a truck and a tractor as well as how to do ranch chores, ride horseback, and shoot. Deciding that the schools in their ranch's area were not adequate for their bright daughter, the Days sent Sandra to live with her grandmother in El Paso for school. Later, she attended Stanford University, majoring in economics. As a senior, she took several law courses, liked them, applied to the selective law school, and was admitted. There she met her future husband, **John O'Connor,** as well as classmate **William Rehnquist,** future Chief Justice of the Supreme Court.

Graduating third in her class of 102 (Rehnquist ranked first), O'Connor went job hunting. Gibson, Dunn and Crutcher, a leading Los Angeles firm, offered her a job—as a legal secretary. She turned that down and worked instead as a deputy attorney for San Mateo County in northern California, advising local agencies such as the police and fire departments. Later, while raising her three sons in Phoenix, where the O'Connors had moved, she was active in local Republican Party committee work. In 1965, she returned to full-time work as an assistant attorney general representing state agencies. In 1969, the Arizona governor appointed her to fill a vacancy in the state senate. She soon won election in her own right and served five years in the senate, becoming its majority leader in 1973. During this period, she supported the Equal Rights Amendment, which failed to win passage in Arizona; she also engineered passage of change in the law that had said that husbands controlled all property of a married couple. In 1974, O'Connor ran successfully for a post as a trial judge on the Maricopa County Superior Court, and in 1979 Governor **Bruce Babbitt,** a Democrat, named her to the Arizona Court of Appeals. At a conference on women in the Constitution in 1988, Kansas State University scholar Orma Linford reported that O'Connor's legislative and state and local judicial experiences gave rise to two guiding principles: "respect for the products of the legislative process" and rejection "of the notion that federal judges are somehow better than state judges."

When nominated for the Supreme Court in 1981, O'Connor faced opposition from antiabortion groups that felt she was not staunchly in their corner. Yet she said she personally opposed abortion. "I'm not going to be pregnant anymore," she said, explaining that perhaps that made it easier to hold that position. Under persistent questioning from conservatives on the Senate Judiciary Committee, she declined to make any prejudgments on the issue. She was confirmed on a 99–0 vote by the Senate.

O'Connor's court record in the field of sex discrimination is uneven, but more often than not she has voted for the person charging the discrimination. Writing for the majority in *Mississippi University for Women v. Hogan,* she argued strongly against sex stereotyping in a case that involved a man whose application had been rejected by the school of nursing. The school's rule barring male applicants, O'Connor wrote, "lends credibility to the old view that women, not men, should become nurses." In November 1993, O'Connor wrote for a unanimous court in the case of *Harris v. Forklift Systems* that those charging sexual harassment need not prove psychological injury to collect damages. Federal law, she said, "comes into play before the harassing conduct leads to a nervous breakdown."

Born in Brooklyn, Ruth Bader Ginsburg was encouraged toward independence and achievement by her mother, who had been unable to attend college because she had to work to put her brother through school. Her mother died of cervical cancer the day before Ruth's high school graduation. She excelled at Cornell University, where she met her future husband. First **Martin Ginsburg** went to Harvard Law School, then after the birth of their daughter, Ruth did. One of nine women in a class of four hundred, she suffered the indignities of the day, such as being called on in class for supposed comic relief and discovering that not all sections of the library were open to her. When her husband got a job in New York, she transferred to Columbia University Law School, graduating first in her class in 1959.

Like O'Connor, Ginsburg applied for jobs at law firms but only two interviewed her; neither would hire her. As she wrote later, "In the Fifties, the traditional law firms were just beginning to turn around on hiring Jews. But to be a woman, a Jew and a mother to boot—that combination was a bit too much." She clerked for U.S. District Court Judge **Edmund L. Palmieri,** then taught law at Rutgers and became the first female law professor at Columbia University School of Law in 1972. She worked *pro bono* for the American Civil Liberties Union's Women's Rights Project, arguing six cases before the Supreme Court and winning five. Later she was appointed to the U.S. Appeals Court in Washington.

At a Rose Garden ceremony at which her Supreme Court nomination was announced, Ginsburg said that she hoped her selection would move the country toward "the end of the days when women, at least half the talent pool in our society, appear in high places only as one-at-a-time performers." She paid tribute to her mother as well, saying, "I pray that I may be all that she would have been had she lived in an age when women could aspire and achieve and daughters are cherished as much as sons."

In one of the first legal arguments that she heard as a new justice, Ginsburg tried to bring clarity to the attempt to define sexual harassment in the *Harris v. Forklift Systems* case. Couldn't such harassment simply be defined as conduct based on the sex of an employee that makes it more difficult for one person than another to perform a job? "Is it really more complex?" she asked. "The terms and conditions of employment are not equal if one person is being called names and the other isn't." If "one sex has to put up with something that the other sex doesn't have to put up with," that could prove sexual harassment, she said. Ginsburg concurred with O'Connor's opinion when it was issued a month later.

In 1988, while Ginsburg was still a federal Court of Appeals judge in Washington, she was asked about O'Connor's influence on the Supreme Court. "O'Connor is a daily reminder [to her fellow justices]," Ginsburg replied, "that women are people who can think—that paternalistic care for one's wife or daughter is no longer the only way women want to be treated."

Why did Anita Hill's charge of sexual harassment reverberate so loudly?

Anita F. Hill, a law professor at the University of Oklahoma, told Senate Judiciary Committee investigators in September 1991 that the man President **George Bush** had nominated for the U.S. Supreme Court—**Clarence Thomas**—had harassed her while both worked at the Department of Education and then at the Equal Employment Opportunity Commission. Initially, the Judiciary Committee, conducting confirmation hearings for the court appointee, paid little attention to the charge. However, when it leaked to National Public Radio and *Newsday,* women across the country bombarded the Senate with demands that Hill be heard. Seven women from the House of Representatives stormed up the Senate steps and insisted on being heard by the Democratic caucus. They were not allowed into the meeting; the only woman present was the lone female Senate Democrat, **Barbara Mikulski** of Maryland. It was clear from the initial reactions of many U.S. senators (**Alan Simpson** of Wyoming called it "this sexual harassment crap") that they didn't "get it," that they did not understand the sensitivity among women to the issue.

After dithering for several days, the committee relented and called Hill as a witness. She testified that while she worked for Thomas, he not only pressed her to go out with him but also described pornography to her, talked about the size of his penis, and made other offensive remarks. Thomas refused to address the specific charges and angrily denounced the proceedings as a "high-tech lynching." Hill, described by associates as a conservative who had supported the failed Supreme Court nomination of **Robert Bork,** appeared unflappable as she was asked repeatedly about the nature of the harassment and why she had not reported it and had continued working for Thomas. Other witnesses said that she had told them about the harassment as early as 1982 and that was why she had left the government. The atmosphere was supercharged because of the element of race. African-Americans found themselves divided over supporting one of their own for the nation's highest court or believing a woman who said she had faced circumstances with which many women were familiar.

Equally provocative as the charges, in many women's eyes, was the questioning by an all-male panel at best indifferent and uninformed on the nature of sexual harassment and at worst hostile and hectoring. The senators backing Thomas attacked Hill's character and speculated that she had fantasized the harassment. She stood her ground but had no strong defenders on the panel, which included Senator **Edward M. Kennedy** of Massachusetts, a liberal whose own reputation because of the death of **Mary Jo Kopechne** years earlier in questionable circumstances rendered him virtually silent.

Whatever the truth of the charges—and many women quickly sported buttons saying, "I Believe Anita Hill"—the hearings dramatized women's lack of political presence in the U.S. Senate. Women's political organizations and individual women decided to try to put more women in the Senate. **Lynne Wolsey** in Pennsylvania challenged **Arlen Specter,** one of Hill's harshest questioners, who was up for reelection the following fall. She lost. **Carol Moseley Braun,** then controller in Chicago, decided while watching the hearings to run for the Illinois Senate seat and knocked off incumbent **Alan Dixon** in the primary. In the fall 1992 elections she won, becoming the first African-

American woman in the Senate. **Patty Murray,** who described herself as a mom in tennis shoes, also became a candidate as a direct result of the Hill–Thomas hearings and was elected from Washington State. Both **Barbara Boxer** and **Dianne Feinstein** capitalized on the anger and feelings of powerlessness that surfaced as a result of the hearings during their successful 1992 U.S. Senate campaigns in California.

Why have women in the White House always been First Ladies, not Commanders in Chief?

A century apart—in 1872 and 1972—two women campaigned for the presidency. Neither candidacy had a chance to succeed. The first, because the candidate was an Equal Rights Party candidate, **Victoria Woodhull,** in an era in which women decidedly did not have equal rights. In fact, they didn't even have the right to vote. The second, because the candidate was an outspoken African-American woman, Congresswoman **Shirley Chisholm,** who lacked broad-based support in a political world still dominated by white males. She was unable to secure her party's nomination. Senator **Margaret Chase Smith** of Maine had actually been the first woman to contend for a major party nomination, vying unsuccessfully on the Republican side in 1964. Only one woman has ever carried a major party's nomination for vice president—Democrat **Geraldine Ferraro** in 1984—and none has been elected.

Victoria Woodhull (1838–1927), the child of a medicine-show operator, was a spiritualist who claimed both clairvoyancy and the right "to love whomever I may . . . to change that love every day if I please." She mounted her unsuccessful presidential campaign in 1872. A stockbroker and editor of a wide-ranging weekly reform newsletter, Woodhull had become the darling of the national women's suffrage leadership only a year earlier. She had argued before the House Judiciary Committee that no constitutional amendment was necessary to give women the right to vote because women already had the franchise under the Fourteenth and Fifteenth Amendments, passed at the end of the Civil War, then less than a decade earlier. Eventually, Woodhull's emphasis on free love and her self-aggrandizing courtship of the press cost her the support of suffragist **Susan B. Anthony.** Her presidential campaign, the creation of an Equal Rights Party that she had established, quickly faltered as financial supporters withdrew.

Shirley Chisholm (b. 1924) began her political career in the 1950s in the state legislature in New York. In 1969, she became the first black woman ever elected to the U.S. Congress. Either revered or feared, this Brooklyn-based politician billed herself as *Unbought and Unbossed,* writing an outspoken autobiography of that title. An advocate of the poor, Chisholm sought fairer wages for domestic workers and improved education and employment programs. She mounted a quixotic attempt to secure the Democratic presidential nomination in 1972, doomed to fail because she had never been the type to do the politicking within her party that any potential nominee needed to do. She served in the House until 1982. In 1993, President Clinton nominated her to be ambassador to Jamaica, but she had to withdraw because of an eye ailment.

Who was the first female member of Congress?

Jeannette Rankin (1880–1973) was elected to the U.S. House of Representatives in 1916 after working in campaigns for women's suffrage in her home state of Montana as well as Washington State, New York, California, and Ohio. She campaigned on a platform calling for women's suffrage nationally, an eight-hour day for working women, and prohibition. She had the distinction of being the only member of Congress to vote against American entry into both World War I and World War II, her first vote coming only four days after she entered Congress. She served only the one term in the first quarter of the century, then lobbied and organized for the National Consumers' League and the Women's International League for Peace and Freedom. She was elected again to Congress in 1940, just in time to be the sole dissenting vote in the declaration of war against Japan after the bombing of Pearl Harbor.

Who were the nation's first female governors?

Nellie Tayloe Ross of Wyoming and **Miriam Amanda "Ma" Ferguson** of Texas were elected as the nation's first female governors in 1924. Ross succeeded her husband, who had died. "Ma" Ferguson was the more controversial because she had run for office after impeachment and conviction of her husband, Texas Governor **Jim Ferguson.** Running on a slogan of "Two Governors for the Price of One," "Ma" Ferguson appealed to the common people of Texas and was an ardent foe of the Ku Klux Klan. She ran unsuccessfully for nomination to a second term in 1926 but was elected and served again from 1932 to 1934 as a strong supporter of President **Franklin D. Roosevelt.**

By 1993, there was another woman governor of Texas—**Ann Richards,** victor in both bitter primary and general elections in 1990—and the first female governor of New Jersey, **Christine Todd Whitman,** as well as women governors of Oregon (**Barbara Roberts**) and Kansas (**Joan Finney**). In the intervening seventy years, women had been governors of only seven other states: Alabama, Arizona, Connecticut, Kentucky, Nebraska, Vermont, and Washington.

Why was 1992 "The Year of the Woman" in politics?

Tripling the number of women in the U.S. Senate in the 1992 election sounds better than it was because only two women—Republican **Nancy Kassebaum** of Kansas and Democrat **Barbara Mikulski** of Maryland—already were senators. But women had never before made such a breakthrough; they also significantly increased their numbers in the House of Representatives, going from twenty-nine to forty-eight female members. The new senators included the first African-American woman, **Carol Moseley Braun** of Illinois. Among the new House members were the first Mexican-American and Puerto Rican women. The gains occurred because many House seats were open following reapportionment, because women had learned political fund-raising skills, because women had served in state offices to build up experience, and because many voters were angry at the U.S. Senate Judiciary Committee's handling of **Anita Hill**'s charges of sexual harassment against Supreme Court nominee **Clarence Thomas.**

Women didn't emerge from nowhere to serve in these numbers in 1992. Ever since **Jeannette Rankin**'s election in 1916, they had been gravitating, often in infinitesimal numbers, toward Washington. Among the key figures:

Margaret Chase Smith succeeded her husband in the House of Representatives in 1940, but she was hardly a novice politician. She had been a Republican state committeewoman from Maine's Somerset County and president of the statewide Federation of Business and Professional Women's Clubs before her marriage. She worked as her husband's secretary until he died in 1940. Elected to the U.S. Senate in 1948, she issued a famous "declaration of conscience" challenging her party to renounce Senator **Joseph McCarthy**'s infringements on free speech and association. A woman of many political firsts, she became half of the first all-female Senate contest in Maine in 1960 when former schoolteacher **Lucy Cormier** was her Democratic opponent. Smith won then and again in 1966 but was defeated in 1972.

Attorney **Martha Griffiths** was elected twice to the Michigan legislature and, starting in 1955, served twenty years in the U.S. House of Representatives. A leading congressional advocate for an equal rights amendment for women, she was responsible for changing the wording of the 1964 Civil Rights Act so that sex discrimination was banned along with that against race, religion, color, or national origin. She also worked for improved pensions for widows. After her congressional service, she was elected to two terms as lieutenant governor of Michigan.

A founder of Women's Strike for Peace, New York City attorney **Bella Abzug** was elected to Congress in 1970 as an activist against the Vietnam War. Almost immediately she introduced a resolution calling for U.S. troops to be withdrawn from Vietnam within six months. Abzug, a founder of the National Women's Political Caucus, served for six years.

Barbara Jordan, a Texas Democrat, may have served only three terms in Congress, but her voice has resonated in history because of her forceful presentation during the House Judiciary Committee hearings about impeaching President **Richard M. Nixon.** She had been a state legislator from Houston when she was elected to Congress in 1972. In 1976, she gave the keynote address at the Democratic National Convention. After leaving Congress, she taught at the University of Texas.

The dean of the congressional women by 1993 was **Patricia Schroeder** of Colorado, elected in 1972. She helped establish the Congressional Caucus on Women's Issues in 1977 and became an expert on women's economic and health concerns. She was the lead sponsor of the Family and Medical Leave Bill, signed in 1993 by President **Bill Clinton.** Schroeder rose in seniority on the House Armed Services Committee, advocating that America's allies share more of the military defense burden while also championing women's advancement in the military. In 1987, she explored the possibility of running for president. When she announced she would not run, she shed tears that led to much meaningless blather over whether women were too emotional to be chief executive. Schroeder, who stuck **Ronald Reagan** with the phrase "Teflon president," has always been ready with the good quote. Asked once if she was "running as a woman," she replied, "Do I have a choice?"

The first woman ever elected to the U.S. Senate not as a successor to her husband was Nancy Kassebaum of Kansas, daughter of **Alf Landon,** the Republican candidate swamped by President **Franklin D. Roosevelt**'s landslide reelection in 1936.

Kassebaum, first elected in 1978, became a respected voice in the Senate on foreign affairs. She helped establish the Republican Majority Coalition in 1992 to fight the power of the religious right.

Kassebaum's lone counterpart on the Democratic side of the Senate as the 1992 election approached was Barbara Mikulski of Maryland. The word most frequently used to describe the former Baltimore social worker, city councilwoman, and member of Congress is "feisty." Daughter of an East Baltimore bakery owner, Mikulski got her political start in a successful fight to block a freeway through her urban immigrant neighborhood. She chaired the Democratic Party's committee that wrote the rules for selecting delegates to the 1972 convention, ran unsuccessfully but well for the U.S. Senate against the popular incumbent **Charles Mathias** in 1974, then won election to the House in 1976. She served ten years, then defeated Republican **Linda Chavez** in a nasty race for the Senate in 1986. She was reelected in 1992 and joined by four new female colleagues, all Democrats. In 1993, Texas Republican **Kay Bailey Hutchison** was elected as the seventh female senator.

Did Hillary Rodham Clinton bring First Ladydom a new look?

Presidential wives have always done more than just wearing those fancy ball gowns we see at the Smithsonian. **John Adams** confided often in his wife **Abigail,** writing her once, "I think women better than men, in general, and I know that you can keep a secret as well as any man whatever." Nonetheless, she became an issue in his reelection campaign in 1800 because critics said she had too much influence over her husband. (The Constitution, it should be noted, contains no mention of presidential wives, and certainly never anticipated presidential husbands; the term First Lady was not used until 1877, when **Lucy Hayes** was so described by a magazine writer.)

Dolley Madison convinced husband James not to move the

nation's Capitol to Philadelphia after it was burned by the British during the War of 1812, but instead to rebuild in Washington. **Sarah Polk** was her husband James's private secretary and principal assistant when he was president. Congress investigated whether **Mary Todd Lincoln,** coming from a Southern family, might have been a spy during the Civil War. Lucy Hayes was called "Lemonade Lucy" because she believed that people should not consume alcoholic beverages and would not allow any—not even wine—to be served at the White House. **Helen Taft,** whose husband **William Howard Taft** was president from 1909 to 1913, sat in on Cabinet meetings, not so much to influence him but to wake him up when he fell asleep. **Edith Wilson,** one of only three women to marry men already serving as president, virtually ran the country when her husband, **Woodrow Wilson,** had a debilitating stroke in 1919 yet did not resign. Critics said that she kept him so isolated that he didn't know how intensely the U.S. Senate disliked the idea of a League of Nations to try to keep the peace after World War I. He wouldn't compromise and the United States never joined. Even **Lou Hoover,** rarely heard from in history, was national president of the Girl Scouts and presided over significant growth for that organization.

Eleanor Roosevelt served as a rallying point for liberal causes as well as a stand-in for her husband, Franklin, as she traveled the country during the Depression, then visited troops during World War II. Activism became more acceptable (at least among some segments of the American population) for First Ladies as a result. Still, **Bess Truman** and **Mamie Eisenhower** played more traditional roles, although President **Harry Truman** insisted that he always consulted Bess on major decisions such as bombing Japan and fighting the Korean War.

In the early 1960s, **Jacqueline Kennedy** showed her flair for restoring the White House historically and supporting the arts, while **Lady Bird Johnson** enhanced the beauty of the nation's capital and many other regions by her emphasis on planting flowers and preserving the environment. Her husband, **Lyndon,** was faced with the candidacy of **Margaret Chase Smith** in 1964—although his real rival was sure to be the conservative

Senator **Barry Goldwater** of Arizona. Johnson claimed that Smith had "misunderstood" his pledge to put more women in federal jobs. "I was referring to an echelon lower than my own," he said in protest.

Pat Nixon was a force of steely quiet behind her husband's controversial political career. **Betty Ford** underwent personal traumas and emerged encouraging increased public attention to breast cancer as well as drug and alcohol addiction. A treatment center was later created in her name. **Rosalynn Carter,** who sometimes sat in on Cabinet meetings with her husband, Jimmy, in the late 1970s, was honorary chair of the President's Commission on Mental Health and the moving force behind its work. She testified before the Senate on its report, which led to increased federal spending on mental health treatment. **Nancy Reagan,** who had been an actress when she met actor **Ronald Reagan,** worked to combat increasing drug use and looked out for her husband's welfare. Run afoul of her, and you were out. She was criticized for buying fancy china for the White House and accepting gifts of designer clothing. **Barbara Bush** had a more grandmotherly image and was considered more popular in some circles than her husband, George. But "Bar" could unleash barbs of her own, for example, when she talked about **Geraldine Ferraro** and said she couldn't use a particular word, but it rhymed with "rich." (Get it?)

With attorney **Hillary Rodham Clinton** working on health care reform, the nation finally faced the debate of a spouse's role when a two-career family enters the executive mansion. Truman once wrote that he hoped someday the true role of the wife of a president—and the contributions she makes—would be evaluated. The evaluation is ongoing; it is a constant one as the world changes beneath our feet.

Acknowledgments

This book relies on the scholarship of dozens of women and men who are writing women back into history. Their works are cited in the list of sources; without them, this book would not exist. My purpose is to bring the gist of this work to you, the reader, in hopes that you will pursue the original studies that interest you.

A few people need special acknowledgment, especially my editor, Deb Brody, because this book was her idea, and my agent, Diane Cleaver.

How many people have thanked Estelle Freedman of Stanford University for guidance with their own work? She started my systematic—and exhilarating—exploration of women's history with two courses years ago and remains a source of great encouragement.

When I first mentioned this book to Elaine Tyler May of the University of Minnesota, she went to her study and started filling my arms with books to read. For similar generous spirit of encouragement, for answers to specific reference questions, and for suggestions on sources or women to include I should also thank Linda Kerber of the University of Iowa; Vicki Ruiz of the Claremont Colleges; Jane Bernard Powers of San Francisco State University; Susan Henry of California State University–Northridge; Beverly Guy-Sheftall of Spelman College; Margaret W. Rossiter of Cornell University; Nell Irvin Painter of

Princeton University; Lois Banner, Bryce Nelson, and Barrie Thorne of the University of Southern California; Stephanie Ridder of George Washington University Law School; Valerie Matsumoto of UCLA; Ruth Fitzpatrick of the Women's Ordination Conference; Donna Lenhoff of the Women's Legal Defense Fund; Ruth Mandel and Susan Carroll of the Center for the American Woman and Politics at Rutgers University; Marianne Alexander of the Public Leadership Education Network; Kathy Bonk and Emily Tynes of the Communications Consortium; Nancy Woodhull and Susan Lowell Butler of the National Women's Hall of Fame; Patricia M. Gormley of the Women's Research and Education Institute; Janet Lundblad of the *Los Angeles Times* editorial library; Juana Kennedy and her book group in Los Angeles; authors Suzanne Gordon and Celia Morris; and attorney Carlisle Herbert.

Then there is moral support—an ear to listen when the going was lonely, a tennis game to play when the body needed exercise, a meal to eat when my soul craved good company. Many friends, both in California and across the country, deserve such thanks and the knowledge that they, too, made this book happen. As did my mother, Mary S. Mills, who so many years ago introduced me to my history and my possibilities.

Sources

General

Lois Banner, *Women in Modern America: A Brief History* (San Diego: Harcourt, Brace, Jovanovich, 1984).

Dorothy M. Brown, *Setting a Course: American Women in the 1920s* (Boston: Twayne Publishers, 1987).

Susan Brownmiller, *Femininity* (New York: Linden Press/Simon & Schuster, 1984).

Toni Carabillo, Judith Meuli, and June Bundy Csida, *Feminist Chronicles, 1953–1993* (Los Angeles: Women's Graphics, 1993).

Flora Davis, *Moving the Mountain: The Women's Movement in America Since 1960* (New York: Simon & Schuster, 1981).

Sara Evans, *Born for Liberty: A History of Women in America* (New York: The Free Press, 1989).

Susan Faludi, *Backlash: The Undeclared War Against American Women* (New York: Crown Publishers, 1991).

Eleanor Flexner, *Century of Struggle: The Woman's Rights Movement in the United States* (New York: Atheneum, 1974).

Cynthia Harrison, *On Account of Sex: The Politics of Women's Issues, 1945–1968* (Berkeley, Calif.: University of California Press, 1988).

Darlene Clark Hine, ed., *Black Women in America: An Historical Encyclopedia* (Brooklyn, N.Y.: Carlson Publishing Inc., 1993).

Toyomi Igus, ed., *Great Women in the Struggle* (New York: Scholastic Inc., 1991).

Edward T. James, ed., Janet Wilson James, assoc. ed., and Paul S. Boyer, assist. ed., *Notable American Women, 1607–1950* (Cambridge, Mass.: Belknap Press, 1971), three volumes.

Alice Rossi, ed., *The Feminist Papers* (New York: Bantam, 1973).

Barbara Sicherman and Carol Hurd Green, eds., *Notable American Women: The Modern Period* (Cambridge, Mass.: Belknap Press, 1980).

Ronald Takaki, *A Different Mirror: A History of Multicultural America* (Boston: Little, Brown, 1993).

————, *Strangers from a Different Shore: The History of Asian Americans* (Boston: Little, Brown, 1989).

Susan Ware, *Holding Their Own: American Women in the 1930s* (Boston: Twayne Publishers, 1982).

Early America

Carol F. Karlsen, *The Devil in the Shape of a Woman: Witchcraft in Colonial New England* (New York: Vintage, 1989).

Linda K. Kerber, *Women of the Republic: Intellect and Ideology in Revolutionary America* (Chapel Hill, N.C.: University of North Carolina Press, 1980).

Edmund S. Morgan, *The Puritan Dilemma: The Story of John Winthrop* (Boston: Little, Brown, 1958).

Mary Beth Norton, *Liberty's Daughters: The Revolutionary Experience of American Women, 1750–1800* (Boston: Little, Brown, 1980).

Laurel Thatcher Ulrich, *A Midwife's Tale: The Life of Martha Ballard, Based on Her Diary, 1785–1812* (New York: Vintage, 1991).

Slavery

Angela Y. Davis, *Women, Race & Class* (New York: Random House, 1981).

Elizabeth Fox-Genovese, *Within the Plantation Household: Black and White Women of the Old South* (Chapel Hill, N.C.: University of North Carolina Press, 1988).

Eugene D. Genovese, *Roll, Jordan, Roll: The World the Slaves Made* (New York: Random House, 1974).

Leon F. Litwack, *Been in the Storm So Long: The Aftermath of Slavery* (New York: Alfred A. Knopf, 1979).

Frontier

Peggy Pascoe, *Relations of Rescue: The Search for Female Moral Authority in the American West, 1874–1939* (New York: Oxford University Press, 1990).

Glenda Riley, *The Female Frontier: A Comparative View of Women on the Prairie and the Plains* (Lawrence, Kans.: University Press of Kansas, 1988).

Joanna Stratton, *Pioneer Women* (New York: Simon & Schuster, 1981).

Work

Rosalyn Baxandall, Linda Gordon, and Susan Reverby, eds., *America's Working Women: A Documentary History—1600 to the Present* (New York: Vintage, 1976).

Susan Bianchi-Sand, "Pay Equity: A Top Concern of Women," *The Professional Communicator,* February–March 1993, pp. 18–21.

Laurie Coyle, Gail Hershatter, and Emily Honig, "Women at Farah: An Unfinished Story," *Mexican Women in the United States: Struggles Past and Present,* edited by Magdalena Mora and Adelaida R. del Castillo (Los Angeles: Chicano Studies Research Center Publications, University of California, Los Angeles, 1980), pp. 117–143.

Sara M. Evans and Barbara J. Nelson, *Wage Justice: Comparable Worth and the Paradox of Technocratic Reform* (Chicago: University of Chicago Press, 1989).

Evelyn Nakano Glenn, *Issei, Nisei, War Bride: Three Generations of Japanese American Women in Domestic Service* (Philadelphia, Pa.: Temple University Press, 1986).

Rosalinda M. Gonzalez, "Chicanas and Mexican Immigrant Families 1920–1940: Women's Subordination and Family Exploitation," *Decades of Discontent: The Women's Movement,*

1920–1940, Lois Scharf and Joan M. Jensen, eds. (Westport, Conn.: Greenwood Press, 1983).

Joan M. Jensen, *With These Hands: Women Working on the Land* (Old Westbury, N.Y.: The Feminist Press, 1981).

Jacqueline Jones, *Labor of Love, Labor of Sorrow: Black Women, Work and the Family, from Slavery to the Present* (New York: Basic Books, 1985).

Lucie K. Kelly, "Nursing," *Encyclopedia Americana* (Danbury, Conn.: Grolier, 1994).

Alice Kessler-Harris, *Out to Work: A History of Wage-Earning Women in the United States* (New York: Oxford University Press, 1982).

Alfredo Mirande and Evangelina Enriquez, eds., *La Chicana: The Mexican-American Woman* (Chicago: University of Chicago Press, 1979).

Sylvia Nasar, "Women's Progress Stalled? Just Not So," *The New York Times,* October 18, 1992.

National Women's History Project, *Las Mujeres: Mexican American/Chicana Women* (Windsor, Calif.: National Women's History Project, 1991).

Vicki L. Ruiz, *Cannery Women, Cannery Lives: Mexican Women, Unionization and the California Food Processing Industry, 1930–1950* (Albuquerque, N.M.: University of New Mexico Press, 1987).

———, "Luisa Moreno: A Fighter for Social Justice," *Nuestra Cosa,* Claremont Colleges, Spring, 1993.

Leon Stein, *The Triangle Fire* (Philadelphia: J. B. Lippincott, 1962).

Nancy Woloch, *Women and the American Experience* (New York: Alfred A. Knopf, 1984).

Judy Yung, *Chinese Women of America: A Pictorial History* (Seattle, Wash.: University of Washington Press, 1986).

Education

American Council on Education, "More Women Leading Higher Ed Institutions," *Higher Education and National Affairs,* Volume 41, Number 11, June 8, 1992.

Peter Applebome, "Duke University Installs Woman as Its President," *The New York Times,* October 24, 1993.

Mariam K. Chamberlain, ed., *Women in Academe: Progress and Prospects* (New York: Russell Sage Foundation, 1988).

Beverly Guy-Sheftall, *Daughters of Sorrow* (Brooklyn, N.Y.: Carlson Publishing Inc., 1990).

William H. Honan, "Woman Is Penn President; The First in the Ivy League," *The New York Times,* December 7, 1993.

Regina Markell Morantz-Sanchez, *Sympathy and Science: Women Physicians in American Medicine* (New York: Oxford University Press, 1985).

Jane Bernard Powers, *The "Girl Question" in Education: Vocational Education for Young Women in the Progressive Era* (London: Falmer Press, 1992).

Margaret W. Rossiter, *Women Scientists in America: Struggles and Strategies to 1940* (Baltimore, Md.: Johns Hopkins University Press, 1982).

Thomas D. Snyder, project director, National Center for Education Statistics, U.S. Department of Education, *Digest of Education Statistics, 1993* (Washington, D.C.: U.S. Government Printing Office, October 1993).

Judith G. Touchton and Lynne Davis, *Fact Book on Women in Higher Education* (New York: American Council on Education and Macmillan Publishing Co., 1991).

Associations

Cynthia Neverdon-Morton, *Afro-American Women of the South and the Advancement of the Race, 1895–1925* (Knoxville, Tenn.: University of Tennessee Press, 1989).

Anne Firor Scott, *Natural Allies: Women's Associations in American History* (Urbana, Ill.: University of Illinois Press, 1991).

Suffrage and Politics

Hope Chamberlin, *A Minority of Members: Women in the U.S. Congress* (New York: Praeger, 1973).

Nancy F. Cott, *The Grounding of Modern Feminism* (New Haven, Conn.: Yale University Press, 1987).

Ellen Carol DuBois, *Feminism and Suffrage: The Emergence of an*

Independent Women's Movement in America, 1848–1869 (Ithaca, N.Y.: Cornell University Press, 1978).

Inez Haynes Irwin, *The Story of Alice Paul and the National Woman's Party* (Fairfax, Va.: Denlinger's Publishers, 1977).

Aileen S. Kraditor, *The Ideas of the Woman Suffrage Movement, 1890–1920* (Garden City, N.Y.: Anchor Books, 1971).

Marianne Means, "Presidents' Ladies," *The 1964 Democratic National Convention* (Washington, D.C.: Democratic Convention Program Book Committee, 1964), pp. 116–119.

Anne F. Scott and Andrew M. Scott, *One Half the People: The Fight for Woman Suffrage* (Philadelphia, Pa.: J. B. Lippincott, 1975).

Rosalyn Terborg-Penn, "Discontented Black Feminists: Prelude and Postscript to the Passage of the Nineteenth Amendment," *Decades of Discontent: The Women's Movement, 1920–1940,* Lois Scharf and Joan M. Jensen, eds. (Westport, Conn.: Greenwood Press, 1983).

Linda Witt, Karen M. Paget, and Glenna Matthews, *Running As a Woman: Gender and Power in American Politics* (New York: The Free Press, 1993).

Civil Rights

Cynthia Stokes Brown, ed., *Septima Clark and the Civil Rights Movement* (Navarro, Calif.: Wild Trees Press, 1986).

Vicki L. Crawford, Jacqueline Anne Rouse, and Barbara Woods, eds., *Women in the Civil Rights Movement: Trailblazers and Torchbearers, 1941–1965* (Brooklyn, N.Y.: Carlson Publishing Inc., 1990).

Paula Giddings, *When and Where I Enter: The Impact of Black Women on Race and Sex in America* (New York: William Morrow, 1984).

Jacquelyn Dowd Hall, *Revolt Against Chivalry: Jessie Daniel Ames and the Women's Campaign Against Lynching* (New York: Columbia University Press, 1979).

Gerda Lerner, ed., *Black Women in White America* (New York: Pantheon, 1972).

Kay Mills, *This Little Light of Mine: The Life of Fannie Lou Hamer* (New York: Dutton, 1993).

Harvard Sitkoff, *A New Deal for Blacks: The Emergence of Civil*

Rights as a National Issue, Vol I: The Depression Decade (New York: Oxford University Press, 1978).

Native American Women

Associated Press, "Cherokee Losing Chief Who Revitalized Tribe," *The New York Times,* April 6, 1994.

Connie Koenenn, "Heart of a Nation," *Los Angeles Times,* November 1,1993.

Terry R. Reynolds, "Women, Pottery, and Economics at Acoma Pueblo," *New Mexico Women: Intercultural Perspectives,* Joan M. Jensen and Darlis A. Miller, eds. (Albuquerque, N.M.: University of New Mexico Press, 1986).

Janet Spector, *What This Awl Means: Feminist Archaeology at a Wahpeton Dakota Village* (St. Paul, Minn.: Minnesota Historical Society Press, 1993).

Robert A. Trennert, "Educating Indian Girls at Nonreservation Boarding Schools, 1878–1920," *Unequal Sisters: A Multi-Cultural Reader in U.S. Women's History,* Ellen Carol DuBois and Vicki L. Ruiz, eds. (New York: Routledge, 1990), pp. 224–237.

Sam Howe Verhovek, "One Woman's 'Trail of Tears' Ends, With Honor, Back Home," *The New York Times,* November 4, 1993.

Zitkala-Sa, "The School Days of an Indian Girl," *Women's America: Refocusing the Past,* Linda K. Kerber and Jane Sherron De Hart, eds. (New York: Oxford University Press, 1991), pp. 286–289.

Lesbian Life

Lillian Faderman, *Odd Girls and Twilight Lovers: A History of Lesbian Life in Twentieth-Century America* (New York: Columbia University Press, 1991).

Media

Judith Coburn, "Women Take *The New York Times* to Court," *New Times,* October 2, 1978, pp. 20–27.

Jane Hall, "Chung's Making News Tonight," *Los Angeles Times,* June 1, 1993.

Susan Henry, "Sarah Goddard: Gentlewoman Printer," *Journalism Quarterly* vol. 57, no. 1 (spring 1980), pp. 23–30.

David H. Hosley and Gayle K. Yamada, *Hard News: Women in Broadcast Journalism* (Westport, Conn.: Greenwood Press, 1987).

Marion Marzolf, *Up from the Footnote: A History of Women Journalists* (New York: Hastings House Publishers, 1977).

Kay Mills, *A Place in the News: From the Women's Pages to the Front Page* (New York: Columbia University Press, 1990).

Sharon M. Murphy, "Mary Katherine Goddard," in Madelon Golden Schilpp and Sharon M. Murphy, *Great Women of the Press* (Carbondale: Southern Illinois University Press, 1983).

"*New York Times* Settled with Its Women Employees as They Were Preparing for Trial," *Media Report to Women*, November 1, 1978, pp. 1, 5.

Nan Robertson, *The Girls in the Balcony* (New York: Random House, 1992).

"The Media and Women Without Apology," *Media Studies Journal*, Winter/Spring 1993 issue, the Freedom Forum Media Studies Center at Columbia University.

Birth Control and Abortion

David Anderson, *Newsroom Guide to Abortion and Family Planning* (Washington, D.C.: Communications Consortium Media Center, 1993).

Ellen Chesler, *Woman of Valor: Margaret Sanger and the Birth Control Movement in America* (New York: Simon & Schuster, 1992).

Marian Faux, *Roe v. Wade: The Untold Story of the Landmark Supreme Court Decision That Made Abortion Legal* (New York: Macmillan, 1988).

Linda Gordon, *Woman's Body, Woman's Right: Birth Control in America* (New York: Penguin, 1990).

Rickie Solinger, *Wake Up Little Susie: Single Pregnancy and Race Before Roe v. Wade* (New York: Routledge, 1992).

Law and Prisons

Associated Press, "Drawing the Line on Sexual Harassment of Workers," *The Washington Post,* November 10, 1993.

Geraldine Baum, "Storming the Citadel," *Los Angeles Times,* February 13, 1994.

Mary Becker, Cynthia Grant Bowman, and Morrison Torrey, *Feminist Jurisprudence: Taking Women Seriously* (St. Paul, Minn.: West Publishing Co., 1994).

Susan D. Becker, *The Origins of the Equal Rights Amendment: American Feminism Between the Wars* (Westport, Conn.: Greenwood Press, 1981).

Joan Biskupic, "Sexual Harassment Protections Bolstered; Unanimous High Court Rules Plaintiff Need Not Prove Psychological Injury," *The Washington Post,* November 10, 1993.

Estelle Freedman, *Their Sisters' Keepers: Women's Prison Reform in America, 1830–1930* (Ann Arbor, Mich.: The University of Michigan Press, 1981).

Leslie Friedman Goldstein, *The Constitutional Rights of Women: Cases in Law and Social Change* (Madison, Wis.: University of Wisconsin Press, 1988).

Linda Greenhouse, "Abortion Clinics Upheld by Court on Rackets Suit," *The New York Times,* January 25, 1994.

———, "High Court Bars Sex as Standard in Picking Jurors," *The New York Times,* April 20, 1994.

———, "Plain Talk Puts Ginsburg at Fore of Court Debates," *The New York Times,* October 14, 1993.

Guy Gugliotta and Eleanor Randolph, "A Mentor, Role Model and Heroine of Feminist Lawyers," *The Washington Post,* June 15, 1993.

Herma Hill Kay, *Sex-Based Discrimination* (St. Paul, Minn.: West Publishing Co., 1988).

———, *1992 Supplement to Sex-Based Discrimination* (St. Paul, Minn.: West Publishing Co., 1992).

J. Ralph Lindgren and Nadine Taub, *The Law of Sex Discrimination* (St. Paul, Minn.: West Publishing Co., 1988).

Jane J. Mansbridge, *Why We Lost the ERA* (Chicago: University of Chicago Press, 1986).

Ruth Marcus, "Judge Ruth Ginsburg Named to High Court;

Clinton's Unexpected Choice Is Women's Rights Pioneer," *The Washington Post,* June 15, 1993.

David Margolick, "Judge Ginsburg's Life a Trial by Adversity," *The New York Times,* June 25, 1993.

Kay Mills, "A Woman Sitting on the Supreme Court: History's Place for Sandra Day O'Connor," *Los Angeles Times,* February 28, 1988.

Deborah L. Rhode, *Justice and Gender: Sex Discrimination and the Law* (Cambridge, Mass.: Harvard University Press, 1989).

Gilbert Y. Steiner, *Constitutional Inequality: The Political Fortunes of the Equal Rights Amendment* (Washington, D.C.: The Brookings Institution, 1985).

Religion

Alan Cowell, "Pope Rules Out Debate on Women as Priests," *The New York Times,* May 31, 1994.

Antoinette Iadarola, "The American Catholic Bishops and Woman: From the Nineteenth Amendment to ERA," *Women, Religion and Social Change,* Yvonne Yazbeck Haddad and Ellison Banks Findly, eds. (Albany, N.Y.: State University of New York Press, 1985).

Janet Wilson James, ed., *Women in American Religion* (Philadelphia: University of Pennsylvania Press, 1980). Especially useful were the overview article by Janet Wilson James and articles by Virginia Lieson Brereton and Christa Ressmeyer Klein on American women in the Protestant ministry, James J. Kenneally on American Catholicism and women, and Norma Fain Pratt on Jewish American women.

Richard N. Ostling, "The Second Reformation," *Time,* November 23, 1992, pp. 52–58.

Betsy Covington Smith, *Breakthrough: Women in Religion* (New York: Walker and Co., 1978).

Barbara Welter, "The Feminization of American Religion: 1800–1860," *Clio's Consciousness Raised: New Perspectives on the History of Women,* Mary Hartman and Lois W. Banner, eds. (New York: Harper and Row, 1974).

Military

Associated Press, "Woman Officer Tells of Assault as a Gulf POW," *Los Angeles Times,* June 11, 1992.

Carol Barkalow, "Let Women in the Military 'Be All That We Can Be,' " *Los Angeles Times,* July, 28, 1991.

Maureen Dowd, "Senate Approves a 4-Star Rank for Admiral in Tailhook Affair," *The New York Times,* April 20, 1994.

Ellen Goodman, "Military Women Fight the Enemy Within," *Los Angeles Times,* July 7, 1992.

Melissa Healy, "140 Officers Faulted in Tailhook Sex Scandal," *Los Angeles Times,* April 24, 1993.

Jeanne Holm, *Women in the Military: An Unfinished Revolution* (Novato, Calif.: Presidio Press, 1992).

John Lancaster, "Army, Marines Resisting Combat Role for Women," *The Washington Post,* June 18, 1993.

Laura Palmer, "How to Bandage a War; The Nurses of Vietnam Still Wounded," *The New York Times Magazine,* November 7, 1993.

Judy Pasternak, "Sky's the Limit for Squadron," *Los Angeles Times,* May 11, 1993.

Eric Schmitt, "Navy Women Bringing New Era on Carriers," *The New York Times,* February 21, 1994.

Dorothy and Carl J. Schneider, *Sound Off: American Military Women Speak Out* (New York: Dutton, 1988).

Elaine Sciolino, "Female P.O.W. Is Abused, Kindling Debate," *The New York Times,* June 29, 1992.

Richard Serrano, "33 Top Officers Disciplined in Tailhook Case," *Los Angeles Times,* October 16, 1993.

Judith Hicks Stiehm, *Arms and the Enlisted Woman* (Philadelphia, Pa.: Temple University Press, 1989).

Women's Research and Education Institute, "Facts About Women in the Military, 1980–1990," Washington, D.C., June 1990.

———, "Facts About Women in the U.S. Armed Services: The War in the Persian Gulf," Washington, D.C., March 1991.

Sports

Nathan Aaseng, *Winning Women of Tennis* (Minneapolis, Minn.: Lerner Publications, 1981).

Mike DiGiovanna, "Gender Equity Gets Boost," *Los Angeles Times,* October 22, 1993.

"Ensuring Fair Play for Women and Men," editorial in *Los Angeles Times,* September 19, 1993.

"Fairness Isn't Boosterism," editorial in *Los Angeles Times,* August 7, 1984.

Barbara Gregorich, "Women, Baseball and Dodger Blue," *Dodgers Magazine,* vol. 6, no. 4, August 1993.

Earl Gustkey, "USC Names Miller as Women's Coach," *Los Angeles Times,* September 3, 1993.

Allen Guttmann, *Women's Sports: A History* (New York: Columbia University Press, 1991).

Karl Hente, "Miller Puts in Time on USC Bench," *The Washington Post,* January 2, 1994.

Martha Weinman Lear,' "She's No Jockette," *The New York Times Magazine,* July 25, 1993.

Alice Marble with Dale Leatherman, *Courting Danger* (New York: St. Martin's, 1991).

Mariah Burton Nelson, *Are We Winning Yet? How Women Are Changing Sports and Sports Are Changing Women* (New York: Random House, 1991).

Ruth M. Sparhawk, Mary E. Leslie, Phyllis V. Turbow, and Zina R. Rose, *American Women in Sport, 1887–1987: A 100-Year Chronology* (Metuchen, N.J.: Scarecrow, 1989).

Entertainment

Gail Lumet Buckley, "Dorothy's Surrender," *Premiere,* Special Issue 1993, pp. 84–89.

Burt A. Folkart, "Myrna Loy, Star of 'Thin Man' Films, Dies at 88," *Los Angeles Times,* December 15, 1993.

Richard Griffith and Arthur Mayer, *The Movies* (New York: Simon & Schuster, 1970).

Molly Haskell, "Mae West's Bawdy Spirit Spans the Gay '90s," *The New York Times,* August 15, 1993.

Jim Koch, "A Way with Words," *The New York Times,* August 15, 1993.

James Monaco, *The Encyclopedia of Film* (New York: Perigee Books, 1991).

Literature and Theater

Joan Acocella, "After the Laughs," *The New Yorker,* August 16, 1993, pp. 76–81.

Teresa Carpenter, "Back to the Round Table with Dorothy Parker and Pals . . . ," *The New York Times,* August 29, 1993.

Helen Krich Chinoy and Linda Walsh Jenkins, eds., *Women in American Theatre* (New York: Theatre Communications Group, Inc., 1987).

Thomas H. Johnson, ed., *The Complete Poems of Emily Dickinson* (Boston: Little, Brown, 1929, 1957).

Katharine M. Rogers, ed., *Early American Women Writers: From Anne Bradstreet to Louisa May Alcott, 1650–1865* (New York: Meridian, 1991).

Ann Allen Shockley, *Afro-American Women Writers, 1746–1933: An Anthology and Critical Guide* (New York: Meridian, 1988).

Edith Wharton, *The Age of Innocence* (New York: D. Appleton, 1920), edition with R. W. B. Lewis introduction (New York: Macmillan, 1992).

Biographies, Biographical Sketches, and Memoirs

Jane Addams, *Twenty Years at Hull House* (New York: New American Library, 1961).

Jack Anderson, "Agnes de Mille, 88, Dance Visionary, Is Dead," *The New York Times,* October 8, 1993.

Edith Evans Asbury, "Georgia O'Keeffe Dead at 98; Shaper of Modern Art in U.S.," *The New York Times,* March 7, 1986.

Linda Atkinson, *Mother Jones: The Most Dangerous Woman in America* (New York: Crown, 1978).

Kathleen Barry, *Susan B. Anthony: A Biography of a Singular Feminist* (New York: Ballantine, 1988).

Carolyn Blacknall, *Sally Ride: America's First Woman in Space* (New York: Dillon Press, 1984).

Eleanor Blau, "Pauline Frederick, 84, Network News Pioneer, Dies," *The New York Times,* May 11, 1990.

Van Wyck Brooks, *Helen Keller: Sketch for a Portrait* (New York: Dutton, 1956).

Gae Whitney Canfield, *Sarah Winnemucca of the Northern Paiutes* (Norman, Okla.: University of Oklahoma Press, 1983).

John C. Farrell, *Beloved Lady: A History of Jane Addams' Ideas on Reform and Peace* (Baltimore, Md.: The Johns Hopkins Press, 1967).

Dale Fetherling, *Mother Jones: The Miners' Angel* (Carbondale, Ill.: Southern Illinois University Press, 1974).

Marshall W. Fishwick, *Illustrious Americans: Clara Barton* (Morristown, N.J.: Silver Burdett Co., 1966).

Lucy Freeman and Alma Bond, *America's First Woman Warrior: The Courage of Deborah Sampson* (New York: Paragon House, 1992).

Jean Fritz, *The Double Life of Pocahontas* (New York: G. P. Putnam's Sons, 1983).

Noel B. Gerson, *Harriet Beecher Stowe* (New York: Praeger, 1976).

Elisabeth Griffith, *In Her Own Right: The Life of Elizabeth Cady Stanton* (New York: Oxford University Press, 1984).

Joan D. Hedrick, *Harriet Beecher Stowe: A Life* (New York: Oxford University Press, 1994).

Eric J. Ierardi, *Gravesend: The Home of Coney Island* (New York: Vantage Press, 1974).

Sheryl James, "Crowd Pleaser: After 60 years of grunt work for human rights, Michigan's Millie Jeffrey is an icon. And she's not finished yet," *Detroit's Free Press Magazine,* January 23, 1994.

Lauren Kessler, *Stubborn Twig: Three Generations in the Life of a Japanese American Family* (New York: Random House, 1993).

Akemi Kikumura, *Through Harsh Winters: The Life of a Japanese Immigrant Woman* (Novato, Calif.: Chandler & Sharp Publishers, 1981).

Gerda Lerner, *The Grimké Sisters from South Carolina: Rebels Against Slavery* (Boston: Houghton Mifflin, 1967).

Mary S. Lovell, *The Sound of Wings* (New York: St. Martin's Press, 1989).

Carleton Mabee with Susan Mabee Newhouse, *Sojourner Truth: Slave, Prophet, Legend* (New York: New York University Press, 1993).

Wilma Mankiller and Michael Wallis, *Mankiller: A Chief and Her People* (New York: St. Martin's, 1993).

"Maria Povera Martinez, Potter, 94," *The New York Times,* July 22, 1980.

George Martin, *Madam Secretary: Frances Perkins* (Boston: Houghton Mifflin, 1976).

Nancy Mowll Mathews, *Mary Cassatt: A Life* (New York: Villard, 1994).

Susan E. Meyer, *Mary Cassatt* (New York: Harry N. Abrams, Inc., 1990).

Kay Mills, "Aging Women: Don't Agonize, Organize," *Los Angeles Times,* November 21, 1982.

———, "Literature By Lode and By Lore: Hong Kingston Mines Identity," *Los Angeles Times,* August 25, 1985.

———, "Working to Set the Record Right on a Native California Heritage," *Los Angeles Times,* April 8, 1984.

Celia Morris, *Fanny Wright: Rebel in America* (Cambridge, Mass.: Harvard University Press, 1984).

Nell Irvin Painter, "Representing Truth: Sojourner Truth's Knowing and Becoming Known," paper presented at the Berkshire Women's History Conference, June 1993.

Susan Peterson, *The Living Tradition of Maria Martinez* (New York: Kodansha International/USA Ltd., 1989).

John Russell, "An Artist Inspired by New Mexico's Landscape," *The New York Times,* March 7, 1986.

John Anthony Scott, *Woman Against Slavery: The Story of Harriet Beecher Stowe* (New York: Thomas Y. Crowell Co., 1978).

Kathryn Kish Sklar, *Catharine Beecher: A Study in American Domesticity* (New York: W. W. Norton, 1976).

Jessie Carney Smith, ed., *Epic Lives: One Hundred Black Women Who Made a Difference* (Detroit, Mich.: Visible Ink Press, 1993).

Richard L. Spivey, *Maria* (Flagstaff, Ariz.: Northland Press, 1979).

Susan Ware, *Still Missing: Amelia Earhart and the Search for Modern Feminism* (New York: W. W. Norton, 1993).

Alice Wexler, *Emma Goldman: An Intimate Life* (New York: Pantheon, 1984).

Lynne Withey, *Dearest Friend: A Life of Abigail Adams* (New York: The Free Press, 1981).

Cynthia Griffin Wolff, *Emily Dickinson* (New York: Alfred A. Knopf, 1986).

James Woodress, *Willa Cather: A Literary Life* (Lincoln, Neb.: University of Nebraska Press, 1987).

Harold and Geraldine Woods, *Equal Justice: A Biography of Sandra Day O'Connor* (Minneapolis: Dillon Press, 1985).

Index